THE CRISIS IN WORLD POPULATION

J. O. HERTZLER

THE CRISIS

IN WORLD POPULATION

A Sociological Examination

with Special Reference to the Underdeveloped Areas

LINCOLN : UNIVERSITY OF NEBRASKA PRESS : 1956

Preface

This book is the outgrowth of an interdisciplinary seminar on International Relations, devoted specifically to Population in International Affairs, given in the spring semester of 1953 and led by the present writer in cooperation with colleagues from various departments. The keen interest evidenced in the subject by the members, who were selected seniors and graduate students from the departments of anthropology, economics, geography, history, political science, and sociology, indicated the pertinence of the subject in their various disciplines. The semester's experience led to the suggestion that the type of systematic treatment developed in the seminar be made available to a wider audience.

This is not a book for experts. Rather, it seeks in a somewhat general way to set forth some of the main features of the world population situation in a social scientific manner for college students and interested laymen, many of whom seem to be sublimely unaware of the gravity of this situation. It is not primarily a statistical or socio-biological treatment of demographic details. The publications of the Population Commission of the United Nations, as well as those of other United Nations organizations such as the Food and Agricultural Organization and the World Health Organization, carry copious statistical data and are readily available and fairly inexpensive. A number of recent semi-popular works, mentioned below, also provide a wealth of such detail.

Some attention will be paid, nevertheless, to the persistent historical increase of world population and especially to the phenomenal burgeoning of population in recent centuries. But primary consideration will be given to the underlying factors and processes involved, the social scientific principles relating to the changes, some of their more apparent and serious effects, the play of human culture in all its ramifications both as cause and effect, the national and international problems which the situation poses, and especially some of the proposed instrumentalities for coping with the situation. In all candor, "solutions," in this latter connection, are not available; only "possibilities" based on the best knowledge available, and couched in the form of hypotheses, can be presented. Special attention is given throughout to the so-called underdeveloped peoples, constituting approximately two-thirds of the world's population, among whom conditions are most serious.

Population—and its treatment—is always an area of heated controversy; there is frequent disagreement over objectives, over the interpretation of international population facts, over proposed and current methods of dealing with the situations. The problems are sometimes met with an almost juvenile lack of concern. This, however, is not a highly optimistic treatment. When there are five more persons in the world every four seconds, the finiteness of the earth becomes a matter of paramount concern, regardless of man's ingenuity and laboriousness in utilizing its resources. The part of wisdom and prudence would seem to be to assume a cautious, restrained, and responsible attitude. The safety of the human race in the future must be assured. If the actual future situation *for the whole world* with respect to the balance between population and decent means of existence should exceed our anticipations, and things turn out well, it is all to the good. But if we are foolishly and irresponsibly optimistic, the burden of blame—and of disaster—is upon us of the present.

Some of the works referred to, either in the text or in the general bibliographies, are readily available semi-popular and semi-technical books which, nonetheless, are based on sound scientific data and reflect the conclusions of experts and other widely observant and well-informed students. Particularly notable in this respect are those by Fairchild, Thompson, Osborn, Cook, Darwin, Russell, Bliven, Brown, Bates, and Henshaw. Occasional reference is also made to valuable symposia, highly recommended to the reader, such as those edited by Bowman, Joerg, Linton, Hatt, Schultz, Spicer, Hoselitz, Thayer, Ruopp, and Mead, those presented by the Milbank Memorial Fund and the American Philosophical Society, and those published in the *Annals of the American Academy of Political and Social Science*. Most, however, are technical treatments by specialists.

An indispensable companion volume to this present work is the publication of the Department of Social Affairs of the United Nations Population Commission: *The Determinants and Consequences of Population Trends: A Summary of the Findings of Studies on the Relationships between Population Changes and Economic and Social Conditions* (Population Studies, No. 17; New York, 1953). This is an extremely cautious work, but it presents in exhaustive manner an enormous volume of information regarding population growth and trends, population theories, factors affecting mortality, fertility, migration, age structure and distribution, the effects of population changes, and the implications of population trends in both highly industrialized and in underdeveloped countries. The various and often conflicting viewpoints and interpretations of innumerable students of many countries are impartially examined. The bibliography, of some fifty double-column pages in fine print, offers an elaborate and diversified supply of references. The *Demographic Yearbooks,* published annually by the Population Commission of the United Nations, present the most definitive and detailed data, by country, region, and for the world as a whole, and year by year, and indicate the "flow" of population changes. The work by W. S. and E. S. Woytinsky, *World Population and Production: Trends and Outlook* (New York: Twentieth Century Fund, 1953) is also an exhaustive compendium of pertinent data.

Sources referred to in the text or in footnotes by author or organization issuing them are, unless otherwise indicated, to be found alphabetically arranged in the bibliographies accompanying each chapter except the first. These references give complete data regarding the works, including pertinent pagination.

Some ideas are expressed several times in successive chapters. But the repetitions are significant in a particular theoretical context, or as applied to a particular problem or area.

A deep obligation is hereby expressed to the students in my population courses during the last quarter of a century for good "give and take," to various colleagues for helpful suggestion of sources, for certain facts and principles, and for constructive criticism, to the staff of the University of Nebraska Press for various editorial services, and to my wife for her never-failing encouragement in this as in many other enterprises and for her secretarial assistance.

J. O. HERTZLER

Contents

1

Our World

The setting for our study is the contracting, interrelated, and interlocking world of today—the new world that has emerged without plan and intention and has become, recently and quickly, in fact, a single communicating area. It is a world in which each of us must now admit with Zeno of the fourth century B. C., "I am a citizen of the world!" With the development of transportation its various spatial portions are as accessible to each other as were those of a small state a century ago. Time too has shrunk: the jet airplane has brought even remote nations within hours and even minutes of each other. Its inhabitants can communicate with each other as rapidly and readily as was possible in a small city at the turn of the century; the world has come to be a vast whispering gallery. Its inhabitants can even see their fellow men at great distances.

All of its peoples and nations are more dependent upon each other for the good material things of life than were the inhabitants of a village a hundred years ago; it is a share-the-wealth world, one in which we all have to run next door for many necessities, one in which for most nations "the wealth of the nation depends upon the wealth of nations." The "curtains"—Iron, Bamboo, Dollar—only accentuate and illuminate this fact.

1

From the standpoint of health the whole world is a shrinking arena in which vicious endemic and epidemic diseases can readily spread; bacteria, bacilli, and parasites have become cosmopolitan and international even if human beings have not. Culturally, many of the residues of the intellectual, humanistic, religious, political, commercial, scientific-technological, and agricultural-industrial revolutions of the Western World since 1450 have come to penetrate and increasingly to influence all of the rest of the world. Many of the peoples of the world are at least as dependent upon each other for their precious cultural and spiritual satisfactions as were the inhabitants of a village a century ago.

In our world what happens anywhere has its inevitable reverberations everywhere, though in varying degree and with varying effect and time lag. This "one world" has arrived at the point where regional problems cannot be solved piecemeal and in isolation; even national problems and actions are the intimate and vital concern of every other nation. For its individual citizens the world has broadened; its peoples, nations, and regions are tied one to another by exchange of goods, services, and ideas, by their mutual friendships and mutual suspicions, by their very antagonisms and conflicts.

Finally, our geographic world has become finite. The seven seas are charted highways and the open spaces of the six continents have been explored and utilized to the extent that present technology and present economic and political conditions permit. There are no frontiers or unknown parts of the world into which to expand. The discoveries and the frontiers are now of a scientific-technological and a sociological-economic-political, rather than a geographical, nature.

A WORLD OF DIFFERENCES

In spite of the oneness of the world vast disparities and inequalities exist among its peoples and nations. There are glaring differences in amount and quality of land and other resources, in total and per capita wealth and income, in access to raw materials and finished products, in level and degree of economic development and opportunity, and in standards of living. Great differences prevail in cultural level and context, especially with respect to dominating values and ends, and the folkways, traditions, customs, and social institutions which instrumentalize these. The peoples differ in their comprehension of and outlook upon the world. They abide by sharply contrasting and often conflicting political, economic, and religious ideologies. Great differences in political sophistication and stability, in international political status and power, and in political independence are sources of frustration and tension which militate against cooperation and peace. The "Great Divides" of language, race, and nationality, along with other cultural and minority-majority situations, produce discriminations, exclusions, and persecutions, which create inequalities of opportunity and privilege.

The very developments of the last century which have augmented international communication, caused the interpenetration of cultures, increased international cooperation along certain lines, and tended to bring the entire human race into one vast community have at the same time also increased the opportunities for friction. The world has become less stable in many respects, and tensions have increased. Two *world* wars in the present century have been tragic demonstrations of the divisive and destructive potentialities inherent in the world situation. The technological processes that have been responsible for the shrinkage of the world have also augmented its capacity to annihilate itself. Furthermore, because of the imminent threat of greater wars it seems to be a world whose national resources are drained off more and more into the production of military matériel. Created for destructive purposes and usually lost if used in war, military production is a subtraction from the material products for good living.

All have a concern in this one, divided, and troubled world. Can the effects of the differences be alleviated, the inequalities adjusted, and the tensions relieved? Can the long siege of poverty be ended? Can policies, controls, and organizations be established and effectively utilized to resolve these crucial problems—and soon enough?

At the same time some of the diversities, especially those of a unique and rich "cultural" nature—music, the graphic arts, poetry, philosophy, religions—should not be lost or distorted, for they are aspects of the world's spiritual capital. The peoples of the one world, like all the separate personalities, would suffer immeasurable loss if they became all of a piece. Can the peoples and their cultures be, not melted together, but joined into a symphony of many different but harmonious themes?

A WORLD IN FERMENT

The non-European peoples, constituting more than two-thirds of the world's inhabitants, are those with lesser wealth, privilege, opportunity, and power. These peoples, especially those in Asia, Africa, and parts of Latin America, are waking up; new forces are operating among them, and a new life is pulsating within them. They are coming to be keenly aware of the fact that they are part —and a weighty part—of the one world. The signs of ferment have long been discernible, but the course of events since the beginning of World War II has accentuated and accelerated a combination of changes that even the profoundest of observers could hardly have foreseen a quarter of a century earlier. A strange new world is coming into being.

These peoples are experiencing scientific, technological, and economic development in varying degree as the result of penetration from the West. The impact of the West has been sufficient to enable them to realize their technical retardation and limitations, their underproduction, underemployment, and poverty, their limited participation in the commerce of the world, and their sparing enjoyment of its wealth. Some of them are becoming aware of their sharply contrasting chronic states of malnutrition, their burden of endemic disease, their lack of public sanitation, and their other substandard health conditions. Most are concerned about the vast illiteracy that prevails among them, and at least their elites see the relationship of this to their inferior states of wealth and health and political proficiency. There is among them, in every quarter, an increased yearning and a demand for a greater share of material things and of other benefits to be derived from the new ways of doing things. Moreover, they feel—or believe—that improvement is within their reach.

To this technological and economic dynamism must be added the political dynamism in the traditionally slumbering areas. After centuries of colonialism and feudalism, they are coming to independence and are seeking to establish representative government and legal equality. In the short space of ten years since the end of the Pacific war, eight Asian nations with a population of over

600 million have attained independence; six of them—India, Pakistan, Burma, Ceylon, Indonesia, and the Philippines—are in southeastern Asia. Nationalistic movements thrive and multiply among almost all of the other underdeveloped peoples.

There is among them also a growing sense of the inescapable part they are called upon to play in the future of the world. They are insisting upon adequate recognition of their importance in the counsels of nations. They refuse, increasingly and insistently, to be the instruments for the ends of powerful nations. As Indian ambassador Mehta has put it: "We want to be friends, not satellites."[1] Many of them have come to be conscious of their international powerlessness and are anxious to achieve a place in the sun.

Culturally, some of them are becoming proudly conscious of their rich heritages, with their many magnificent, millennia-old religions, their ethical systems, their aesthetic expressions, and other precious fruits of the spirit. But disturbing elements of Western civilization—ideas of equality, liberty, individualism, change and progress, the ways of rationalism and secularism that inevitably accompany industrialization and urbanization—are penetrating the very fabric of their value systems and their institutions. At the same time, since these profound changes are causing in varying degree a disorganization of the matrix of their culture, they are bound to bring some disillusionment to the people. The new civilization is destroying many elements that made their long-established life worth living.

Societally, as modern technology appears among them, there is a tendency toward a dissolution of their old, stable, agrarian peasant societies, with their accepted patterns of social organization and social behavior. New and alien ways of life and work are being tried, and new and alien incentives confuse them and goad them on.

The horizons of these peoples have been immeasurably expanded in a quarter of a century. They are undergoing processes of material and spiritual change of more revolutionary significance than ever before experienced in their history. Because they have awakened late to the possibilities opened up by modern science and

---

[1] G. L. Mehta, "India and the United States: Democracy East and West." *Annals Am. Acad. Pol. & Soc. Sci.*, 294 (July, 1954): 124-130.

technology and government, they are "peoples in a hurry"—peoples
in the grip of what someone has called "the revolution of rising
expectations." But they want to develop their own systems and
economies on their own terms and without domination from the
outside.

A WORLD OF PEOPLE

All social action, and for that matter all individual reaction,
since individuals do not behave in a vacuum, involves people. They
are the agents; all else is neutral nature operating according to
natural laws. Human activity is for people—for their well-being
as they interpret it.

When the needs of the people, in any ultimate sense, are under
consideration, they almost always involve human fertility and
mortality, the composition of the population, the currents and possibilities of migration, and the trends of population growth and
distribution.

The study of population, even on the local level, and vastly more
so on the national and international levels, ties together and requires the closest cooperation of all the sciences and philosophies.
The physical and biological sciences and technologies (including
particularly physical engineering, geology and geography, chemistry, and bacteriology), all primary, secondary, and tertiary production, medicine and public health play an important part in the
understanding of demographic phenomena. Most of the physical
and social changes have profound demographic effects. All analysis
and action related to the social sciences—history, anthropology,
economics, political science, psychology and social psychology,
sociology—are unavoidably concerned with population facts. Religion and ethics, and the bodies of beliefs, sanctions, and ends of
peoples, are reciprocally related to their population situation, past
and present. Population is, in fact, the keystone of societal analysis.

Population, in general perspective, involves or is involved in:

Historical conditions: contacts, migrations, dominations, expan-
    sions and wars;
Physical and ecological factors: land, climate, physical resources,
    location and "standing room" of peoples;
Biological factors: externally all the fauna and flora affecting
    man's life for weal or woe; and, with respect to man himself,

his fertility, morbidity, mortality, age groups, sex and sex ratios, and expectancy of life;

The utilization of all resources, topographical, physical, and biological, and the production and exchange of commodities in all stages of processing and of the innumerable and essential "services";

Local, national, and international political organization, especially legislation and national and international ideologies, policies, and practices;

The personal and social attitudes and habits of people concerning marriage and children and philo-progenitive practices, such as abortion, infanticide, gerontocide, and contraception;

The folkways, mores, traditions, customs, and institutions, as they regulate and motivate individual and social behavior;

The societal makeup, its groups and communities, its differentiated and stratified structuring, and the level and efficiency of its social functioning ("folk" society or industrialized-urbanized society);

The size and make-up of the labor force, that is, the population in the economically and socially productive period of life, as against the proportions of young and aged dependents;

The ethnic and other minority-majority group relations both within and between peoples;

The value-systems, the myths, the religious and other creeds, the ethical systems, the language and meaning systems, the goal and purpose systems.

Thus, population—the stock of human beings—is the material and stuff out of which human affairs come; and population problems underlie almost every other human problem.

Population is in continual process, a dynamic "flow." Change is occurring in the vital processes of reproduction and mortality, in the proportions of the people in the sex and age groups and other crucial categories, in physical movement within and into and out of given societies. These processes have dynamic effects. The increase or decrease of numbers means a changing adjustment to the physical environment, altered potentialities of social organization in that it opens up new possibilities or imposes new limitations, and changing relationships to other societies. A change in the composition of the population means notable shifts in the economy, the available labor force, and various institutional arrangements. Changes in areal distribution, as those from country to city or region to region, affect a vast array of functions and relationships.

There has always been some attempt to manipulate the various demographic processes to conform to changing needs, changing values and ideologies, and new modes of social organization by utilizing available technologies. Today man's technologies enable him to control the population processes as never before. More and more, population facts are of his own making. Whether he likes it or not, he must assume a large measure of responsibility for his destiny. In turn, learning how to control demographic processes enables him to determine in some degree not only the size but also the organization and functioning of a nation, and some of the relationships between nations.[2] Hence, a study of international population offers a unique and indispensable approach to an understanding of world affairs.

In this present study we shall try, as far as possible, concisely to summarize, synthesize, and interpret the best current scientific facts and thinking on:

Population as a world condition.

The factors and processes involved in world population conditions and trends.

Population as it is inextricably involved in the well-being, security, peace, and prosperity of the peoples of the world: the economic, technological, political, sociological, and cultural problems involved.

Especially, the presumed solutions: procedures and instrumentalities.

---

[2] On demographic processes see J. O. Hertzler, *Society in Action: A Study of Basic Social Processes* (New York: Dryden, 1954), pp. 108-110.

The Increase of People

THE PRESENT RATE OF POPULATION INCREASE

In 1950 the population of the world was placed at roughly 2,400 million, and now probably more than 2,500 million people[1] are contriving to live together and share the world's resources, always limited at any given time. The rate of growth of the world's population is greater than ever before in history, and the successive net additions, period by period, are breath-taking. In the mid-twenties the annual increase was approximately 17 million per year, and in 1950 it amounted to some 25 million. But the rate has accelerated. As of 1953 the annual world increase was estimated to be above 30 million. This means that there are five more persons every four seconds, and around 90,000 more every 24 hours. At the 1953 rate of increase of about 1.2 per cent per year, the world's population will double in about 58 years, other factors permitting, and the same old earth will have on it five billion human beings instead of the present two and a half billion.

This rate of growth has become a critical matter. To be sure, there are people everywhere with ostrich-like mental attitudes which cause them to avoid facing the simple, inescapable facts of population growth. But the present vast, world-wide problems relating to it, and the probability of even more horrendous ones ahead, are

---

[1] United Nations (Statistical Office, Department of Economic Affairs), *Demographic Yearbook, 1954* (New York, 1955), p. 111.

forcing honest and socially conscious people to pay attention to them. Demographic arithmetic is beginning to be crucially important. In view of the interlocking nature of the modern world, its problems, all of which involve population in considerable degree, are world-wide in significance and effect; they can only be realistically examined and treated *on a world scale.*

ELEMENTAL BALANCE, THE SURVIVAL DRIVE, AND MAN'S MANIPULATIVE ABILITY

Every species in nature, plant or animal, high or low, is equipped with a "biological urge," a capacity to multiply at a rate so great that it could overcrowd the earth in a very short time if there were nothing to stop it. But, with a fixed amount of standing room and a limited immediate food supply, the total amount of life that can exist on earth at any given time is strictly fixed. Thus, every species in nature increases in number up to the supporting power of its habitat, in consideration of other species struggling for existence in it. While fertility of the species may be prodigious, its deaths keep it in check. Barring some great cosmic change, as in topography or climate, or modifications in physical characteristics, giving one or the other species an advantage, the number of members of every species, over the long stretch of time, remains relatively constant. This is the *elemental balance of nature.* The reproduction rate and the death rate are approximately equal in the long run.

New forms of life may come into the habitat. They may increase at first, but eventually, usually rather soon, they will achieve this balance in relation to all other forms of life and the available supply of food. The English sparrows imported into the United States provide a notable example. At first they increased at a tremendous rate, but now they are in balance with all other birds, with all of their predators, and with the food supply.

The species *Homo sapiens,* however, has the ability to disturb this elemental equilibrium directly. He is much more flexible in adaptive ability. He has been able to move to every continent from his supposed place of origin in central Asia and to survive under very different topographies, climates, and food supplies. He has intelligence and contrivance; he has readiness to experiment; he not only learns from experience, but also passes on this knowledge to his successors. Hence, he has been able to protect himself against, or to circumvent, many hostile forces of nature, and has been able to utilize, manipulate, even transform natural physical and biological substances. He is able to invent resourceful ways of acting. In short, he is characterized by that distinctly human expedient, culture, and, particularly significant for our study, technological-economic culture, a contrived social organization, values, and institutionalized ways of behaving. In general, then, man has been able to increase the supplies essential to his existence; he has been able to manipulate the natural forces, develop new techniques, and produce new combinations of substances. He has been able within expanding limits to control his births and deaths if he wished.[2]

The survival drive is found among all creatures. Among men it has been rationally recognized, elevated above the instinctive level, incorporated into their body of values, and made a supreme end. Great value has been attached, universally and at all times, to both individual and group survival; and all societies have welcomed anything which improved their life chances. Folkways, mores, customs, and institutions have instrumentalized this deep-seated, dominant, and precious end. Since survival depends directly and finally upon mortality and fertility, the attitudes toward these and social action respecting them demonstrates the point. The reduction of mortality by saving and prolonging life is universally considered as an end in itself, an essential humane endeavor. No particular group has deliberately permitted for itself higher death rates as a means of demographic adjustment. However, the conquests, deliberate exterminations, and wars of groups of men against other groups have taken a frightful toll.

Conversely, a high fertility, with all the cultural devices that maintain it, has almost universally been considered as an automatic good. All pre-modern societies, having to face heavy mortality, had to have high fertility to survive. But in modern societies, too, even among the most advanced and secure, with high proficiency in death control, the value of high fertility for group survival still

---

[2] Relatively untouched primitives have been able to contrive and maintain an equilibrium on their own terms. See the monumental study of Ludwick Krzywicki, *Primitive Society and Its Vital Statistics* (London: Macmillan, 1934). For later developments among primitives see S. F. Cook, "Demographic Consequences of European Contact with Primitive Peoples," *Annals Am. Acad. Pol. & Soc. Sci.*, 237 (Jan., 1935): 107-111; S. F. Cook; E. N. Palmer, "Culture Contacts and Population Growth," *Am. Jour. Soc.*, 53 (Jan., 1948): 258-262.

persists. The injunction to the folk to be fruitful and multiply and replenish the earth in order that they might inherit it is still widely respected. High fertility, looked upon as a sign of individual and national vitality, is encouraged by all sorts of means —financial, legal, religious, and honorific. Most Americans—the most prosperous people on earth—cheer their census statistics.

The upshot of this preliminary discussion is this: What we need to understand is that man's demographic problems are primarily of his own making, and that, likewise, he has the sole responsibility and means for solving them. No benevolent nature will solve them for him.

ESTIMATES OF HISTORICAL WORLD POPULATION INCREASE

The vast population of the world and the stupendous rate of growth, indicated at the beginning of this chapter, are very recent developments in the long history of man on earth. Through the first 99 per cent of man's career on earth population increased with infinitesimal slowness and remained extremely sparse.

THE DIFFICULTIES REGARDING DATA

Statements about the population of the world at any specified time are, of course, subject to great uncertainty. Historical studies of population growth are handicapped by a shortage of reliable data which grows more serious as the investigations are carried further back into time. Censuses, that is, fairly systematic counts of population, are quite old; but ancient governments resorted to them, not as a comprehensive inventory of population, but for particular purposes, some of which made the censuses unpopular and hence resulted in much evasion and in inadequate reporting. For example, many of the censuses in ancient times foreshadowed unpleasant events, being enumerations for the purpose of conscripting males for military purposes, for *corvées* for the construction of great public works, for levying higher taxes, or for seaching out owners of land and houses. Only adult males were included in some of these censuses. The Roman censuses were restricted to "citizens," an expanding category as citizenship rights were extended to various conquered peoples. Counts have also been based on such representative evidences of human beings as the number of hearths and chimneys. Even at the present time in many parts of the world censuses are sporadic and piecemeal, or lacking altogether. In general, they vary greatly in quality, coverage, and availability. Today the statistical records of population are well developed in the United States and most of Europe. But information is either lacking or very inadequate for many countries of Latin America, the Middle East, Asia, and Africa. The Bureau of the Census takes no position as to the accuracy of the recent Chinese Communist census. The Soviet Union has released no statistics regarding the number of its people since 1939.[3]

Throughout history, and even at present, world population figures have been based in considerable part on estimates. But these estimates are not entirely a matter of random guessing. Scientifically established data and principles regarding climatic conditions and resources of an area and an era, the productive ability of the people based on their degree and level of technical proficiency (the state of the "arts"), and their social organization enable us to determine approximate population-carrying capacity and gives us a fairly reliable basis for population estimates. Reasonable inferences can be drawn from various kinds of archeological evidence. Pre-modern censuses, properly oriented and evaluated, and data from ancient manuscripts provide fairly reliable information. Finally, increasing reliance can be placed upon modern statistical procedures of reporting, sampling, and estimating; these bring even more refined data to the demographer and close some of the gaps in our knowledge.

WORLD POPULATION INCREASE AND CULTURAL ADVANCE

The population trends from earliest human times to the present have been neither continuous nor uniform. For the world they have varied for peoples, areas, and eras. They have fluctuated widely not only from one region to another, but also at different times within a region, because of physical calamities—droughts and floods, famines and epidemics, climate cycles—and social disorders and breakdowns—rebellions, invasions, conquests, and wars. For the world and for certain regions there have been periods of stagnation, and of alternating increases and decreases.[4] Many peoples

---

[3] United Nations, *Determinants and Consequences*, p. 19; R. C. Cook.

[4] For example, Ta Chen's study of Chinese population indicates that it fluctuated widely between the Han period (206 B.C.-201 A.D.) and the beginning of the Manchu Empire (1644 A.D.). In fact, its history can be described as a

doubtless have disappeared entirely. The ecology and distribution of population has also varied greatly.[5]

In general, however, when we take the long view and smooth the world's population curve, we note an increase, very slow at first, but accelerating progressively until it reaches the explosive state during the last three centuries.

We will note below the very evident general relationship between cultural development, especially in technology and social organization, and population changes. Population increased or decreased as the means and techniques of existence rose or fell. For purposes of conciseness this relationship will be presented in the form of a chart. The left column indicates the course of world population increase by eras. In the right column is the approximate stage of cultural development of the era, particularly the level of technological-economic development. Before the early modern period the materials of both columns are approximations at best, and equally reliable experts might differ within rather broad limits both as to the approximate time of the population indicated and the parallel set of cultural developments.[6]

series of cycles of growth and decline. "Population in Modern China," *Am. Jour. Soc.,* 52 (July, 1946): Part 2. The demographic history of India also shows marked advances and regressions. Its population was about the same at the beginning of the modern era as it was 2000 years earlier. Cf. K. Davis, *The Population of India and Pakistan* (Princeton: Princeton Univ. Press, 1951), pp. 23-24. Similar variations in time are noted by competent students for many other areas. See United Nations, *Determinants and Consequences,* pp. 8-10. The uneven nature of population growth is well brought out in this United Nations report: "The imperfect information that is now available makes it evident that the numerical expansion of the human race has been sporadic. In every inhabited region of the earth there have been periods when the population grew at a comparatively rapid rate, and other periods when it remained nearly stationary or decreased. The cycles of growth have not been synchronous in different areas. Diversity in the patterns of economic and social change has been matched by a diversity of population trends." Pp. 19-20.

[5] For example, large aggregations of people lived in Asia, especially India and China, at a time when most of Europe and America had only few and widely scattered inhabitants. In pre-Columbian days all of North America may have had little more than a million persons as against some 200 million in 1953. Cf. W. S. and E. S. Woytinsky, *World Population and Production: Trends and Outlook* (New York: Twentieth Century Fund, 1953), pp. 33-34; United Nations, *Demographic Yearbook, 1953,* pp. 104-106.

[6] Our sources are Bennett, Borrie, Carr-Saunders, Huxley, Kroeber, Kuczynski, Pearl, Reed, Thompson (1944), Willcox, and the United Nations publications. For information on the early revolutions that created new techniques and

The long career of man on earth divides itself roughly into general epochs. Each successive age is a "new age" ushered in by a higher level of knowledge and of technical skill and attainment, providing a superior way of obtaining livelihood and resulting in an expansion of the economy and increasing complexity of the social and cultural organizaton. These changes produce a succession of "revolutions" in the broader sense. With each revolution comes a corresponding increase of the human species.

It might be pointed out that the innovations and advances usually originate only in certain areas, because of a favorable combination of geographical and cultural factors. Hence, they appear in different regions at different times, sometimes with a lapse of thousands of years. The ages are not absolute. However, as Childe points out,[7] in most instances at least the earlier ages followed each other in much the same order. But they did not begin or end simultaneously all over the world. Until recently there were remnants of the Paleolithic period in central Australia and the Arctic, and Neolithic features are still widespread in many of the more isolated and retarded areas of the earth. The actual location in time of particular innovations and discoveries before the modern period is at best a matter of rough approximation.

The revolutions of the period 1450-1950 had the effect of producing a demographic revolution. In fact, world population has mushroomed like the explosion of a hydrogen bomb. It has increased by nearly five times in the last three centuries. Different peoples and continents have been affected in varying degree and rate, but eventually all have shown marked increases in population.[8] The number of people actually added to the world's population in the half century between 1900 and 1950 (798 million) is about 60 per cent of the number added in the nine centuries between 1000 and 1900 A. D. (1,333 million), and this number is over

economies which furthered the increase of the human species, we will draw in part upon V. Gordon Childe, *Man Makes Himself* (London: Watts, 1937). See also his *What Happened in History* (Harmondsworth, Middlesex: Penguin, 1942), his *Social Evolution* (London: Watts, 1951), and the critical review of Childe by Robert Redfield, *The Primitive World and Its Transformation* (Ithaca: Cornell Univ. Press, 1953), pp. ix-x, 1-53.

[7] *Man Makes Himself*, p. 49.

[8] The demographic effects of these later and other time-related revolutions will be further examined in the next chapter.

TABLE 1

WORLD POPULATION GROWTH BY ERA
AND STAGE OF CULTURAL DEVELOPMENT

Population Estimates by Period. (Estimates very rough before 165 A. D.)	*Cultural, especially Technological-Economic, Situation Prevailing during Period.*
The Paleolithic period, constituting about 99 per cent of man's first million years.	Food supply restricted to that provided by nature, and acquired by hunting, fishing, and gathering.
Probably achieved a maximum of 5 million, with 2 or 3 million as the lower limit. (Huxley)	Only rude tools and weapons of chipped stone and wood.
Notable increase with retreat of the last great ice-cap about 25,000 B. C., after about 200,000 years of the Ice Age.	Transportation on foot.
	Toward the end of the period the revolutionary effects of the ability to make and control fire.
	Enabled men to spread to wider and often more productive regions.
	Protection against wild beasts.
	The cooking of heretofore indigestible substances, and corresponding expansion of food supply.
	Limited handicrafts.
Beginning about 8000 B.C. to 5500 B.C.	Organized hunting.
The beginning of the Neolithic period.	Greatly improved tools and weapons.
A population of 10 million with 5 million as the lower limit, and 20 million as the upper. (Huxley)	Great advances in agriculture and appearance of more scattered and shifting resident populations (villages). Due to:
	Marked improvement in spade-and-hoe agriculture.
	The "agricultural revolution," i.e., the ability to select and cultivate useful plants and domesticate certain a n i m a l s: cattle (6000 B.C.), sheep, goats, hogs, fowl (4900 B.C.). Used as food, and some used for power and transportation. ("Mixed farming.")

TABLE 1.—*Continued*

	Utilization of floods creating fresh soil and beginning of irrigation, and draining of marshes. Protection against floods by building dykes.
	Extension of handicrafts. Improved pottery. Spinning and weaving of cloth with animal and vegetable fibers.
	Improved storage facilities.
The two millennia preceding and following 3500 B.C. Population of about 30 million, with 20 million as the lower limit and 40 million as the absolute top limit. (Huxley)	The beginning of "civilization." Great advances in the domestication of plants and animals. Settled agriculture and expanded exchange of agricultural products. Some organization of the storage of food. The "metallurgical revolution" with the knowledge of the properties of metallic ores, the development of mining, and the discovery of smelting processes (the use of heat under blast). *The Bronze Age* (4000 B.C. and following): Advances in agriculture and trade providing a food surplus to support bodies of miners, smelters, and smiths. More durable and efficient tools and weapons. *The Iron Age* (1300 B.C. and following): Use of a widely distributed, a b u n d a n t, and easily worked mineral. Iron tools and weapons much superior to bronze. Cheap iron tools allowed cultivation of fresh lands, clearing of f o r e s t s, improved drainage and irrigation, etc.

TABLE 1.—*Continued*

	Wheeled vehicles (3500 B.C.) drawn by oxen, donkeys, and horses (Asia *c.* 3500 B.C.) and the revolution in land transport.
	Plank sailing vessels (Egypt, *c.* 3500 B.C and East Mediterranean *c.* 3000 B.C.) and vast improvement of fluvial and maritime transportation.
	Great extension of area of exchange of raw materials and finished products, and increase in mobility of men.
	Use of the inclined plane, the roller, and the lever.
	Increase in number and size of towns and cities, beginning in some areas as early as 5000 B.C. (the first "urban revolution"), due to surpluses of primary production and development of supply facilities; the expansion of secondary and tertiary production, the extension of trade, the engineering ability to construct and maintain cities, etc.
	Invention of writing and the keeping of accounts.
	The multiplication of various handicrafts, professions, and social classes.
	The development of somewhat extended, stable areal governments with centralized administration.
	Beginning of great "public works" based on slavery and the *corvée.*
1000 B.C. to 250 A.D. 100 million was certainly passed during this period. "The 200 million mark must have been passed during the early or middle Roman Empire." (Huxley)	The extension of agriculture to new areas and its intensification in older areas. The extension and improvement of manufactures and the extension of trade with greater conquests and empires.

TABLE 1.—*Continued*

According to Julius Beloch, as revised by Eduard Meyer, the population of the Roman Empire in Europe, Africa, and Asia totaled approximately 55 million about 30 A.D.

The Woytinskys state: "All in all, the population of the earth at the beginning of the Christian era may have been between 210 and 250 million, with the most populous areas in the Far East." (Huxley, p. 34)

Social-political-economic organization over ever wider areas (e.g., with the Roman Republic and Empire, the Alexandrian Empire and its successors in the Near and Middle East, the Han Empire in China).

Reduction of mortality in some parts of the world due to the reduction of intertribal wars.

250-1500 A.D.

Slow increase to around 300 million, but population often stationary and even declining.

In 1000 A.D. the population of the world was somewhere around 275 million. (Bennett, p. 7)

Dessication in Asia.

Vast migrations and chronic wars.

Barbarian invasions and "milling" of peoples in Europe.

Recurrent famines and pestilences (e.g., "Black Death" in Europe and in other parts of the world.)

By the seventeenth century data are more plentiful and more accurate. There are excellent world estimates from 1650 to 1950. (Population estimates as synthesized and summarized by Carr-Saunders, the UN publications, and Willcox.)

A.D.	Population in millions	
1650	545	The "Revolutions" (1450-1950).
1700	623	*The Geographic Explorations and Discoveries Beginning in the Late 1400's.*
1750	728	
1800	906	Access to rich unexplored lands and opening up of vast new lands as good as or better than those previously exploited.
1850	1,194	
1900	1,608	
1920	1,834	
1930	2,008	
1940	2,216	*The Commercial Revolution, Well under Way in the 1500's.*
1950	2,406	
1980*	3,523	Development of the modern corporation (capitalized joint-stock company) and modern finance, vast extension and acceleration of transcontinental commerce, and beginning of oceanic transportation and commerce.

* At 1946-48 rate of increase, according to UN estimate in 1951.

TABLE 1.—*Continued*

T h e Scientific - Technological - Economic Revolutions, beginning to be impressive 1750-1800 and continuing unabated ever since.

The revolution in medicine, hygiene, sanitation, and public health.
  Morbidity and mortality reduction and increasing control.
  C o n t r o l of endemic and epidemic diseases.
  Sanitary garbage and sewage disposal.
  Safeguarding water and food supplies.
  Private hygiene.
  Extension of therapeutic services.
  Hygienic housing.
  Organized catastrophe control.

The revolution in communication and transportation.
  Application of mineral power to transportation and communication.
  Wider information as to "good" places and cheaper and more efficient means of going to them.
  Faster and wider access to and exchange of raw and processed materials (including the diminution of effects of hunger and famine).
  Internal, international, and intercontinental m o b i l i t y of peoples—and the occupation of the "open spaces" of the earth.

The revolution in agriculture.
  Improved tillage and land management.
  Genetics: improved breeds of plants and animals.

TABLE 1.—*Continued*

	Commercial fertilizers.
	Mechanical power and efficient machinery.
	Fewer people needed to produce food, thus freeing the majority for other economic activities.
	Extension of cultivated areas.
	Soil conservation, drainage, and irrigation.
	World-wide commercial agriculture.
	The Industrial Revolution
	Increased division of labor and specialization of function.
	Development of new sources of power—water power, coal, steam, electricity.
	Efficient and labor-saving power for more efficient extraction of nature's wealth and manufacture of goods.
	The factory system and extension of secondary production beyond handicrafts.
	Astounding gain and diversification in human productive efficiency.
	Widespread conversion of unutilized and heretofore unknown resources into human utilities.
	Increase of wealth and creation of surplus wealth for capital development.
	Higher economic levels for all segments of the population.
	Application of scientific principles and engineering techniques to housing and to the development and physical maintenance of cities.

Figure 1
Historical Growth of World Population
by eras of Cultural Development

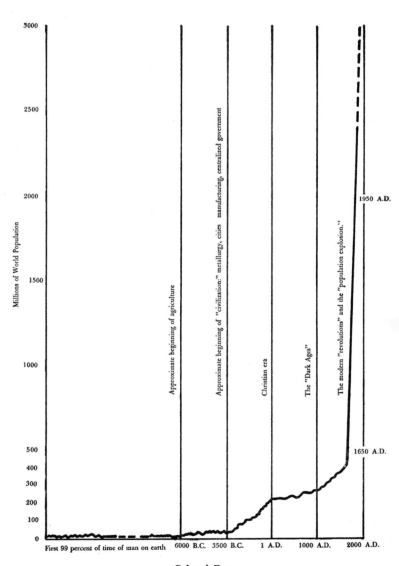

Cultural Eras

8. Suggested by the graph of L. Dudley Stamp,
Land for Tomorrow: The Underdeveloped World
(Bloomington, Indiana Univ. Press, 1952) p. 23

80 per cent of those added between 1000 and 1800 A. D. (899 million).

The United Nations Population Division points out that the *rate of increase* of world population has been accelerating during the last 300 years.[9]

Between 1650 and 1850, the estimates indicate an average annual increase of about 4 per thousand; between 1850 and 1900, they show an annual growth of 7 per thousand; and between 1900 and 1950, 9 per thousand. Although these are only rough approximations, they leave little room for doubt that the rate of growth has been substantially higher since 1850 than it ever was before.

TABLE 2

ESTIMATES OF THE POPULATION OF THE WORLD AND
OF THE CONTINENTS, 1650-1950[10]

CONTINENT	NUMERICAL DISTRIBUTION					
	1650	*1750*	*1800*	*1850*	*1900*	*1950*
	Millions					
Europe	100	140	187	266	401	541
North America (Canada and United States)	1	1.3	5.7	26	81	166
Central and South America	12	11.1	18.9	33	63	162
Oceania	2	2	2	2	6	13
Africa	100	95	90	95	120	198
Asia	330	479	602	749	937	1320
World Total	545	728	906	1171	1608	2400
	Percentage Distribution					
Europe	18.3	19.2	20.7	22.7	24.9	22.5
North America	0.2	0.1	0.7	2.3	5.1	6.9
Central and South America	2.2	1.5	2.1	2.8	3.9	6.8
Oceania	0.4	0.3	0.2	0.2	0.4	0.5
Africa	18.3	13.1	9.9	8.1	7.4	8.3
Asia	60.6	65.8	66.4	63.9	58.3	55.0
World Total	100.0	100.0	100.0	100.0	100.0	100.0

[9] *Population Bulletin*, No. 1, p. 2.

[10] From Landis, p. 21. As to sources and procedure, Landis states: "Data for all years except 1950 are from A. M. Carr-Saunders, *World Population* (Oxford: The Clarendon Press, 1936), p. 42. These figures are a revision of W. F. Willcox's data. Data for 1950 are from the United Nations, *Demographic Yearbook, 1951*, table 1A, p. 103. Population of the U.S.S.R. is assigned as three-fourths to Europe and one-fourth to Asia. North America includes only Canada and the United States."

It might be pointed out that a rate of 1 per cent per year causes a doubling of population in about 72 years, and a rate of 0.75 per cent, a doubling in about 92 years. On the other hand, a rate of 3.2 per cent, such as Mexico had for 1952, results in a doubling every 22 years.

The trends of population increase, however, have not been parallel in different parts of the world during the last three centuries. These variations are indicated in Table 2.

 The United Nations *Demographic Yearbook, 1954* changes its "mid-value" of total world population for 1950 to 2,455 million Depending upon a population estimate for the U.S.S.R. of 207 million, allocated three-fourths to Europe and one-fourth to Asia, its mid-value figures for 1953 are as follows:

TABLE 3

		Millions
Europe		559
North America		177
Central and South America		174
Oceania		14
Africa		208
Asia		1,415
	World Total	2,547

The crucial and sinister fact revealed in our examination of world population trends is this: thus far in man's history world population, and indeed that of every continent, in spite of temporary ups and downs, has persistently and consistently expanded into every gain resulting from scientific-technological-economic-humanistic advance. Man's spread over the globe and his almost continuous increase is parallel to, correlated with, and possibly caused by these developments. Every extension of communication has given him information about new good lands and new good ways of life. Every improvement in transportation has enabled him to spread to new habitable areas, gain access to new supplies, and conduct exchange over wider areas. Every material, technological, and social innovation making for improved production of wealth and an advance in social organization has resulted in more people. Every bit of knowledge and every procedure making for reduction of morbidity and mortality—every "death gain"—has been grasped and utilized, and has further augmented numbers.

DIFFERENTIAL POPULATION INCREASE WITH VARIANCE IN
CULTURAL MEANS

The means for this stupendous increase have not been diffused the world over at the same rate and have not become available at the same time. During the last 300 years the population of Asia increased about 400 per cent as compared with the world increase of 440 per cent, and the population of Africa, until recently the Dark Continent, increased only 98 per cent. By contrast, the increase of Europe and among the peoples of European descent overseas has been tremendous.

The revolutions (1450-1950) had their beginnings in Europe, and their fullest effects to date among Europeans and European peoples of the world. The expansion of Europe has been the dominating feature of modern history. This has expressed itself significantly in the extraordinary growth of European population both at home and overseas in physical environments very similar to Europe. In 1650 the population of Europe was considerably less than one-fifth of the population of the world. During the next three centuries European stocks spread mainly to the Americas and Oceania, where today they make up the preponderant portions of the population. As Figure 1 shows, Europeans at home increased from 100 to 541 million, or 541 per cent, while world population as a whole was increasing by 440 per cent. The population of Europe alone is now almost equal to that of the entire world three centuries ago. The population of the Americas and Oceania has increased from approximately 15 million to around 341 million, of which at least 200 million can be considered to be mainly of European descent. In other words, in 300 years Europeans and European-descended stocks increased by about 645 per cent. Now nearly one-third of the population of the world is European or predominantly of European descent. Will such increases occur in Asia and Africa as the Western-style technological-economic and social revolutions make their way among these peoples?

While, as just noted, the factors associated with the West's phenomenal upsurge were not present in the other regions of the earth during most of the last three centuries, the last half century has been marked by a considerable extension of these Western incitements to the other peoples. Concomitantly, all regions have experienced sharp, though not equal, increases in population during the last fifty years.

FUTURE WORLD POPULATION

Various persons and groups have hazarded the extension of human population growth curves into the future on the basis of recent and present trends, the resources of the earth, and man's techniques as applied to them—wars and other man-made calamities, of course, permitting. Notestein, after estimating component projections for the major regions of the earth, states:

> Summing the hypothetical figures for the year 2000, we have a world total of 3.3 billion. On the assumption of general order and the spread of modern techniques of production, the figure is probably conservative.[11]

According to the United Nations study,

> The world's people will increase by at least 500 million and perhaps by as much as 1,200 million during the period 1950 to 1980, in the absence of major wars or other calamities. On this basis the world population will rise from 2,400 million in 1950 to between 2, 976 million and 3,636 million in 1980.[12]

Harrison Brown makes certain plausible assumptions regarding the probable population performance of the demographically diverse regions of the earth. By applying these assumptions, he finds that the growth of the world population will be about as follows during the course of the next century:

TABLE 4

	Billions
1950	2.4
1975	3.4
2000	4.8
2025	6.0
2050	6.7

[11] F. W. Notestein, "Population—The Long View," in T. W. Schultz (ed.), *Food for the World* (Chicago: Univ. of Chicago Press, 1945), pp. 36-57.
[12] *Determinants and Consequences*, pp. 160-161.

He continues:

> It is difficult to visualize any reasonable combination of circum-
> stances not involving catastrophe which could lead to a popula-
> tion increase of less than twofold during the next century. It
> seems far more likely that we can expect the world to be popu-
> lated by at least 5 billion persons and perhaps 10 billion persons
> by the time another 100 years have passed.[13]

While there are divergences among these estimates of future
world population, they are unanimous in one respect: in the absence of serious hindrances, and unless population controls become
rather widely effective, the increase of world population in the very
near future is likely to be tremendous.

NATURAL INCREASE, BIRTH AND DEATH RATES, REGIONAL DIFFERENTIALS

A knowledge of fertility and mortality, that is, of births and
deaths and the relative rates of each, is the basic requisite for an
understanding of population growth. The natural increase (or decrease) is the margin or gap between births and deaths. For a
particular population at any given time, of course, there is also
the effect of migration in and out of its area. But the two determining variable elements in increase or decrease in the world are fertility and mortality. All the factors, whether geographical, biological, or sociological, must take effect through these.

Up to the beginning of the nineteenth century both birth rates
and death rates (the number of each per thousand of population
per year) must have been very high almost everywhere. Birth rates
probably ranged normally between 35 and 50, and were fairly constant year after year. Death rates ranged between 30 and 45, and
fluctuated greatly. Recurrently in certain areas death rates exceeded birth rates as a result of natural holocausts such as floods,
earthquakes, drought, volcanic disturbances, famines, and epidemics,
and of social catastrophes such as wars, rebellions, feuds, and deliberate extermination.

During the last century and a half, both birth rates and death
rates have changed very unevenly in the different parts of the world.
In countries where technological-economic advance has been most

[13] Pp. 98-99.

rapid, birth rates have shown a tendency to decline very considerably and at an accelerated, though also fluctuating, rate. Since
the mid-thirties, to be sure, some of these countries have experienced
an increased fertility. There is good reason, however, for thinking
that this may be a temporary phenomenon occasioned by the de-
ferment of marriages and births during the depression of the thirties
and during the war. It is also due in part to the unprecedented
post-war full employment and economic prosperity of all social
classes, and, in some cases, to the easing of life through foreign
financial and technical assistance. In western Europe and among
west European stocks elsewhere birth rates have declined as much
as one-half during the last century and a half, though at present
they stand at two-thirds to three-fourths of what they were. In
the more primitive and the underdeveloped peasant societies, where
the penetration of Western civilization has been more limited, birth
rates are generally high and relatively rigid. The Population Commission of the United Nations indicates that according to available
information present birth rates in most of Asia, Africa, and Latin
America are generally somewhat higher than those of western
Europe around 1800.[14] Moreover, in some instances they may
actually have expanded in recent times with the slight improvement
of the physical conditions of life. Asian, African, and most of the
Latin American birth rates, if they fall, will fall slowly for reasons
to be noted in later chapters.

The decline of the death rate during the last century and a
half, though at first slow and gradual, has been more pronounced
and more universal and has shown great flexibility and great
responsiveness to every "death gain." In the Western countries it
has declined to what appears to be its lowest possible point because
of the increasing proportion of the aged and the rising average age
of the population. In general, this decline has been great enough
not only to compensate for the loss in fertility, but also to accelerate
the rate of natural increase. Mortality conditions in much of Asia
and Africa and in some areas of Latin America at present are
probably similar to those which prevailed in western Europe 200

[14] *Findings of Studies on the Relationships between Population Trends and
Economic and Social Factors.* Part Three: Summary of Principle Findings Relevant to Economic Development of Under-Developed Areas (E/C N. 9/55/Add.
2, 2 May 1950) , p. 8.

years ago. In these other parts of the world, while the death rates
are still high, they also seem to be declining and in an unprecedented manner, for reasons to be examined later. The comparative situation as to birth rates and death rates for the different
regions of the world is brought out in the following table prepared
by the United Nations.[15]

TABLE 5

ESTIMATED VITAL RATES FOR THE REGIONS OF THE WORLD
1936-1938 AND 1946-1948

| REGIONS | Rate per thousand population | | | | | |
| | 1936–1938 | | | 1946–1948 | | |
	BIRTHS	DEATHS	NATURAL INCREASE	BIRTHS	DEATHS	NATURAL INCREASE
World Total	34–38	24–27	8–13	35–37	22–25	11–14
Africa	40–45	30–35	7–13	40–45	25–30	12–18
America						
North of Rio Grande	17	11	6	25	10	15
South of Rio Grande	45–45	20–25	17–23	40	17	23
Asia (exclusive of Asiatic U.S.S.R.)						
Near East	40–45	30–30	7–13	40–45	30–35	7–13
South-central Asia	40–45	30–35	7–13	40–45	25–30	12–18
Japan	28	17	11	31	15	16
Remaining Far East	40–45	30–35	7–13	40–45	30–35	7–13
Europe and Asiatic U.S.S.R.						
Northwest-central Europe	17	13	4	19	12	7
Southern Europe	23	16	7	23	12	11
Eastern Europe and Asiatic U.S.S.R.	30–40	17–21	11–15	28	18	10
Oceania	20	11	9	28	12	16

On the basis of the table it will be noted that the birth rates of
1946-1948 were low in northwest-central Europe (with a range of
19 to 23 per thousand) and somewhat higher in southern and eastern
Europe, the United States and Canada, and Australia and New
Zealand (with a range of 23 to 25). They were considerably higher

[15] *Population Bulletin,* Table III, p. 3. See also United Nations, *Preliminary
Report on the World Social Situation,* pp. 6-17, for vital rates for the world
and for many selected and regionally distributed countries.

in Japan (31) and exceedingly high in Latin America and the agrarian countries of the Orient (40 to 45). The regions of lowest mortality were America north of the Rio Grande, northwest-central and southern Europe, and Oceania, wtih death rates in the range of 10 to 12 per thousand. Latin America, eastern Europe, and Japan had intermediate mortality (with a range of 15 to 18 per thousand). Asia and Africa had the highest rates; in most areas of these continents the death rate ranged upward from 25 to as high as 35 per thousand.

It may be pointed out that until about 150 years ago in the Western world, fluctuations in over-all economic and social well-being were reflected in oscillations of the death rate, the birth rate remaining constantly high. Now death rates remain relatively constant, but birth rates are extremely sensitive barometers of economic and social change. In a goodly portion of the rest of the world today, the Western situation of 150 years ago still largely prevails.

In general, however, the world over, mortality has tended to decline more rapidly than fertility; the spread between birth rates and death rates has been becoming greater. The tremendous expansion of population, therefore, must be attributed to declining death rates as the major cause. Over the last century and a half, among the various countries, death rates generally have fallen to about one-half of what they were, and in some cases to one-third. Lowered mortality has been highly attractive, and one of the most readily exportable and eagerly accepted of all technological products.

A widespread conclusion is that if fertility declines do occur in the more underdeveloped areas, it is nearly certain that they will lag behind the declines in mortality, surely in the initial stages of technical-economic development and probably for a very considerable period of time.

The ever-greater number of stomachs that need to be filled as the result of annual world population increase can best be realized, and located, in the estimated yearly natural increase expressed in absolute figures. This the United Nations Department of Social Affairs has done for around 1947.[16]

---

[16] *Preliminary Report,* p. 18.

TABLE 6

ESTIMATED YEARLY NATURAL INCREASE IN
ABSOLUTE FIGURES, AROUND 1947

	Millions
World	26–32
Africa	2.5–3
America	
North America	2.3
Latin America	3.5
Asia	12–18
Europe	5.3
Oceania	0.2

In the next two chapters we will examine in some detail the conditions and factors which appear to have a bearing upon these unprecedented changes in fertility and mortality and upon the appearance of these marked regional differentials.

BIBLIOGRAPHY

BATES, MARSTON. *The Prevalence of People.* New York: Scribners, 1955. Pp. 9-27.

BENNETT, M. K. *The World's Food: A Study of the Interrelations of World Populations, National Diets, and Food Potentials.* New York: Harpers, 1954. Pp. 3-22.

BLIVEN, BRUCE. *Preview for Tomorrow: The Unfinished Business of Science.* New York: Knopf, 1953. Pp. 3-35.

BORRIE, W. D. *Population Trends and Policies.* Sydney: Australian Pub. Co., 1948. Pp. 1-30.

BROWN, HARRISON. *The Challenge of Man's Future.* New York: Viking, 1954. Pp. 3-45, 68-86.

CARR-SAUNDERS, A. M. *World Population.* Oxford: Clarendon Press, 1936. Pp. 1-45.

COOK, R. C. "World Population Round-Up." *Population Bull.* 10 (Jan., 1954): 1-9.

COOK, S. F. "Survivorship in Aboriginal Populations." *Human Biol.* 19 (Feb., 1947) : 83-89.

DAVIS, KINGSLEY. "The World Demographic Transition." *Annals Am. Acad. Pol. & Soc. Sci.,* 237 (Jan., 1945): 1-11.

FAWCETT, C. B. "The Numbers and Distribution of Mankind: A Study in Comparative Civilization." *Scientific Monthly,* 64 (May, 1947) : 389-396.

JEFFERSON, M. "Distribution of the World's City Folk." *Geog. Rev.,* 31 (July, 1931): 446-465.

HAUSER, PHILIP M. "World Population Trends." *Soc. & Soc. Res.,* 39 (Nov.-Dec., 1954). 73-80.

HENSHAW, P. S. *Adaptive Human Fertility.* New York: McGraw-Hill, 1955. Pp. 24-56.

HUXLEY, JULIAN. "Population and Human Destiny." *Harper's* 201 (Sept., 1950): 38-46; or *World Rev.,* Jan., 1950: 7-14.

KROEBER, A. L. *Anthropology.* New York: Harcourt Brace, 1948. Pp. 625-732.

KUCZYNSKI, R. R. "Population: History and Statistics." *Encyc. Soc. Sci.*, New York: Macmillan, 1934. Vol. 12, pp. 240-248.

LANDIS, P. H. *Population Problems: A Cultural Interpretation* (2nd ed. by P. K. Hatt) . New York: American Book, 1954. Pp. 18-30.

LORIMER, FRANK, *et al.* "Capacity for Procreation and Levels of Fertility," in *Culture and Human Fertility: A Study of the Relation of Cultural Conditions to Fertility in Non-industrial and Transitional Societies.* Paris: UNESCO (New York: Columbia Univ. Press), 1955. Chap. I, pp. 22-57.

ORR, SIR JOHN BOYD. *The White Man's Dilemma.* London: Allen & Unwin, 1953. Pp. 52-60.

OSBORN, FAIRFIELD. *The Limits of the Earth.* Boston: Little, Brown, 1953. Pp. 207-219.

PEARL, R. S. *The Natural History of Population.* New York: Oxford Univ. Press, 1939.

PEARSON, S. V. *The Growth and Distribution of Population.* London: Allen & Unwin, 1935.

Population Bulletin (Population Reference Bureau, Washington): "Speculations in Population Growth," 4 (May, 1948) : 9-14; "The Speed-Up in Population Growth," 8 (June, 1952): 9-13; "World Population Round-Up," 10 (Jan., 1954) : 1-9; "A New Science Emerges," 10 (July, 1954): 57-68.

REED, S. W."World Population Trends," in Ralph Linton (ed.), *Most of the World: The Peoples of Africa, Latin America, and the East Today.* New York: Columbia Univ. Press, 1949. Pp. 94-155, esp. pp. 94-112.

THOMPSON, W. S. *Plenty of People.* Lancaster, Pa.: Jacques Cattell Press, 1944. Pp. 1-24.

—————. "Population." *Scientific American,* 182 (Feb., 1950): 11-15.

UNITED NATIONS, Department of Social Affairs. *Preliminary Report on the World Social Situation.* New York, 1952. Pp. 5-21.

—————, Department of Social Affairs. *World Population Trends, 1920-1947.* New York, 1949.

—————, Population Division, Department of Social Affairs. *The Determinants and Consequences of Population Trends: A Summary of the Findings of Studies on the Relationships between Population Changes and Economic and Social Conditions* (Population Studies, No. 17). New York, 1953. Chap II, "Historical Outline of World Population Growth," pp. 5-20; Chap. IV, "Economic and Social Factors Affecting Mortality," pp. 47-70; Chap. V, "Economic and Social Factors Affecting Fertlity," pp. 71-97.

—————, Population Division, Department of Social Affairs. *Population Bulletin,* No. 1 (Dec., 1951). New York, 1952.

UNITED STATES DEPARTMENT OF COMMERCE, *Population Estimates and Forecasts for Selected Countries: January 1, 1950 to 1954* (Series P-91, No. 1). March 16, 1953.

WILLCOX, W. F. *Studies in American Demography.* Ithaca: Cornell Univ. Press, 1940. Pp. 22-51.

WOLFE, A. B. "Fecundity and Fertility of Early Man." *Human Biol.,* 5 (Feb., 1953) : 36-39.

WOYTINSKY, W. S. and E. S. *World Population and Production: Trends and Outlook.* New York: Twentieth Century Fund, 1953. Pp. 32-49, 241-264.

3

The Modernization Pattern
and Modern Demographic Balance

Thus far we have noted the stupendous increase of the world's population, especially in very recent times, and the great variations in fertility and mortality control in the different areas of the globe. In the present chapter an attempt will be made to spell out the conditions and the man-made, Western-originated socio-cultural factors invariably closely associated with, and probably actually responsible for, these demographic changes and trends. An understanding of these factors, and of their possible universal applicability, is imperative since they have been directly related to the achievement of the physiologically and humanely more economical population balance (between births and deaths) in the Western world. They certainly will be involved more and more, not only in the solution of the population problems, but also in the political-military problems that need to be alleviated among the writhing, grinding, poverty-striken peoples that make up the population of most of the rest of the world.

THE REVOLUTIONS THAT HAVE AFFECTED THE DEMOGRAPHIC REVOLUTION

As a background we need to review briefly the nature and effects of the revolutions indicated in the schematic presentation of the preceding chapter, as well as certain other ones occurring since 1450. While all these more recent revolutions started in Europe and have had their most marked effects to date among European and European-descended peoples, the knowledge of them and their influence has spread to every nook and cranny of the world in some degree, in varying tempo, and with perceptible though often dissimilar effects. Present indications are that this process will continue with ever greater acceleration and intensification. Many of the characteristic elements of these revolutions are highly contagious upon contact and are looked upon as "great goods."

The Renaissance, long in gestation, but well under way in the fifteenth century, is one of these revolutions. It was far more than a revival of "classical" Graeco-Roman civilization—its philosophy, usages, and manners. Men struck out along new paths of thought and action. While the humanistic and scientific phases cannot be divorced, in each, distinctive new insights were gained and rich new contributions to freer, larger living were made.

The humanistic phase was characterized by intellectual curiosity and exploration. The humanists were not satisfied with ancient knowledge; they wanted to know *why* things are so; they demanded proofs or reasonable explanations. Their investigations led them into new paths, to discovery of new truths regarding the physical universe and the nature of man and his works. They came to new conclusions as to his destiny. It was a critical age; men questioned ancient and accepted axioms and institutions. There was an efflorescence of the spirit and a new freedom of thought as men emancipated themselves from dogmatism, determinism, and sacerdotalism. The movement was characterized by intense individualism, in sharp contrast to medieval devotion to fixed social position and institutional controls; Renaissance men had a keen appreciation for the worth of the individual; they strove for personal development, prestige, and social advancement. People did not feel that they were forced to accept the notion of a fixed, pre-established "fate" or destiny. They were less concerned with future penalties and rewards, seeking full satisfaction in this world, here and now. A humanitarianism developed; there were reformist tendencies in the criticism and correction of social evils, and a reaching out for enhanced well-being; men propounded Utopias with blueprints of how these luminous anticipations were to come into being.

The scientific phase was much more than an appropriation and improvement of the compass, maps, gunpowder, paper, and printing from China. The scientific spirit reached new levels. Factual knowledge was achieved through objectivity, induction and experimentation. A new understanding of nature and man and society came into being; men developed ways of manipulating and, in a measure, of controlling nature. The urge to know led to new scientific discoveries, to new inventions along mechanical lines, and to geographical explorations. Superstition and magic were giving way to scientific facts and techniques, enhancing the knowledge of morphology and physiology and of the treatment of the ills of the human body. Galileo and others developed a new physics; Copernicus demonstrated the sobering reality of a heliocentric instead of a geocentric universe. Astrology gave way to astronomy and alchemy to chemistry.

The humanistic developments prepared the way for, and then gave an impetus to, religious reform movements that culminated in several countries in the Protestant Reformation. Aside from its schismatic results, the Reformation had definite effects in the way of breaking away from authoritarian dogmas and interpretations; it emphasized individual thinking and salvation; it was a revolt against clerical tutelage and against the dominance of political by ecclesiastical institutions.

The geographic explorations and discoveries of the sixteenth century were a direct result of the scientific phase of the Renaissance. They were made possible by the compass, the astrolobe, the quadrant and sextant, better maps, and the Copernican knowledge of the nature of the earth. The discovery of the route to India and to the whole Pacific area around the Cape of Good Hope and the discovery of the great American Continents brought the world well on the way to being physically one. There was access to vast new and good lands. Intercontinental trade in goods was expanded by means of cheaper oceanic transportation as compared with expensive overland trade. Europeans spread to the Americas and to many of the newly discovered areas as extenders of European empires and exploiters of the resources and the indigenous peoples. The very exploitation, even the slave traffic involving these peoples made for the diffusion of European ways and things.

The economic effects of the Geographic Revolution gave new impetus to the Commercial Revolution, which was well under way in the sixteenth century. The European traders and bankers were prosperous as the result of the vast extension of both transcontinental and oceanic transportation and the resultant increase of both exports and imports. Capital accumulated for further expansion. Manufactures increased with the expenditures of wealthy individuals and the Mercantilist-Kameralist governments. As the guild system declined, the modern capitalist system arose. There was a switch from barter to money economy. The modern limited-liability corporation in banking, mining, and trade, and the credit system appeared. While most of these institutions had already existed in some form among the great ancient civilizations, they now took on a new efficiency and universality. All this led to a search for colonies, for raw materials, for cheap labor, and for markets. People and products were to be poured through each other; competition and conflict were to burgeon everywhere.

The English revolutions of the seventeenth century, the American and French revolutions, and the parallel eighteenth-century "Enlightenment" in social thinking, along with great democratic developments of the nineteenth century in the rest of Europe and in the Americas, added further revolutionary elements that were to reverberate around the world. The seminal democratic notions inherent in the bills of rights and the declarations of the rights of man—Liberty, Equality, and Fraternity—were planted, began to germinate and to spread. The explosive notion that one man was as good as another began to spread from class to class and from people to people. A new importance attached to the individual: to his dignity, uniqueness, self-determination, initiative, health, welfare, and advancement. Social liberty came into being; there was the equal freedom and right of each man to think for himself, the privilege to experiment and behave according to his own conception of expediency, to act on his own. Impetus was given to the breakdown of the rigid systems of social stratification and to the movement toward "open class" systems. Institutions were *for* men, and not the reverse. The state began to be seen as of, for, and by the people, and a great upsurge of representative government developed. There was the rise of "secularism"—what is expedient and profitable in the light of the present situation— as against the "sacred"—the ancient traditional beliefs and values and the customary ways. Man came to be viewed as master of his own destiny, in fact, as assuming responsibility for it and bringing about continual progress. Today everyone is committed to some interpreta-tion of democracy; even the Communist regimes pay lip service to it and have to make "democratic" gestures to their subjugated masses.

Concomitant with these later revolutions came the great scientific advance of the seventeenth, eighteenth, and later centuries, such as the discoveries of Kepler, Newton, Franklin, Boyle, Harvey, and Jenner, the new stress laid on experimentation, the development of investigative and constructive technics and techniques, and the amazing body of new facts and principles. These advances led to the rapid development of new technologies, which soon had revolu-tionary significance. Notable was the vast progress in medicine, hygiene, sanitation, and public health, the revolution in communi-cation and transportation due to electricity and steam, the revolu-tion in agriculture, and especially the Industrial Revolution.

It can be pointed out, however, that, like the features of the other revolutions, the new tools and machines, the new technical procedures, and the new ways of life inevitably related to them have high diffusional capacity and are in varying degree and with varying selection of elements to be found almost everywhere in the world today. Machines have almost become the mark of modern "civilization." Furthermore, the very development of technology depends in considerable measure upon emancipation from super-stitions, from many sanctified ideas, beliefs, and values, from ancient class and other power systems. Modernization is interrelated with freedom of thought, freedom of science, and freedom of action. If the people generally do not have these freedoms, as in totalitarian regimes, special individuals and groups must exercise these freedoms for them in a paternalistic manner if at least the material advan-tages of modernization are to be developed among them. Finally, the combination of intellectual and material revolutions of recent centuries has resulted in the appearance of the concept of altering human existence by deliberate intention and design.

Since these revolutions had their main inception in Europe and their early and main diffusion and effects among European peoples, these peoples "swarmed" before any others. They swarmed first geo-graphically, expanding into far areas; first politically, in conquest and colonization; first scientifically, technologically, and economical-ly, in life-saving, production, and the increase of wealth; first demo-

cratically, with rights and freedoms and aspirations; first ideo-
logically, in secularization and rationalization; and first demographically, in their numbers.

The effect of the revolutions just examined was a process of
technological, economic, social-organizational, social-psychological,
and spiritual change which will be here referred to as "modernization." The process, realistically and comprehensively viewed, involves more than is included in the widely used terms "industrialization" or "industrialization-urbanization," though these are basic
processes. Involved also are an array of political, psychological, and
sociological innovations and their effects. The operation of "modernization" among a people means that they are in process of transition from what the anthropologists and sociologists refer to as a
"folk," or "folk-agrarian," to a "modern" society.

From one-half to two-thirds of the people of the world still live
in predominantly folk societies. The economies of these societies
are agrarian, in some instances with as high as 90 per cent of the
population engaged in agriculture—in most cases mainly subsistence
agriculture. What manufacturing exists largely takes the form of
village handicrafts. The factory system and its correlates vary in
degree of development among these peoples; most of them are still
in the incipient stages, and the factories are confined mainly to the
large cities. Capital equipment is limited, and for most of the
productive operations consists largely of fairly simple tools and
implements. The exchange of the vast village populations occurs
largely by means of barter, without extensive use of money, though
money is necessary among them for the payment of taxes and fees.
The great bulk of the population is illiterate. Communication is
largely of the intimate face-to-face variety. Life is lived mainly
within the self-sufficient community, and communities are relatively isolated. The population of the communities is homogeneous, a
strong sense of solidarity pervailing among the members. The "extended" family is the basic unit of production, and, with the village,
is the basic unit of social organization as well. There is very little
mobility, either physical or social. These are essentially "sacred"
societies in the sense that behavior is dominated by ancient, sanctified values, traditions, and customs; social control is largely through

superstitions, folkways, and mores, and is enforced by informal but extremely effective community opinion and sanctions.

Such societies are archaic, with long-standing, deeply rooted culture systems; they are also static and change-resistant, especially along certain lines.[1] The political structures vary greatly; some are still tribal or village societies with a remote colonial "father" government collecting taxes and exercising other occasional influence; others are mainly feudal in character. Where there is independent and centralized government, it is usually a rather new experience for the people. If it is democratic, it is groping and hesitant. Much of the new political organization, because of lack of political sophistication among the people, is rather totalitarian in nature.

The modernization pattern of societal change rests upon advances in science and technology and includes the increasing use of power and machines in production and transportation, the factory system and urbanization, the increase of wealth and income, and the elevation of the level of economic life. But it involves also a profound modification of the social psychology and the ethos of a people, an ideological shift reflected in new types of attitudes, interests, beliefs, and values and affecting the policies and programs of endeavor of the people. These changes in turn affect not only their economic but also their familial, political, educational, and religious institutions, bringing marked changes in the structures and functions of the entire social system. All these changes blend together to produce a distinctly modern way of life.

Along technical-economic lines the pattern, of course, involves the use of physical power derived from coal, oil, natural gas, or hydroelectric energy. It is used in all stages of production to drive machines and appliances and in transportation. The machines used in large-scale secondary production are grouped in assembly lines. The production processes require special buildings and other expensive and complicated capital equipment, division of labor, technical specialization of function, increase of output per worker, the diversification of output of the factory system, the concentration of labor at the points of primary and secondary production and of transportation, commercial and marketing operations (mainly in

[1] See Chap. VI, p. 129.

large towns, cities, and metropolitan areas), an elaborate financial
and credit system with the operating funds drawn from a multiplicity of risk-taking contributors, and usually the manufacturing,
transporting, marketing, financing, and credit activities conducted
by corporate organizations. Economic and many other relations are
of a contractual rather than a customary nature. Monetary considerations come to prevail in almost every department of life. In
agriculture there is also increasing mechanization and labor-saving,
and consequently the release of rural labor for urban pursuits and
an increasing agricultural productivity per man-hour.

This brings various changes in the way of life of the people. The
improvement of all productive techniques means an increase in per-
capita wealth and income, a rise in the level of living, and some
reduction of worry regarding the bare necessities of existence. In
the western world, and here and there elsewhere, when wealth and
income have reached the point of adequacy, there has been evidence
of the operation of the standard-of-living factor. Attention shifts
from production and bare subsistence to varieties and qualities of
consumption—"embroidered" consumption. There is an increasing
desire for (1) greater material comforts and conveniences, especially
in the way of housing, living conditions, and labor-saving and com-
fort-enhancing appliances; (2) leisure and recreation; (3) better
health and diet and cleanliness; (4) educational and "cultural"
opportunities and satisfactions; (5) social, economic and political
opportunity; (6) the satisfactions flowing from social achievement;
(7) better care of children and greater opportunity for child development; (8) the satisfactions flowing from the opportunities of
wealth ("conspicuous display" in consumption); and (9) higher
social status, involving the development of ambition and social
striving.

In the shift from primary agricultural and simple handicraft
pursuits to manufacturing, merchandising, finance and marketing,
and personal and professional services, there is a proliferation of
occupations requiring special kinds of knowledge and skill. This
array of occupations, falling along a scale of values, creates a vast
diversity of interests. In addition to the occupations, there are innumerable ways of acting to meet needs and survive in a mechanized
society—telephoning, driving a car, operating household gadgets,
for instance. The occupations and these other ways Odum ap-

propriately calls "technic-ways, . . . the ways of a technological civilization . . . basic to technological culture." [2]

Part of the modernization process is the development of more and better education. This is absolutely essential if the increasingly complex technological system, in all its economic, political, and social phases, is to be efficient, and if the individual is to be successful in it. But it also means more information and a greater awareness of social conditions and opportunities and access to new values and aids for more and more of the population. Usually education is accompanied by the restriction of child labor and concomitant compulsory school attendance at higher ages.

Urbanization, or the movement of population from rural areas and villages to metropolitan areas and the concentration of population in cities, is correlated with industrialization. It is in the cities that the very great bulk of the multiple activities which characterize an industrial civilization take place. The cities also become the center of "cultural" activities (in the narrower sense) and of mass communication. As an increasing proportion of the population lives under urban conditions, urban ways of life and interests tend to pervade the whole civilization. In the cities the population is heterogeneous, often as to race and nationality, as well as in cultural origins and geographic backgrounds. Human relationships are increasingly impersonal, anonymous, superficial, transitory, formal, and contractual. People participate less and less in local, intimate, neighborhood groups; in fact, they are alienated from them, being attracted to segmental, special-interest groups or to large, diffuse secondary groups. Individuals and families tend to be isolated from the kin group. There is both *individualization,* that is, the freeing of the individual from many of the pressures of the clan, the local community, and other traditional authority, and *individuation,* or the tendency to develop the unique capacities and potentialities of each individual. There is a shift from a family-centered to an individual-centered culture correlated with a new kind of motivation. Personal interests and aspirations are important factors in individual life. As the Germans put it: "Stadtluft macht frei!" There is also a lack of cultural unity in the urbanized society; but an overall standardization of externals comes about through the agencies

[2] Odum.

of mass communication. People abide by easily comprehended symbols mainly taking the form of overt patterns of behavior in speech, dress, and recreation. In urbanized, in contrast to agrarian, societies the family, while retaining its lessened reproductive functions, ceases to be the basic productive unit and operates mainly as a consumption unit.

With increasing modernization the "sacred" traditions, customs, and proprieties, and the sanctions of behavior resting on conservative mores give way to utilitarian and rationalistic considerations. Not only in industry and commerce, but also in personal and family behavior, there is a strict and systematic adaptation of means to the achievement of monetary, prestige, or efficiency ends. There is a great increase in spatial mobility. This is possible through communication, which provides knowledge of alternative opportunities elsewhere, and to the availability of far-reaching, efficient, cheap, and rapid means of transportation. This mobility is necessary because of the constant variation of economic and social opportunities from place to place, of which people often must avail themselves. This means less locational stability and less community rootage of reputation and status. Social mobility comes to be a characteristic phenomenon as people attempt to achieve higher positions in the social scale by utilizing educational and occupational opportunities, exercising talent, and conspicuously displaying wealth, leisure, and other prestigeful cultural acquisitions and activities. This is encouraged by lessening rigidity of the stratification system of the society and the development for most population elements of an "open-class" system. In general, because of the higher levels of literacy, physical and social mobility, the weakening of clan and local community ties and pressures, individualization, anonymity, cosmopolitanism, and utilitarian emphasis, life becomes secularized. People become reluctant to accept many things on traditional faith or authority; the sanction for much action rests on personal tastes, momentary perferences, and sophisticated viewpoints. Formal, deliberately organized social control affects more and more of the social behavior of individuals, instead of the age-old informal, traditional, primary group controls.

An efficient political system operating over the entire societal area must develop. Rebellion and serious dissension cannot be permitted. Transportation, communication, the exploitation of resources, and the conduct of all productive, monetary, financing, and marketing agencies must be regulated; the security and safe internal movement of the people must be assured. As the formal political agencies regulate the action of the people, the "state-ways," along with the "technic-ways," come to supplant the folkways.

Modernization this side of the Iron Curtain is correlated and interdependent with democracy. Behind the Iron Curtain modernization to the extent of its technological and economic features seems to be moving apace by means of the absolutistic and forceful manipulation of persons and organizations, but it is a truncated modernization. For a society to operate efficiently and enduringly, with full realization of its individual and social potentialities, most people free to observe and choose conclude that there must be general freedoms (social, intellectual, religious), equality of opportunity, guarantee of civil rights, and government of, for, and by the people. Modernized society works best when individuals are self-acting, self-developing, self-determining, self-governing; when there is free will, free choice, free movement, free responsibility; when people are free to initiate, experiment, and invent; when people participate, mutually and reciprocally, according to freely formed aims and aspirations and the freely revised institutions of their society; when individuals act as responsible citizens, and not as lethargic or reluctant subjects. There must also be a free system of social selection of talented personnel, the widespread voluntary utilization of learning, research, and all manner of utilitarian practices, and the critical weighing of prevailing values, facts, and principles.

Finally, with scientific and technological development, there come, very soon, medical and sanitary advances which bring new controls over the ravaging diseases, both endemic and epidemic, and engineering advances which utilize and enhance the physical environment for the life-saving and death-controlling of the people.

In general, modernization produces an economy and correlated ways of life which are economically and culturally productive and expansive, tending toward higher levels of living and the development of higher standards of aspiration and achievement. These standards move downward and outward from person to person, class to class, race to race, nation to nation, continent to continent. Modernized societies, and societies on the way to modernization, are innovative, fluid, dynamic, and ever-different. They are characterized by changes in techniques and equipment, changes in production, trade, and consumption, changes in societal structure and operation, changes in all their institutions, changes in attitudes, values, and motivations, and changes in population composition as the continual sorting and re-sorting of population proceed.

THE DEMOGRAPHIC EFFECTS OF MODERNIZATION

The tremendous increase in population in the last three centuries suggests profound changes in the circumstances governing rates of growth. The modernization process appears to be the key factor, or it presents a combination of factors, affecting both death rates and birth rates. It seems to be involved in effecting the more economical and humane "modern" demographic balance in those countries where it is well advanced, and, because of its limited and partial development in most of the world, it is liable to bring about the vast population increase among peoples least capable of coping with this increase. We will examine its immediate and long-range effects on death rates and birth rates.

A change in almost any social phenomenon is the result of changes in several variables rather than in a single one. It should be pointed out, therefore, that population change due to variations in births and deaths is always the result of a combination of interdependent variables. Physical and biological forces and processes are always the ultimate factors in achieving the "elemental balance"; but men have seldom been completely at the mercy of these elemental factors; they have sidestepped them or controlled them in various ways. Human population changes are always bound up, in cause-and-effect relations, with technological, social-economic, psychological, political and ideological factors. In the great majority of instances the gains and the dilemmas are created by men.

THE EFFECT ON DEATH RATES

The decline of death rates is the first perceptible, and the most quickly, persistently, and consistently operative demographic effect. Even with incipient modernization the death rates begin to lose some of the highly fluctuating tendencies which they have in primitive and underdeveloped societies. As modernization proceeds, this tendency toward stabilization continues.

As already pointed out, life-saving is a universal desire supported by almost all value systems. Even in primitive societies the efforts of Westerners to limit native mortality are far more generally accepted than their efforts to limit fertility. There can be considerable reduction of mortality without individual or family intelligence, knowledge, or inclination. The means can be applied with little or no interference in the daily ways of life of the people. Such changes as are required do not conflict with established social attitudes, values and customs. The technical means are relatively cheap and apply mainly to the impersonal and external aspects of life. Deaths can be greatly reduced by governmental control of water supply and waste disposal, by the control of noxious and infectious insects, bacteria, germs, or animals which cause or transmit disease, and by governmental action in the improvement of transportation and the distribution of food to areas threatened with famine. Measures such as these do not require much cooperation on the part of the individual or community beneficiaries.

Several features of the modernization pattern have been particularly potent in reducing deaths.

Medical science, in all its departments and various applications, has been a primary factor. The increasing knowledge of the cause and control of disease, the expansion of public health facilities making for community sanitation, such as refuse removal and sewage disposal, the protection and purification of water supplies, and more effective drainage have greatly reduced deaths caused by both endemic and epidemic diseases. As a result of improvements in disease control and advances in sanitation, mortality from typhus cholera, bubonic plague, smallpox, dysentery, diarrhea, and enteritis have declined to a small fraction of former levels. In the highly modernized societies the frightful plagues of history are almost unknown. An interest in personal hygiene also appears; personal cleanliness is enhanced through the availability of water and soap. Medical progress, as it affects both community and private action, has been cheaper and easier to accomplish among underdeveloped peoples than any other aspect of modern technology.

Even at an early stage of modernization there are improvements in agriculture and agricultural enginering (for example, irrigation), as well as some manufacturing itself, which increase the quantity and improve the quality of food, thus reducing the likelihood of famine. The increased production of crops for commerce, that is, for export, also operates as a local reserve against bad times.

Superior living facilities, such as eradication of rural and urban slums, and the provision of better housing and clothing, mean protection against physical hardships, and reduce the susceptibility to disease.

Improved facilities for transportation, storage, and distribution of foodstuffs tend to eliminate local famines.

The improved productivity provides a surplus of wealth that can be devoted to public uses, not only to public health controls, but also to popular education, to better medical training and research, and to provision of hospital systems.

The influence of various social reforms becomes effective in the course of modernization. Public health laws are enacted and state health agencies are established following surveys of health and sanitation. Regulations governing the work of all, but especially that of children and women, come into being. There are general improvements of the physical working environment.

Finally, certain beneficent political conditions become operative. Internal peace and order are increased by the reduction of war, rebellion, feuds, and banditry as the result of stronger government, whether democratically or absolutistically imposed. Centralized governments are better able to mitigate the more drastic effects of crop failures, famines, epidemics, and other natural calamities. They are also capable of erecting a more stable foundation for the individual's right to life through rudimentary programs for social welfare. In fact, better governmental agencies, once established, supply or supervise most of the other death-controlling factors.

THE EFFECT ON BIRTH RATES

The relation between modernization and the control and decline of fertility is not yet a matter of universally valid principles, as is the case with the reduction of mortality. We are still dependent upon hypotheses; but the evidence is accumulating, based on experience, not only in the West but elsewhere (in Japan, for example), that these hypotheses have increasing general validity.

The effects of modernization on the birth rate come about slowly, causing changes in the birth rate to lag behind those of the death rate. The first tendency of the birth rate is often slightly upward. A comparison of estimated birth rates of 1934-35 and 1947-49 of peoples in the early stages of industrialization, such as in the Belgian Congo, Honduras, Malay Federation, Nicaragua, South and Southwest Africa, shows increases of as much as 7 per cent. This is probably due to some easing of the food supply, some improvement in general living conditions, and a somewhat improved vitality making for greater likelihood of conception and live births. The long-range tendency is downward, but very slow. In the first place, industrial progress and extensive urbanization— with which declining and controlled fertility are directly related—are complex processes, vast in scope, and arduous and expensive. Medical progress, on the other hand, is smaller in scope, can occur without much industrialization, and is cheaper and easier to accomplish.

Furthermore, the decline of the birth rate comes so slowly because, unlike the decline of the death rate, which is occasioned mainly by external actions and agencies, the fall of the birth rate involves not only a host of external changes, but also subtle inner changes in the culture as a whole and in actual and potential parents. As a sociological phenomenon reproductive behavior is greatly affected by values, attitudes, ideologies, habits and customs which harness, regulate, define and even institutionalize its patterns. At the same time reproduction is a private practice, and general modifications of it involve changed privately held interests and wishes. It is a matter of motivation, and motivation must be taken into account in all forms of voluntary behavior. But the motivating factors in human behavior are resident in the above-mentioned features of the culture.

As noted early in the preceding chapter, the necessity for survival in man's long history has fixed in the religious admonitions, the moral and legal codes, the popular customs, the thought-ways, habits, and family organizations of most peoples the importance of high fertility. The change in reproductive practice bringing a decline in the birth rate involves changes in social attitudes, changes in the valuations of family and reproduction, changes in almost all habitual and planned institutional behavior, all of which usually come slowly. To bring these changes, there must develop a rational as against a "sacred" ideology, powerful social incentives and individual motivations to change the reproductive practices, accompanied by individual initiative and adaptability.

One of the key operative elements in the downward trend of the birth rate is the standard-of-living factor. With the increase in wealth and income, people develop desires for greater quantity and quality of material and social satisfactions. They aspire to have and display the evidences of success; they seek to enjoy enhanced prestige and opportunity. In the more economically secure cultures, pleasure patterns as well as competitive-success patterns are also in effect. As Nitti put it, such people find that "children are a heavy baggage to carry up the social ladder." To compete successfully and to achieve higher levels put heavy economic penalties on the large family. Children contribute less and less to family income, and the cost of maintaining them and giving them the extending range of opportunities increases. Furthermore, children are looked upon and cherished as ends in themselves; the family desires only the number that can be given the culture's best advantages. The parents also view themselves not merely as reproductive organisms, but as developing individuals.

Urban life particularly makes children a luxury, and to some extent an inconvenience and a liability. Child labor legislation, invariably and of necessity accompanied by compulsory school attendance laws, adds to the burden of child maintenance. The emancipation of women has changed old roles and has been accompanied by many new ones. Both unmarried and married women are increasingly employed outside the home. They also participate in various other activities which are relatively incompatible with continuous child bearing.

The development of popular education, the increasing need for more education at ever higher levels for all segments of a modernized population, and the wider horizons and more expensive cultural aspirations opened up by education also tend to restrict fertility.

Most of the material, social-organizational, social-psychological, and spiritual changes related to industrialization, urbanization, and democratization, discussed above as aspects of modernization, bring about profound modification of the compulsive cultural norms and of the patterns of behavior and, among many other effects, also tend to diminish fertility. There develop the small-family ideal and the small-family system.

Finally, as part of the general technological advance, come the increasing diffusion of knowledge of, and the increasing availability and use of, contraceptive techniques and materials. The social and cultural situation and individual and family motivations cause more and more people to resort to these. They make possible also the controlled-family system, since fertility is a matter of choice and of relatively effective manipulation. This tends to produce a somewhat fluctuating birth rate among the "modernized" peoples, though withal at a modest level. The birth rate goes up when the people have community security and economic prosperity, and down when social and economic times are hard.

BIBLIOGRAPHY

Bowen, E. *An Hypothesis of Population Growth*. New York: Columbia Univ. Press, 1931.

Brown, Harrison. *The Challenge of Man's Future*. New York: Viking, 1954. Pp. 3-45.

Burchard, J. E. (ed.) *Mid-Century: The Social Implications of Scientific Progress*. New York: Wiley, 1950.

Cowgill, D. O. "The Theory of Population Growth Cycles." *Am. Jour. Soc.*, 55 (Sept., 1949): 163-170.

Davis, Kingsley. "Puerto Rico: A Crowded Island." *Annals Am. Acad. Pol. & Soc. Sci.*, 285 (Jan., 1953): 116-122.

————. "The Origin and Growth of Urbanization in the World." *Am. Jour. Soc.*, 60 (March, 1955): 429-437.

————. *The Population of India and Pakistan*. Princeton: Princeton Univ. Press, 1951. Pp. 33-90.

————. "The World Demographic Transition." *Annals Am. Acad. Pol. & Soc. Sci.*, 237 (Jan., 1945): 1-11.

———— and H. Hertz. *Pattern of World Urbanization*. New York: Macmillan, 1954.

Deutsch, K. W. "The Growth of Nations: Some Recurrent Patterns of Political and Social Integration." *World Politics*, 5 (Jan., 1953) : 168-195.

Hare, Ronald. *Pomp and Pestilence: Infectious Disease, Its Origins and Conquest*. New York: Philosophical Library, 1955. Esp. pp. 188-201.

Hauser, Philip M. "World Population Trends." *Soc. & Soc. Res.*, 39 (Nov.-Dec., 1954): 73-80, esp. 75-77.

Hayes, S. P., Jr. "Personality and Culture Problems of Point IV," in B. F. Hoselitz (ed.), *The Progress of Underdeveloped Areas*. Chicago: Univ. of Chicago Press, 1952. Pp. 203-219.

Jaffe, A. J. "Urbanization and Fertility." *Am. Jour. Soc.*, 48 (July, 1942): 48-60.

Kirk, Dudley. "Population Changes in the Postwar World." *Am. Soc. Rev.*, 9 (Feb., 1944) : 28-35.

LANDIS, P. H. *Population Problems: A Cultural Interpretation* (2nd ed. by P. K. Hatt). New York: American Book, 1954. Pp. 47-51, 112-196.

LORIMER, FRANK. "Issues of Population Policy." *Annals Am. Acad. Pol. & Soc. Sci.,* 237 (Jan., 1945): 193-203.

————, *et al. Culture and Human Fertility: A Study of the Relation of Cultural Conditions to Fertility in Non-industrial Societies.* Paris: UNESCO (New York: Columbia Univ. Press), 1955.

NOTESTEIN, F. W. "Summary of the Demographic Background of Problems of Undeveloped Areas," in *International Approaches to Problems of Undeveloped Areas.* New York: Milbank Memorial Fund, 1948. Pp. 9-15.

ODUM, H. W. "Folk Sociology as a Subject Field for the Historical Study of Total Human Society and the Empirical Study of Group Behavior." *Soc. Forces,* 31 (March, 1953): 193-223.

PENROSE, E. F. *Population Theories and Their Application.* Stanford, Calif.: Food Research Institute, 1934.

REDFIELD, ROBERT. *The Primitive World and Its Transformation.* Ithaca: Cornell Univ. Press, 1953. Pp. 1-25.

REED, S. W. "World Population Trends," in Ralph Linton (ed.) , *Most of the World: The Peoples of Africa, Latin America, and the East Today.* New York: Columbia Univ. Press, 1949. Pp. 109-112, 137-142.

SIEGEL, I. H. "Technological Change and Long-Run Forecasting." *Jour. of Business of Univ. of Chicago.* 26 (July, 1953): 141-156.

TAEUBER, IRENE B. "The Future of Transitional Areas," in P. K. Hatt (ed.), *World Population and Future Resources.* New York: American Book, 1952. Pp. 25-38.

————. "Migration and the Population Potential of Monsoon Asia," in *Postwar Problems of Migration,* New York: Milbank Memorial Fund, 1947. Pp. 7-29.

THOMPSON, W. S. *Population Problems* (4th ed.) . New York: McGraw-Hill, 1953. Pp. 73-85.

UNITED NATIONS, Population Division, Department of Social Affairs. *The Determinants and Consequences of Population Trends: A Summary of the Findings of Studies on the Relationships between Population Changes and Economic and Social Conditions* (Population Studies, No. 17) . New York, 1953. Pp. 47-97.

4

The Modernization-Demographic Differential

The modernization process has not proceeded uniformly or at the same rate among all peoples. Some—the great bulk, in fact—are still largely in a pre-industrial or incipient industrial state; certain others are intermediately launched in the process; still others are quite typical "modernized" societies. Likewise, there is great variation among peoples with respect to the correlated processes of demographic change, especially changes in birth and death rates, in age structures, and in fertility and mortality controls. A glance at some of the data available by major regions as well as particular countries reveals marked differences. It also indicates, however, that from a world standpoint modernization is still in its infancy.

Because of greatly varying rates and degrees of modernization, the countries of the world can be placed along a continuum with the almost completely modernized countries at one pole and the "pre-modern" or relatively "underdeveloped"[1] countries at the other. World demographers have also noted that the countries of the world can be arranged along a continuum with respect to their birth, death, and natural increase rates, their states of fertility and mortality control, and other significant demographic characteristics.

---

[1] The term "underdeveloped" as applied to a country will be more completely analyzed in the next chapter.

Modernization and these demographic features can be roughly correlated, because the technical-economic-social conditions and the
demographic situation constitute a sort of "bundle" of elements.
There is always a relationship between kind and degree of technological development, kind of economy, amount of communication
and transportation facilities, national per-capita income, material
level of living, level of literacy and education, quantity and quality
of nutrition, degree of secularization and rationalization of life, and
kind of social structure on the one hand and the different kinds
of population densities, birth rates, death rates, infant mortality
rates, longevity, age and sex structure of the population, and fertility and mortality control on the other. Some of the more pertinent features of this "calculus" can be indicated.

To make the comparative analysis more concrete, the countries
of the world have been generally characterized and roughly classified into three groups, here designated as I, II, and III.[2] An examination of these groups will enable us more readily to picture the
general modernization-demographic situation and also to identify
the major "problem spots."

It should be kept in mind that these categories must be regarded
as stages in a continuum. Every classification does some violence

[2] The characteristics of the "groups" here presented, and part of the data
regarding them, come from Thompson (who made the earlier "classic" contribution), Notestein, Piquet, Reed, and Spengler, and from United Nations publications, *Population Bulletin,* No. 1 (December, 1951); *Preliminary Report on the
World Social Situation;* and the *Demographic Yearbooks* for 1953 and 1954. Other
sources of data, used as a basis for compilations and condensations here presented,
will be indicated at the appropriate points. The placement of countries in the
respective groups is in the main a composite of the UN reports and Thompson's
latest conclusions. A few departures are made from these, however, on the basis
of the latest data relating to the main criteria of placement: (1) the degree of
industrialization-urbanization as against agriculturalism, and (2) the apparent
degree of death and birth control. The concept of the three groups will also be
expanded to include a much larger number of characteristic elements than have
been given in the standard treatments. Considerable data will be drawn from
the remarkable statistical compendium by the Woytinskys.

For a recent study, in which twenty-one countries of the world are arrayed
into *seven* types on the basis of the use of the three variables of fertility, mortality, and modernization, see the article by P. K. Hatt, Nellie L. Farr, and
E. Weinstein. Very recently the demographers of the UN Department of Social
Affairs have outlined five different patterns of population growth; see "Framework for Future Population Estimates, 1950-1980," a paper presented in Rome
to the UN World Population Conference, Aug. 30-Sept. 10, 1954.

to truth, but for purposes of comparison and understanding it is always useful to reduce an array of phenomena to a few broad categories. At best each group must be loosely defined. As in all continua, the point of transition from one stage to another is difficult to locate; hence there is a certain overlapping; certain countries can be considered marginal to the adjoining stage. Particular countries also may be somewhat atypical in some respects, and hence can be located only on the basis of a bare preponderance of characteristics. In the main, however, most of the countries fall into one group or another quite clearly.

A similar pattern of treatment will be followed, as far as the available data permit, in the case of each group: first, the position in the modernization process will be indicated by means of some of the most typical technological, economic, and social characteristics of the class of countries; second, the related major critical demographic features of the category will be noted.[3]

GROUP I

The countries, by regions, are those of northwest, central and some of southern Europe, namely, the United Kingdom, France, Belgium, Denmark, Norway, Sweden, the Netherlands, Germany, Switzerland, Czechoslovakia, the Baltic countries of Estonia, Latvia, and Lithuania (now part of the Soviet Union), Finland, and possibly Italy, Austria and Hungary (though the latter two will occasionally be considered in Group II), North America north of the Rio Grande (United States and Canada), and Oceania (Australia and New Zealand). These contain about 20 per cent of the world's population.

TECHNOLOGY, ECONOMY, AND SOCIAL STATE

Though by no means at precisely the same level, these are the highly industrialized-urbanized and, in most instances, the highly democratized countries of the world. A very small porportion of their populations are engaged in agriculture, for example, 15 per cent in the United States (1950), 25 per cent in Canada (1941), 6 per cent in the United Kingdom (1931), 25 per cent in France (1946),

---

[3] For a most revealing earlier study of fifty-three countries of the world, divided into three groups on the basis of per-capita income, with data mainly from 1939, see U.S. Department of State, pp. 92-115.

18 per cent in the Netherlands (1930). This is another way of saying that their populations are predominantly urban. Some of them (the United States, Canada, and Australia) nevertheless produce vast surpluses of some agricultural crops. On the other hand, about three-fifths of the countries have to import part, sometimes a very considerable part, of their food supply and of the raw materials used in their diversified manufacturing operations. But they have access to and the ability to acquire the materials, and to exchange their products in the markets of the world. They are the world's great secondary (manufacturing) and tertiary (trade, transportation, communication, finance, personal and professional services) producers. The people of the Group I countries enjoy the highest level of technological development, the most widespread and far-reaching application of scientific principles and technical procedures, the most highly organized economies, the highest economic levels of living, and have aspirations for ever-higher standards of living.[4] They are also imbued with the democratic philosophy as it applies to the political, economic, and social aspects of life. Most of the countries have run the full course of the process of modernization as we now understand it.

They have the highly efficient surplus-producing economies of the world.[5] Their economies are characterized by the wide use of diversified resources (whether local or imported), by division of labor and specialization of function, by labor highly diversified as to occupation, by the great use of mechanical power, by organized machine production (production lines) and huge capital equipment, by organized finance and credit systems. Their communication and transportation systems (both internal and with other countries) carry to every inhabited section, tying all regions and country and city together into a network of cultural and economic exchange. These countries enjoy cheap and rapid movement of

[4] Throughout this study the terms "level," or "plane," of living, and "standard" of living will be used with distinctive meanings. By "level," or "plane," of living is meant the plane that a population is enabled to live on, in terms of real income, at a given time. By "standard" of living is meant the minimum of real income that a person or group considers indispensable.

[5] "The United States has about 5 per cent of all the people of the world. It uses about 50 per cent of all the world's output of raw materials. It makes about half of the world's manufactured goods—and, roughly, enjoys about half of the earth's wealth." "Personal and Otherwise," *Harper's*, 208 (May, 1954): 14.

goods from primary to secondary and tertiary producers, from producers to consumers, from market to market. Because of ready
communication and transportation, and the necessary favorable
political conditions, there is also the easy flow (physical mobility)
of persons and families within the country between places of differential and changing opportunity.

All three groups have cities, and some areas in each have had
them for millennia. While the present-day world is more urbanized
than ever before, it is still primarily a rural world. A high degree
of urbanization is found in only a few areas of the world. The
definition of "urban areas" differs greatly among the different countries in the world, ranging through "incorporated places of 2,500 or
more inhabitants" (the United States), "incorporated places of all
sizes" (Canada), "cities and towns" (Norway), "municipalities," or
municipalities of a given number of inhabitants, "urban communities," and so on. Therefore, we will place ourselves on more certain ground by comparing the three groups on the basis of their
populations living in cities of 100,000 or more. Such cities are a
fairly sure test of the technological-economic-social advancement;
they imply the ability to support large urban populations through
a food surplus and in secondary and tertiary production; they imply
adequacy of transportation and political control and the ability to
provide the physical facilities for health and sanitation of great con-
centrations of people. The four regions of major urbanization include most of the Group I countries. They consist of northwestern
Europe, Australia-New Zealand, United States-Canada, and southern
South America. While these regions contain only 21 per cent of
the world's people, and 24 per cent of the habitable area, they contain 62 per cent of all the world's population living in cities of
100,000 or over.[6] Typical Group I countries show the following
percentages of people living in cities of 100,000 and over: United
States (1950), 29.5 per cent; Australia (1947), 47.5 per cent; the
Netherlands (1946), 30.3 per cent; Denmark (1945), 32.7 per cent.[7]
It is important to note that the cities of the different groups exercise different kinds and degrees of influence. In Group I countries

[6] K. Davis, as reported in *Population Index*, 17 (July, 1951) : 173.
[7] On world urbanization, with an abundance of specific data, see Woytinsky,
pp. 111-124.

we have not only the stupendous growth of cities and an increasing proportion of the population living and/or working in cities, but —what is especially distinctive of Group I countries—the development throughout their cultures of urban values, interests, and ways of life. For them urbanization means the penetration of almost every aspect of life by these city values and processes. The whole people also enjoys the advantages and amenities (as well as many of the disadvantages) of city activities. It may also be pointed out that the highly urbanized countries usually have relatively low agricultural densities and an agricultural population living at a high economic and social level. The agriculture of North America especially is highly mechanized and commercialized. The use of the tractor is probably the best index of agricultural mechanization. It is estimated that there were 6,130,000 tractors in the world in 1951. Of these, the United States and Canada with 2.2 per cent of the world's farmers had 4,168,000 tractors, or 68 per cent of the total; all of Europe had 971,000; Latin America had 122,000; the Near East had 16,000; the Far East, with half the world's farmers and one-fourth of the world's arable land, had 23,000, or 0.4 per cent of the whole; and Africa had 100,000.

Among the Group I countries, in 1951, the United States had 119 acres of arable land per tractor, Canada had 247, the United Kingdom had 57, Australia had 247, and New Zealand 72.[8]

The proportion of the world income produced by the respective regions is highly significant. While the figures are not available by groups, approximate allocation can be made on the basis of world regions. The world income in 1948 was estimated at $548 billion. Of this North America (United States and Canada) received $235 billion, or 42.9 per cent of the whole; Europe received $145 billion, or 26.4 per cent; and Oceania, $8 billion, or 1.5 per cent. These regions, most of the countries of which are in our Group I, thus received some 70.8 per cent of the world's income. The U.S.S.R. received $35 billion, or 6.4 per cent. On the other hand, with respect to the Group II and III regions, Central and South America received $23 billion, or 4.2 per cent; all of Asia

---

[8] Woytinsky, pp. 515-519. For data on number of tractors by world regions, pre-war to 1953, see United Nations (Food and Agricultural Organization), *The State of Food and Agriculture, 1955* (Rome, 1955), Table IV-4, p. 61.

$86 billion, or 15.7 per cent; and all of Africa $16 billion, or 2.9 per cent—making a total of $125 billion, or 22.8 per cent.[9]

The United Nations, (Department of Social Affairs), using 1950 estimates and relating them to proportional population, states:

> On a regional basis, Asia (not including the Middle East), with approximately half of the world's population, produced but 10 per cent of the world's income in 1950; 7.5 per cent of the world's population in Africa accounted for a little over 2 per cent of the world's income; 4 per cent of the world's population in the Middle East had 1.5 per cent of the world's income; and almost 7 per cent of the world's population in Latin America obtained about 4.5 per cent of the world's income. On the other hand, less than 7 per cent of the world's population in North America (Canada and the United States) produced almost 43 per cent of the world's income; and about one-fourth of the world's population in Europe, U.S.S.R. and Oceania accounted for almost 40 per cent of the world's income.[10]

Claude A. Buss has called attention to the fact, based on the United Nations World Economic Survey for 1950-51, that during those years there was evidence that the gap in income between the advanced and the underdeveloped countries was widening, not narrowing.[11]

The distribution of national income by agricultural origin on the one hand, and by origin in manufacturing, construction, trade, and transportation on the other is also highly indicative of the stage of industrial development. While we do not have estimates by groups, we do have figures for typical countries in each group. Among Group I countries, for example, for the United States in 1950 the proportion of national income derived from agriculture was 7 per cent, with 65 per cent from the other sources; for Canada the percentages (1950) were, respectively, 14 and 64; for Great Britain, 5 and 59; for France, 16 and 61; for Norway, 15 and 65.[12]

Another indication of the nature of the economy and its productive potentialities is found in the labor force, especially its dis-

---

[9] Woytinsky, pp. 392-395.

[10] *Preliminary Report*, p. 131. See also Piquet, p. 154.

[11] "New Relationships: Economics and Democracy in Southeast Asia," in P. W. Thayer (ed.), *Southeast Asia in the Coming World* (Baltimore: Johns Hopkins Press, 1953), pp. 81-95.

[12] Compiled from Woytinsky, p. 430.

tribution as to type of production, and the proportion of the population in the productive age period. Again, while estimates are not
available by groups, we do have some for particular countries in
each group. Among Group I countries, the percentage distribution
as between all primary production (agriculture, mining, forestry,
and fisheries) and all secondary and tertiary production (manufacturing, construction, trade, transportation and communication,
government services, professions, and personal services, and including "other" and "unknown") is as follows: United States
(1940), 20.6 per cent and 79.5 per cent; Great Britain (1931), 12.1
and 87.1; Netherlands (1947), 20.6 and about 75.[13]

Data are now available in the form of fairly reliable estimates
made by United Nations organizations regarding certain other
specific elements that enter into and are highly indicative of the
level of living and the degree of modern development of a people. The three types to follow will also be indicated for Group II
and III below.

On the basis of a recent United Nations study, excluding Italy,
Austria, and Hungary from Group I, the 1949 per-capita income
ranged from $348 for Finland to $1,453 for the United States, with
a median per-capita income of about $635.[14] Furthermore, due to
various kinds of taxes (income, estate, etc.), the spread of education, and other factors, there is a tendency for income and wealth
to become more nearly equalized; the gap between the very rich
and the very poor is closing.

Literacy is an excellent index of modernization. According to
another United Nations study, the countries here included in Group
I have a literacy rate of about 95 per cent of their population.[15]

---

[13] *Ibid.*, pp. 356-357. See also pp. 462-463.

[14] This data on per-capita income for Group I and for the other two groups
is based upon United Nations, *National and Per Capita Incomes*, pp. 14-16. For
a 1950 revision of countries classified by size of per-capita income showing regional divisions, see United Nations, *Preliminary Report*, pp. 130-134. See also
Spengler, 1945. These references to sources of the different types of data will
not be repeated in the treatment of Groups II and III. The reader will recognize
the sources.

[15] United Nations, *Preliminary Report*, pp. 86-98, has compiled data from 146
countries, colonies, protectorates, mandated territories, etc., on percentage of
literacy, on compulsory schooling requirements (if existent), and on school en-
rollment. We are drawing on the literacy data. The concepts of literacy vary
widely in different countries, ranging from merely "literate," to "baptized" (with

Another crucial criterion of development among peoples is the adequacy of their diet. The Food and Agriculture Organization of the United Nations has established as a bench mark of reasonable adequacy a diet that provides 2,750 calories per capita per day. The calories should be derived from starches, sugars, fats, and proteins and should include other nutritive essentials. On the basis of "recent" as distinct from "pre-war" estimates, the United Nations study indicates that all Group I countries have diets above 3000 calories per diem (except Germany, France, and the Netherlands, whose circumstances at the moment are somewhat exceptional), with New Zealand heading the list with 3,250 calories per day, and the United States fifth with 3,130. Tolley also concludes that the Group I countries derive only 30 to 50 per cent of their calories (in most cases 30 to 40 per cent) from cereals and potatoes, indicating diets comparatively rich in both plant and animal fats and proteins.[16] In general, these countries have fairly balanced rations, including the high-energy and the so-called "protective foods"—a variety of vegetables and fruits, and an adequacy of fats and proteins.

Finally, the Group I countries are the healthiest and have, in most respects, a low incidence of disease because of the conquest of many of the children's and endemic diseases and the virtual elimination of the major epidemic diseases. The prevailing major diseases are those of late middle and old age, occasioned largely by the remarkable prolongation of life. The Group I countries have the highest mortality rates among the groups from suicide and

---

the presumption of ability to read), to "able to read" at some specified age, to "population 10 years of age and over able to read and write." The criteria are not indicated at all in some instances, and, of course, no data is available in some instances. For most of the Group I countries the data are based on censuses of 1940 or more recent ones; for Group II countries the data are based in some instances on estimates, and in others on censuses of varying quality and vintage, some going back as far as 1928; for Group III dependence is almost entirely upon estimates. In spite of these variations and complications, the test of the percentage of the population which is "literate"—whatever its meaning in particular cases— enables one very readily to arrange the countries into the three groups.

[16] United Nations, *Preliminary Report,* pp. 51-52; R. H. Tolley, "Agricultural Adjustment and Nutrition," in T. W. Schultz (ed.), *Food for the World* (Chicago: University of Chicago Press, 1945) , pp. 164-176. For an earlier study summarizing and correlating by countries pre-war data on calories per capita, annual income per capita, and death rates, see "Food, Income, and Mortality," *Population Index* (Office of Population Research, Princeton Univ.) , 13 (April, 1947) : 96-103.

industrial and traffic accidents. In the main, however, they seem to have a high rate of control over the environmental factors making for shortness of life and mortality.[17]

THE CORRELATED DEMOGRAPHIC SITUATION

Demographically, Group I consists of countries of relatively low fertility and low mortality, with moderate natural increases, but potentially in a state of stability or even decline of numbers. Fertility and mortality among them have declined to low levels during recent decades. In the period 1946-1948 birth rates averaged around 22 per thousand, and death rates around 12 per thousand, with a natural increase rate of about 10 per thousand.[18] Natural increase rates of some of the countries have again descended to the pre-World War II levels of around 7 or 8 thousand. Birth rates have been as low as 16.8 per thousand of population in the United States in 1935 and 1940, 16.3 in Norway in 1940, and 15.2 in Sweden in 1932. Some of the birth rates for 1953 were United States, 24.7; France, 18.6; Norway, 18.9; United Kingdom, 15.9. By 1954 the birth rate in most of the countries of northwestern Europe had again retreated to the approximate level of the 1930's.

In southern and southeastern Europe the birth rates during the last two decades have generally continued their previous downward trend without the major interruption noted elsewhere in Europe, North America, and Oceania. While the birth rates of these countries taken as a group are still somewhat above the typical level of northern and western European countries, their recent experience suggests the likelihood of a further decline.

[17] For comprehensive treatments by regions and various countries, with data and interpretations on subjects pertinent to the type of analysis of Groups I, II, III, see Woytinsky, as follows: "Health," pp. 196-240; "Consumption and Standards of Living" (including consumptive standards, patterns of nutrition, dietary patterns, clothing, housing, medical and educational services, pp. 282-311; national and per-capita income and related population characteristics, pp. 378-412); "Economic Patterns," pp. 413-447; "Agriculture and World Economy," pp. 451-469.

[18] The vital statistics used in this discussion of groups will be drawn mainly from the recent *Demographic Yearbooks* of the United Nations; United Nations, *Preliminary Report*, pp. 6-21; and the vital statistics section of the *Population Index*, published quarterly by the Office of Population Research (Princeton Univ.) and the Population Association of America. See also Woytinsky, pp. 138-187. On the demographic prospects of the three groups see United Nations, *Determinants and Consequences*, 1953, pp. 151-162.

For most of the countries of this group the birth rates seem to have become mobile, and their fluctuation seems to be related to the mass appraisal of two, also related, sets of social conditions. First, to the state of the economy; a minor economic improvement will raise them, while a depression will lower them. Second, to the state of social security and normality; in time of war or other social confusion and disruption the birth rates come down.

The crude death rates are very low, for example, 9.9 in 1948 and 9.6 in 1953 for the United States, 9.0 in 1950 and 8.6 in 1953 for Canada, 7.7 in 1953 for the Netherlands, 9.0 in 1953 for Australia. Infant mortality rates—the number of deaths during the first year of life per thousand babies born alive during the year—always especially sensitive to technological, economic, political, and social conditions, are exceedingly low and generally falling. In 1953, for example, the United States had a rate of 28 per thousand live births; the United Kingdom, 28; New Zealand, 20 (for European stocks); Australia (1952), 24; the Netherlands, 22; Sweden, 19.

The expectation of life (longevity) is constantly increasing, ranging from 50 to above 70 years at birth, with most of the countries in the sixties. For example, Canada (1947) had 65.18 for males and 69.05 for females; the United States (whites, 1950), 66.6 for males and 72.4 for females; the United Kingdom (1952), 67.06 for males and 72.35 for females; Australia (1946-48), 66.07 for males and 70.63 for females.

In general, for a century the countries of Group I have demonstrated a considerable degree of voluntary control of fertility and there is every likelihood that the control will increase. They have also had, and will continue to have, a large measure of organized and efficient mortality control. In fact, so secure are they in their technical control of the factors making for morbidity and mortality that not only did their death rates not rise in most instances during the Depression and World War II, but actually declined slightly. However, possibilities of further decline of the death rates of northern and western Europe, the United States and Canada, and Oceania are limited; the death rates have reached, or will soon reach, the lowest possible point and then will increase somewhat in spite of further health improvements. But this phenomenon is itself a reflection of the high effectiveness of their death control, as evidenced in the increasing proportion of the aged and the rising average age of the population. For central and southern Europe further declines in the death rate to the northern and western levels can be expected.

The birth rates in most instances can go still lower than they are at present, matching or even falling below those of thirties. Fluctuations in birth rates, related to economic and other security circumstances, rather than fluctuations in death rates cause the changes in the rates of natural increase in Group I countries. Or, put differently, the dominant factor affecting the rates of increase is not the death rate, assuming no great natural or man-made catastrophes, but the birth rate.

The age structure is also a matter of major importance in the demographic situation of any country or group of countries. It is directly affected by the present levels and past trends of both fertility and mortality, and also by migration. The age structure at any given time influences future trends of births, deaths, and natural increase. Its specific significance is that it has immediate economic consequences since it indicates the relative proportions of the population in the naturally dependent (the young and the aged) and the productive age (labor force) periods. There are, of course, various other social consequences, such as child welfare tasks, the economic burden of educating the young, and problems of old-age support, services, and security. The three groups of countries show large differences in the age structure of their populations.

The table below does not conform exactly to our three-group allocation of countries. The reader can, however, readily locate the countries among the regions given.

From the point of view of the proportion of the population in the productive years of life, the Group I countries are at a great advantage. As noted, these are the countries that have had the lowest fertility and mortality rates. At present they have the lowest percentages of children (the category under 15 years of age). Because of increased life expectancy, they have in increasingly larger proportion of those born living through the productive period of life (15-59 years). Very general regional figures show that the United States and Canada have about 25 per cent of their population in the "under-15" age group, and 64 per cent in the "15-to-59" group; for northwest-central Europe the figures are, respectively, 24 per cent and 62 per cent, and for Oceania, 28 and

TABLE 7

ESTIMATED AGE DISTRIBUTION OF WORLD POPULATION
BY REGIONS, 1947[19]

REGION	Per cent of total population			
	Under 15 years	15-19 years	60 years and over	Total
World Total	36	57	7	100
Africa	40	55	5	100
America:				
Northern America (North of Rio Grande)	25	64	11	100
Latin America (including Carribean region)	40	55	5	100
Asia:				
Near East	40	54	6	100
South-central Asia	40	56	4	100
Japan	37	55	8	100
Remaining Far East (excluding Asiatic U,S,S,R,)	40	55	5	100
Europe:				
Northwest-central Europe	24	62	14	100
Southern Europe	30	59	11	100
Eastern Europe (including Asiatic U.S.S.R.)	34	59	7	100
Oceania	28	62	10	100

62. However, also because of longevity, these countries have the highest percentages of aged persons (60 years and over).

The recent increase in the number of births which has taken place in most of the Group I countries has tended to increase the present proportion of children in the population and reduce the ratio of workers to such dependents. The same situation, however, points to an expanded proportion of population in the 15-to-59 age group in the near future, assuming that the birth rates fall, as is likely.[20] At the same time, if life expectancy continues to increase, as is also likely, the proportion of aged dependents will increase.

While the infant mortality rates of Group I countries are low and still falling, they cannot fall much lower, with the result that the

[19] This table is found in the following United Nations publications: *World Population Trends, 1920–1947* (New York, 1949), p. 15; *Determinants and Consequences,* p. 144. In connection with comparative age structures of countries, see the latter, pp. 141-149, 194-200, 213-214, 253-260, 265-267. For data on the percentage of children under 15 years of age for countries representative of all three groups, see Woytinsky, pp. 399-400.

[20] The 1954 figures show that this is actually occurring among most Group I countries.

death factor will in time be stabilized as it affects the proportion of the young dependents.

The Group I countries have been called the "uncoiled" and the "rationally balanced" countries. They have done their "swarming" and passed through most of the expansive portion of the increase cycle of modern times. There is great likelihood that their rate of population growth will be moderate to low in the future.[21] There is also a possibility of the resumption of the tendency toward a stationary or even a declining population, demonstrated by some of the countries prior to World War II, especially if local and/or international conditions impair or threaten to impair their high level of living. They have the knowledge and the latent attitudes for doing so. In general, Group I countries, with their high technological-economic development, show a tendency toward stabilization of their populations on the basis of the high level of living in efficient industrial society and the high proficiency in life saving. They are in a state of "modern balance," or rapidly approaching such a state.

The relatively low birth rates of this group are the result of far-reaching changes in attitudes regarding family size; the small-family ideal, or, perhaps better named, the controlled-family ideal, prevails among them and is unlikely to give way to attitudes that would permit continuous, general high birth rates. Both the knowledge and practice of contraception—itself a signal feature of technological development—has spread, or is spreading, to all groups and classes despite varying religious and political objections to it. These Group I peoples are not likely to increase greatly the total population of the world; in fact, most of the signs, as will be noted below, indicate that they will become a diminishing proportion.

GROUP II

There is less general agreement among international demographers on the list of countries to be included in this group than in Groups I and III. Groups I and III represent the extremes of the continuum, while Group II countries are in an intermediate and transitional state from the point of view of both the technological-

---

[21] As of 1952, most of them show low percentage rates of annual increase, e.g., Norway, 0.93 per cent; France, 0.85 per cent; Sweden, 0.73 per cent; Belgium, 0.32 per cent; the United Kingdom, 0.30 per cent.

economic and the demographic conditions. Hence, as implied, some of the countries at the lower margin of Group I might be considered as upper marginal countries of Group II, and certain upper marginal countries of Group II, like Argentina, could be in Group I. Similarly, some of the more advanced countries in Group III might from some points of view be lower-margin Group II.

Included in Group II are certain countries of central, southern, eastern and southeastern Europe (Poland, Greece, Yugoslavia, Bulgaria, Rumania, Spain, Portugal, the Soviet Union, and possibly, in most respects, Hungary, Austria, and Italy); of Latin America (some of the Caribbean countries, especially Puerto Rico and Cuba, Mexico, Venezuela, Brazil, Argentina, and Uraguay); of Africa (Algeria, Tunis, Morocco, and white South Africa); and of Asia (Japan). They include about 20 per cent of the world's population.

TECHNOLOGY, ECONOMY, AND SOCIAL STATE

The Group II countries are in a broad intermediate stage of transition from a predominantly agrarian to a predominantly industrialized-urbanized economy. While all have undergone a considerable degree of technological-economic advance, some are much farther along than others; many are still mainly agricultural. The economies of these countries are intermediate as to the development of their factory systems, their communication and transportation systems, the proportion of their population in mechanized agriculture and urbanized industry, commerce, the development of urbanization, and of industrial capital equipment, and their finance and credit systems.

As of 1950, all but six of the world's twenty-five largest cities were in Group I and II countries,[22] even though the countries included only about 40 per cent of the world's population. Some of the Group II countries show high urbanization. Argentina in 1947 had 61.4 per cent of its population living in "places of 2,000 or more inhabitants," and in 1948 Japan had 50.9 per cent living in "municipalities of 30,000 or more inhabitants." As to the percentage of total population living in cities of 100,000 or more, the figures on particular countries are as follows: Mexico (1940), 10.2 per cent; Brazil (1940), 15.9 per cent; Argentina (1947), 39.4 per

[22] For their populations see Thompson, 1953, p. 399.

cent; Hungary (1941), 15.4 per cent; Spain (1940), 19.2 per cent; Italy (1936), 16.0 per cent; Union of South Africa (1946), 19.7 per cent; Japan (1936), 25.3 per cent.[23] Among these countries are to be found a sufficient degree of technological advance to provide efficient surplus production, transportation and exchange facilities, construction of buildings and public utilities, and principles and means of large-scale social organization essential to the development of large cities. Here also is the division of labor and specialization of function, and the array of special services that, in their very nature, have to be carried on in cities.

The tractor test of agricultural mechanization applied to certain Group II countries about which data are available shows Mexico with 772 acres of arable land per tractor, Cuba with 608, Venezuela with 482, Brazil with 2,965, Uruguay with 331, Poland with 1,888, Yugoslavia with 2,792, Greece with 1,631, and Turkey with 4,571.[24]

The distribution of national income between that of agricultural origin and that from manufacturing, construction, trade, and transportation also shows an intermediate situation. For particular countries we find the following respective percentages: Colombia (1949), 39 per cent and 38 per cent; Chile (1948), 18 and 46; Argentina (1945), 24 and 58; Poland (1948), 24 and 75; Italy (1950), 30 and 52; Greece (1948), 38 and 42; and Japan (1949), about 28 and 54.[25]

The percentage distribution of total labor force for certain countries between all primary industry on the one hand, and all secondary and tertiary industry on the other, is as follows: Mexico (1940), 67.2 per cent and 30.9 per cent; Chile (1940), 41.1 and 58.6; Portugal (1940), 49.6 and 45.0; Japan (1942), 54.5 and 42.4.[26]

The per-capita yearly incomes, according to the United Nations study, range from $100 for Japan to $346 for Argentina. As other examples, Brazil has $112; Greece, $128; Yugoslavia, $146; Venezuela, $322; Poland, $300; and Portugal, $250. The median is about $190, as against $635 for Group I.

---

[23] Woytinsky, pp. 116-117; Davis, *The Population of India and Pakistan, p.* 129.
[24] Woytinsky, pp. 516-517.
[25] *Ibid.,* pp. 430-433.
[26] *Ibid.,* pp. 356-357.

The literacy rates, where known or estimated, rest upon censuses which are usually older than those for Group I countries, and the definitions of literacy have a wider variation. The percentage of the population counted as "literate" according to some definitions ranges from 43.3 per cent in Brazil to a possible 95 per cent in Japan. For example, Portugal is listed as 51.3 per cent literate; Greece, 59.2 per cent; Mexico, 48.9 per cent; Argentina, 83.4 per cent. The median percentage is about 71, as against 95 for Group I.

As to caloric intake per day, all except Argentina, with 3,190 calories, are below the FAO bench mark, with a low of 2,100 calories in Japan to a high of 2,600 in Greece. The median is around 2,300 calories per person per day as compared with 3,000 for the Group I countries. According to the Tolley study, these peoples obtain 50 to 70 per cent of their calories from cereals and potatoes and need more animal fats and proteins.

Group II countries are also intermediate as to health. Medical and sanitary proficiency is usually somewhat retarded. There is less control of both endemic and epidemic diseases.

THE CORRELATED DEMOGRAPHIC SITUATION

Most of these countries have relatively high fertility and considerably lower and falling mortality, with very rapid natural increase. The technological-economic development has been far more effective in health and death control than in producing the social and psychological phases of economic advance, especially as these eventually affect fertility.

Birth rates vary widely. As peoples emerge from Group III to Group II conditions, and living conditions and physical vigor improve somewhat, their birth rates may actually rise for a time. While the 1946-48 birth rates were as low as 25 per thousand of population for Argentina, 28 in eastern Europe (including Asiatic U.S.S.R.), and 31 in Japan, they have been 25 to 40 for most of the countries of the group, with 35 as a fair median rate. Some of the countries at the upper margin, however, have recently had low rates: for 1953 Poland shows a rate of 23.3, Spain of 20.6, Italy of 17.5, and Japan of 21.5. At the lower margin, on the other hand, for the same year Mexico had a rate of 44.9, Puerto Rico of 35.1 and Venezuela of 46.1.

The death rates, having been reduced to a much greater extent than the birth rates, stand at moderate levels. The 1946-48 rates fell as low as 15 per thousand in Japan, and averaged around 17 for Latin America and 18 for eastern Europe (including Asiatic U.S.S.R.). The median death rate for the group was probably around 17 per thousand. The 1953 rates show amazing declines, however, with that for Mexico reported as 15.4. Venezuela 9.9, Italy 10.0, Portugal 11.3, Spain 9.7, and Japan 8.9.

Present infant mortality rates range upwards from the high forties. For example, for 1951 the rate for Mexico was 100; and the 1953 rate for Japan, 48; for Portugal, 96; for Puerto Rico, 63; for Italy, 59; and for Spain, 60.

The expectation of life at birth, for the latest dates available, ranges upward from the mid-thirties. For example, Bulgaria (1925-28) had an expectation of life at birth of 45.92 years for males and 46.64 for females; Hungary (1941) of 54.92 for males and 58.22 for females; Italy (1930-32) of 53.76 for males and 56.00 for females; Japan (1949-50) of 56.19 for males and 59.61 for females; and Mexico (1940) of 37.92 for males and 36.79 for females.

By virtue of the high birth rates in most of the countries, partly due to the heavy concentration of population in the child-bearing age, the natural increase rate is generally much higher than that of Group I countries. For example, Mexico for 1947-49 had a rate of 28.3 and for 1953 a rate of 29.5; Venezuela for 1950 had a rate of 31.6 and for 1953 of 36.2; Puerto Rico for 1949, a rate of 28.4 and for 1953, of 27.0; and Japan, of 21.2 in 1949. On the other hand, Portugal for 1946-50 had a rate of about 12; for the same period Bulgaria and Argentina averaged, respectively, 11.2 and 15.6; and Japan's rate had dropped to 10.6. The average rate of natural increase is probably 18 to 22. In the main, the annual rate of growth in Group II countries at the present time is about 35 per cent greater than in Group I.

The death rates are still declining and possibilities for further substantial decreases remain. The UN's *Preliminary Report on the World Social Situation* states (page 19): "With their present relatively youthful age structure of population, these countries could achieve crude death rates below those of some of the most advanced countries of Europe, if they reached a comparable level of health." The infant mortality rate is also declining in most instances.

Birth rates seem to be quite rigid and in most cases are at a high level, in only rather exceptional instances (as in Italy and Japan) showing a marked tendency to decline. There is little voluntary fertility control. The death rates, by comparison, are low and falling. This accounts for the prodigious rates of increase. Most of them behave like Group I countries of 40 to 75 years ago.

As to age structure, the Group II countries, because of high birth rates, have a relatively larger proportion of those under 15 as compared with Group I countries, and because of higher death rates and lower life expectancy, a relatively smaller proportion of those of 60 and over, with an intermediate proportion in the 15-to-59 age group—a proportion definitely smaller than that of the Group I countries. The regions in Table 7 having in them many of the Group II countries show the following situation: Latin America, 40 per cent of the population under 15 years and 55 per cent between 15 and 59 years; southern Europe, 30 per cent and 59 per cent, respectively; eastern Europe (including Asiatic U.S.S.R.), 34 and 59; and Japan, 37 and 55. The proportion of the aged (60 years and over) is roughly that of the Group I countries about a quarter of a century ago.

The age structure, like other demographic aspects of these countries, is also in process of considerable modification. If and when birth rates fall, there will be an increasing proportion in the productive period of life, and as death rates decline and the expectancy of life increases, there will be a growing proportion of the aged. In general, the aging of the population of these countries has only recently begun to be noticeable.

The present gap between the birth and death rates seems to point to a continuation of rapid growth for some time to come, even if birth rates decline faster than death rates. The potentialities are inherent in the situation. These are the "expanding" countries experiencing population "explosions" in varying degrees. However, as mechanization and industrialization proceed, the birth rates may begin to come down in characteristic fashion. There is some evidence that they are "uncoiling." Sometimes called "areas of demographic transition," they are in a state of "transitional lag" in achieving an economical balance between births and deaths; birth rates in most instances have not yet begun to fall perceptibly; deaths are increasingly under control, and death rates are relatively low and falling rapidly.[27]

GROUP III

This group consists of all of the remaining people of the world—all of Asia, except the U.S.S.R., Israel, and Japan; most of Africa; most of the Pacific islands; and the most retarded portions of Latin America. It constitutes about 60 per cent of the world's population.

TECHNOLOGY, ECONOMY, AND SOCIAL STATE

The economy of the Group III countries is largely agrarian as it has been for millennia, with more than 80 per cent of the people directly engaged in agriculture. The agriculture is mainly of the bare subsistence variety, carried on by archaic methods and supporting the people at a distressingly low level of living. The density of persons on the agricultural land is sometimes almost unbelievable. In Egypt (1951) there were about 1,336 persons per square mile of habitable land; in India (1950) about 450 per square mile of arable or cultivated land; in Java (1941) about 1,500 and the Philippines (1939) about 1,000 per square mile of cultivated land. The agriculture is conducted on tiny holdings often as small as one and a half acres per cultivator and probably averaging three to four acres.[28] Some of the people in certain areas are also employed all or part of the time on plantations. Insofar as there are commercial crops (sisal, rubber, tea, rice, sugar) beyond the subsistence crops of the peasant agriculture, they are produced mainly under the plantation system, which until recently at least was operated with foreign capital, under foreign management, for foreign profit. Some of the people in Africa and the Middle East are pastoral nomads or are engaged in semi-arid agriculture with conditions of life as precarious as those of the peoples of southern Asia. But the great bulk of them are engaged in simple settled agriculture and live in small villages. Six out of seven inhabitants of India spend their

---

[27] Reed states: "It is logical to assume that, as modernization proceeds, these societies will tend more and more toward the rational balance characterizing the western societies. The rapidity of this development depends directly on the speed of modernization."

[28] In India for 1939-40 the average number of acres per cultivator was 1.9. Davis, *The Population of India and Pakistan*, p. 207.

lifetime within the circumference of one or another of the more than 650,000 peasant settlements, and only one out of every seven Indians lives in a town of 5,000 or more.[29]

Zinkin points out that three-quarters of the population of Asia is today still rural and engaged in peasant agriculture, and that the percentage is dropping only slowly.[30]

While these countries have cities—some of the world's very large cities—the urban population is still a comparatively small part of the total population. Zinkin, without defining "urban," points out that on the basis of scattered estimates of 1930 or thereabouts, Malaya was 29.5 per cent urban, Indo-China 5 to 10 per cent, Indonesia 7.5 per cent, the Philippines 10 per cent, and Thailand 11 per cent.[31] We have figures for India and Egypt only with respect to the percentage of population living in cities of 100,000 or more; India (1941) had 4.1 per cent living in such cities, and Egypt (1937) had 13.3 per cent. A significant feature of urbanization of Group III countries as compared with those of I and II is that the proportion of the population living and working in cities is increasing only very slowly, and the cities are growing very slowly by comparison.

There is still a sharp separation of city and country. The great bulk of the population is still dominated by rural-agrarian small village ideas and ways of life. The people do not carry on to any considerable extent activities based on specialized production and trade; they do not consume or enjoy urbanized forms of recreation, urban-processed foods, urban-developed personal or professional services. In general, as Condliffe points out, "There can be no effective development of urbanism when four people out of every five are needed to grow necessary food supplies for the population."[32]

With the exception of China, all of them have been colonial peoples during the last three centuries, and some of them (for example, most of Africa and the Pacific islands) still are.

The processing operations consist mostly of village handicrafts, using mainly home-grown materials, and for mainly local consump-

---

[29] D. and A. Thorner, "India and Pakistan," in R. Linton (ed.), *Most of the World* (New York: Columbia Univ. Press, 1949), pp. 563, 583.

[30] Maurice Zinkin, *Asia and the West* (London: Chatto & Windus, 1951), pp. 18-31, on "The Peasant World of Asia."

[31] *Ibid.*, pp. 23-24.

[32] P. 46.

tion. Industrialization, however, has made notable beginings among some of them, for example, Egypt, the Middle East, India, and Indonesia.[33] Most of the industrialization that has occurred in these countries has been due to outside influences.

There is only a limited development of mechanical power, though there are notable exceptions with respect to hydroelectric power. Capital equipment, especially mechanical devices for saving labor, is limited in amount. In applying the "tractor test" (1951), Syria has 20,591 acres of arable land per tractor, Iraq 13,096, Iran 3,435, Pakistan 19,691, India 20,398, Indonesia 271,810, the Philippines 9,625, Northern Rhodesia 5,337. In production there has not been great change from hand to machine work, or from craft to factory methods, or from small entrepreneurial to corporate organization of manufacturing and commerce. These countries produce and consume a very small proportion of the world's industrial output.

Because of the lack of surplus and capital, transportation and communication are limited, consisting mainly of major highway, railway, and telephone and telegraph trunk lines. What communication and transportation systems they have do not create the close network of reciprocal relations and of supply, and the exchange of ideas and products, that prevails in Group I and many Group II countries. There is an extreme lack of physical mobility of the population.

The origin of national income shows great dependence upon agriculture, as against origin from manufacturing, construction, trade, transportation, and communication. For the two countries for which we have estimates, India (1948) derived 48 per cent from agriculture and 36 per cent from the other sources, and the Philippines (1948) 62 per cent and 22 per cent, respectively. Without doubt a similar situation prevails among other Group III countries.

The percentage of the total labor force in all primary industry, on the one hand, and in all secondary and tertiary industry, on the other, shows a similar completely reverse ratio as between Group I and III countries. For example, the respective percentages for India

[33] "India stands eighth in the list of the world's industrialized nations, and Tata's are the largest single iron and steel works in the world." W. R. McAuliffe, *Modern Asia Explained* (New York: Philippine Library, 1952), p. 95. Nevertheless, India's industry is almost negligible in its total economy and population.

(1931) were 67.3 and 27.4; for Thailand (1937) 88.7 and 10.9; for the Philippines (1939) 73.6 and 26.2; and for Egypt (1937) 70.9 and 29.1. As will be noted in the discussion of age structure below, these countries are the most deficient of the three groups in the proportion of their populations in the productive (labor force) years of life.

The per-capita income per year (as of 1949) ranged from lows of $25 for Indonesia, $27 for China, $35 for Korea, and $36 for Thailand, to highs of $100 for Peru and Egypt, with the median for the group around $55. A serious factor among the Group III countries is the wide gap in income and wealth between the few very rich and the vast masses of the poor.

According to the United Nations study, the estimated literacy rates run from 9.1 per cent of the population of India (1931), ten years of age and over, 13.8 per cent of Pakistan (1951), and 14.8 per cent of Egypt (1937) able to "read and write," to 61 per cent of the population of the Philippines (1948), ten and over, who are "literate." The median estimate of literates for the countries of Group III is about 32 per cent.

The caloric intake per person per diem, among the peoples where estimates are possible, ranges from about 1,700 for India to 2,400 for Egypt, with about 2,000 calories as the daily median. Between 70 and 90 per cent of the calories of these peoples come from cereals and potatoes; they partake of very limited and only occasional amounts of animal proteins and fats; even their intake of plant fats and proteins is scanty. Their diets are unbalanced and very poor from the point of view of the "protective" elements essential to physical vigor and health.

These countries have made the least advance in health. They have an initial disadvantage in that the countries of the group in South America and the Caribbean, those of central Africa, part of China, and the countries of India, Burma, Ceylon, Indo-China, Thailand, and Indonesia are in the "tropical disease" belt. Some of the most serious endemic, and most of the horrible epidemic diseases have their worst incidence among them. In some parts smallpox, cholera, plague, and leprosy are widespread; others suffer from yellow fever, sleeping sickness, flukes, and tuberculosis. The filth disease, hookworm, is common. There is very limited control over the biological disease-causing factors; public health organization is poor; there is a lack of inoculation. Poverty and lack of education make hygienic and sanitary practices difficult.

These Group III countries are the homes of the vast masses of the world's underdeveloped peoples. But they are beginning to wake up; small elements in their populations and in some instances their own governmental officials are highly alert and keenly conscious of their problems and needs even if the great masses are still deeply entrenched in their archaic ways of life.

THE CORRELATED DEMOGRAPHIC SITUATION

These are countries of high fertility and high mortality, with moderate rates of increase at the present, but with high growth potential. The estimated birth rates for these peoples for the 1946-1948 period were high, mostly in the range from 40 to 45 per thousand. The estimated death rates ranged from around 17 for the Latin American countries (including those in Group 11) and 25 to 30 for Africa (including the Group II areas) and south-central Asia, to 30 to 35 for the Near East and the remaining Far East. Both birth rates and death rates were close to pre-modern standards. The rate of natural increase was 7 to 18, with the average around 12. This indicates a moderate recent and present rate of increase, but an increase achieved by a tremendously wasteful expenditure of births and deaths. In general, they are still in a condition of pre-modern "demographic balance." Neither natality nor mortality are under much voluntary control.[34].

Fertility, as noted, is extremely high. Birth rates show very little variability and persist at a high level. In many areas they cannot go much higher, being near the biological maximum, considering the physiological state of the female population. Because of the almost complete absence of the conditions and incentives that make for fertility reduction, the birth rates are quite stable at this high level, and they are likely to remain high.

The death rates are also high—the highest in the world. In general, death rates are not stable, but fluctuate from year to year, sometimes violently, with the uncontrolled conditions affecting

---

[34] It must be pointed out that the available figures for 1953 show that the birth rates have tended in general to stay up, in some instances actually to increase. The death rates, on the other hand, in the majority of cases have declined, in a few instances (e.g., Ceylon, Taiwan, Malaya) to a startling degree.

lethality—malnutrition and famine, disease and epidemic, physical catastrophe, war and rebellion. Infant mortality is very high. India in 1948 had a rate of 130, but it was down to 116 in 1951; Egypt in 1950 had a rate of 130, and Malaya of 102. Life expectancy at birth averages around 30 years, as against the high sixties for the Group I countries, and upper forties for Group II. In some of the countries, especially the less populous ones, there is some tendency toward decline of death rates with the development of medicine and public health facilities.

The tempo of population increase or decrease is determined, not by the fluctuations of the birth rate in good and bad times, as is the case of Group I countries, but by the performance of the death rate, which is under limited and precarious control. The level of the death rate depends upon the degree of success in coping with the recurrent crises caused by the hazards of weather and bad harvests, by ravaging diseases and epidemics among the people and their plants and animals, and by political disturbances.

The reductions in mortality in some areas point to the fact that social, medical, sanitary, and economic development may give a tremendous impetus to morbidity and mortality control, and in the future may lead to a spectacular lowering of the death rate. Even now the simplest public health provisions (such as waste control or the use of DDT) quickly reduce death rates. If improvements in the death rate come and there is the universally experienced tardiness in the decline of the birth rate, the rate of growth will shoot up. Since the aggregate of population in Group III is huge, the increase in absolute numbers of persons will be tremendous.

In general, therefore, the immediate effect of a drop in the death rate, while the birth rate remains high or even increases, is markedly to increase the population. What is especially a matter of concern is that most of this increase is concentrated in the younger age groups. In the course of time these children and young people enter the reproductive period of life and add greatly to the number of prospective parents. Thus a vast increase in the present foreshadows an even greater future increase. Hence, in such countries, as long as there is no decline in the birth rate, the increase in population, once begun, is cumulative.

As a result of high fertility and mortality rates and low life expectancy, which have prevailed for centuries, and still do, the age structure of Group III countries shows a pattern of high percentages of children (population under 15) and low percentages both of adults of working age (15-59 years) and aged dependents (60 years and over). This pattern appears to have persisted throughout the period for which information is available, except for temporary modifications due to the effects of migration. Estimates for 1947 for specific regions show the Near East as having 40 per cent of its population under 15 years and 54 per cent from 15 to 59 years; for south-central Asia 40 per cent and 56 per cent, respectively; and for the remaining Far East (except Asiatic U.S.S.R.) 40 per cent and 55 per cent. Latin America, consisting primarily of Group III, though also including some Group II countries, had a ratio of 8 persons under 15—and a *combined* ratio of 9 persons under 15 *and* over 59—to only 11 persons in the 15 to 59 range. The United States and Canada, on the other hand, had only 5 children, and about 7 in the dependent ages (below 15 and over 59 years) to 11 productive adults.[35]

There is not likely to be much change in the age structure of the Group III countries during the next few decades unless their birth rates are sharply reduced. But if death rates come down (as noted they show a ready tendency to do so) and birth rates come down (this will occur much more slowly) these countries will have a period when the bulk of the inhabitants will be in the productive years of life.

These are the "unstable" countries. They might also be referred to as the "coiled" countries because of their huge potential for population increase. They are the demographic dynamite of the world ahead or, as Thompson put it as far back as 1929, the major "Danger Spots."

In most instances low birth rates and low death rates are related to abundant available resources, efficient labor, abundant capital equipment, adequate communication and transportation, adequate, balanced nutrition, adequate housing, far-reaching social organization, high level of literacy and education, high levels and standards of living, and among most of the peoples who have achieved these low rates, to democratic, individualistic, and secular ways of life.

---

[35] For a similar comparison between India and the United States see Davis, *The Population of India and Pakistan,* pp. 85-86.

On the other hand, high birth rates and high death rates tend to be related to subsistence-agrarian economy, land crowding, national poverty, low living levels and standards, low per-capita income, malnutrition, inefficient or limited use of resources, low capital equipment, and illiteracy.

The achievement of a more economical population balance for these countries is a matter of tremendous importance, both internally and internationally, but also one of extreme precariousness. The likelihood of an accelerated control of disease and epidemic and many other highly lethal factors is great, and death rates will fall, as they have done so significantly in India and Ceylon.[36] Whether or not they can improve their agriculture, advance in industrialization fast enough and soon enough to elevate the levels of living and produce widespread aspirations for higher standards of living, and bring down fertility rates proportionally, is the burning question. There is a good prospect that growth will continue until the potentialities for increased production are exhausted. Peace and order, and a speedy, thorough, and balanced modernization seem to be the only ways of meeting the situation.

[36] Ceylon is a particularly pertinent example of the demographic effects of health and death control. Extensive applications of DDT have resulted in greatly reduced death rates from malaria and fly-carried infant diarrheas. In the first two years following the introduction of an extensive DDT campaign in 1946 general death rates dropped from 20-22 per thousand of population to 13-14 per thousand, or almost 40 per cent; by 1951 they had declined to 11.6 per thousand of total population. The precipitant decline in mortality was not accompanied by any measurable changes in fertility; the crude birth rate has remained over 40 per thousand. The increase of population in Ceylon between the censuses of 1946 and 1953 was almost 21 per cent. By 1952 the rate of natural increase exceeded 3 per cent per year—an unprecedented level.

The Ceylon experience is being repeated with varying degrees of effectiveness in other localities. Malaria, one of the major killers in India, will probably be brought under essentially complete control in another five or six years. In view of the very remote likelihood of any appreciable reduction of the birth rate, it is likely that in that country, too, population is destined to grow at an unprecedented rate, possibly until other causes of death take hold. For recent treatments of morbidity and death control see Marston Bates, *The Prevalence of People* (New York: Scribners, 1955), pp. 110-125; P. S. Henshaw, *Adaptive Human Fertility* (New York: McGraw-Hill, 1955), pp. 90-95.

BIBLIOGRAPHY

BROWN, HARRISON. *The Challenge of Man's Future*. New York: Viking, 1954. Pp. 46-67, 95-99, 234-235.

BUCHANAN, N. S., and H. S. ELLIS. *Approaches to Economic Development*. New York: Twentieth Century Fund, 1955. Pp. 92-116. See also appendixes, pp. 457-463.

CLARK, COLIN. *Conditions of Economic Progress*. London: Macmillan, 1940.

————. *The Economics of 1960*. London: Macmillan, 1942.

CONDLIFFE, J. B. *The Economic Pattern of World Population* (Planning Pamphlet No. 18). Washington: National Planning Assoc., 1942.

COOK, R. C. (ed.). "Asian Population Roundup." *Population Bull.*, 11 (March, 1955): 1-12.

DAVIS, KINGSLEY. "The Demographic Foundations of National Power," in Meyer Berger, Theodore Abel, and C. H. Page (eds.) *Freedom and Control in Modern Society*. New York: Van Nostrand, 1954. Pp. 206-242.

————. "Population and the Further Spread of Industrial Society." *Proc. Am. Phil. Soc.*, 95 (Feb., 1951): 8-19.

————. *The Population of India and Pakistan*. Princeton: Princeton Univ. Press, 1951. Pp. 85-87.

HATT, P. K., N. L. FARR, and E. WEINSTEIN. "Types of Population Balance." *Am. Soc. Rev.*, 20 (Feb., 1955): 14-21.

HUGHES, E. C. and H. M. *Where Peoples Meet: Racial and Ethnic Frontiers*. Glencoe, Ill.: Free Press, 1952. Pp. 52-60.

JEFFERSON, M. "Distribution of the World's City Folks: A Study in Comparative Civilization." *Geog. Rev.*, 31 (July, 1931): 446-465.

LORIMER, FRANK, *et al*. "The Relation of Cultural Conditions to Demographic Transition," in *Culture and Human Fertility: A Study of the Relation of Cultural Conditions to Fertility in Non-industrial and Transitional Societies*. Paris: UNESCO (New York: Columbia Univ. Press), 1955. Chap. VI, pp. 204-251.

NOTESTEIN, F. W. "Population—The Long View," in T. W. Schultz (ed.), *Food for the World*. Chicago: Univ. of Chicago Press, 1945. Pp. 42-52.

PIQUET, H. S. "Point Four and World Population." *Annals Am. Acad. Pol. & Soc. Sci.*, 268 (March, 1950): 148-159.

REED, S. W. "World Population Trends," in Ralph Linton (ed.), *Most of the World: The Peoples of Africa, Latin America, and the East Today*. New York: Columbia Univ. Press, 1949. Pp. 112-131.

SPENGLER, J. J. "Population and Per Capita Income." *Annals Am. Acad. Pol. & Soc. Sci.*, 237 (Jan., 1945) : 182-192.

————. "The Population Obstacle to Economic Betterment." *Papers and Proceedings of the 63rd Annual Meeting*, Am. Econ. Assoc., Vol. 41, No. 2 (May, 1951) : 243-254.

THOMPSON, W. S. *Plenty of People*. Lancaster, Pa.: Jacques Cattell Press, 1944. Pp. 89-98.

————. "Population." *Scientific American*, 182 (Feb., 1950): 11-15.

————. *Population and Peace in the Pacific*. Chicago: Univ. of Chicago Press, 1946. Pp. 26-35.

―――――. *Population Problems* (4th ed.). New York: McGraw-Hill, 1953. Pp. 267-272.

UNITED NATIONS, Department of Social Affairs. *Preliminary Report on the World Social Situation.* New York, 1952.

UNESCO. *Basic Facts and Figures: Illiteracy, Education, Libraries, Museums, Books, Newspapers, Newsprint, Film, Radio, and Television.* Paris, 1954.

UNITED NATIONS, Population Division, Department of Social Affairs, *The Determinants and Consequences of Population Trends: A Summary of the Findings of Studies on the Relationships between Population Changes and Economic and Social Conditions* (Population Studies, No. 17). New York, 1953. Pp. 44-45, 141-149, 153-162, 194-200, 213-214, 253-260, 265-267.

―――――, Population Division, Department of Social Affairs. *Population Bulletin,* No. 1 (Dec., 1951). New York, 1952. Pp. 4-12.

―――――, Population Division, Department of Social Affairs. *Population Growth and the Standard of Living in Underdeveloped Countries* (Population Studies, No. 20). New York, 1954.

―――――, Statistical Office, Department of Economic Affairs. *National and Per Capita Incomes of Seventy Countries—1949.* New York, 1950. Pp. 14-16.

UNITED STATES DEPARTMENT OF STATE (with technical assistance of the National Advisory Council). *Point Four.* Washington, 1949. Pp. 92-115.

VANCE, RUPERT B. "The Demographic Gap: Dilemma of Modernization Programs," in *Approaches to Problems of High Fertility in Agrarian Societies.* New York: Milbank Memorial Fund, 1953. Pp. 9-17.

WOYTINSKY, W. S. and E. S. *World Population and Production: Trends and Outlook.* New York: Twentieth Century Fund, 1953. Pp. 44-49, 111-124, 196-240, 282-311, 349-469, 513-531.

5

Population Pressure
and the Underdeveloped Countries

We have noted that most of Group II and practically all of Group III countries, constituting close to 80 per cent of the world's population, do not have any appreciable control over their fertility. Their control over mortality, though still limited, is increasing and is producing great and accelerated population expansion. In the case of Group III peoples there is every likelihood that this will produce a stupendous increase in the total number of human beings. At the same time, the Group II and especially the Group III peoples, in the light of their partial or even only incipient modernization, are poorly equipped to cope with these vast and increasing numbers, at least in terms of the standards of production and consumption now accepted almost universally. Indeed, there is substantial evidence that conditions among many Group III peoples have actually been deteriorating in recent decades. This situation, therefore, points to two concepts, "underdeveloped countries" and "population pressure," the essence and significance of which we need to examine briefly.

UNDERDEVELOPMENT AND UNDERDEVELOPED COUNTRIES

The term "underdeveloped" is one adopted by the United Nations to replace the expression "backward." As used now quite generally, in connection with various countries and peoples, it is not a term of opprobrium; nor is it used with an air of condescension or pity. "Underdeveloped" implies mainly that the country or people are technologically and economically underdeveloped or misdeveloped, though other elements of social life are also inevitably involved, as will be noted below.[1] The term signifies that a standard of some sort is used. The standard of "development" is based primarily on the state of technological proficiency, of individual and national economic adequacy, and of general social well-being, as now found (mainly) within the framework of Western civilization and as achieved by the Group I and top-bracket Group II peoples. These presumably favorable conditions serve as ends which the people of the rest of the world want and aspire to as soon as they become conscious of them; the more advanced peoples also deem them essential for the particular peoples and for world peace, prosperity, and progress. The achievement of these conditions is a fundamental aspect of the equalization of opportunity and welfare in the world, and is thought to be crucial in the solution of many of the world's population problems. In brief, "modernization," as discussed in Chapters III and IV above, is a luminous world goal; most of the peoples of the world are anxious to "modernize" though always in a manner consistent with their own cultures.

The lag in modernization in many instances is due to handicaps not imposed upon, or found among, European peoples. Historical, economic, and political circumstances beyond the control of particular peoples may, in part, be responsible—such as suppression, repression, and exploitation by European peoples. Our purpose here, however, is not a review of historical contributory factors, but a scrupulously objective examination of the more general features of the underdevelopment of these people.

It should be pointed out that the term is a limited one. Countries referred to as "underdeveloped" may be highly developed in certain aspects of their culture, such as their philosophy, art, and religion, though these may be mainly for the "few" at the top of the society. The term is also relative; there are almost no peoples or countries that do not have some degree or certain aspects of

---

[1] For treatments involving the concept "underdevelopment" see Bekker, Buchanan and Ellis, Davis (1952), Gerschenkron, Hoselitz, Notestein, Piquet, Spengler, Staley (1954), and Stamp.

technological-economic development. Finally, in order to eliminate looseness of expression, the term is used in connection with a whole country or people, and not particular areas or population segments within a country. We have underdeveloped and underprivileged areas within the so-called highly developed countries, such as the United States. Practically speaking, under the concept, countries are grouped roughly according to their being, in general, developed, partially or intermediately developed, or underdeveloped. Let us indicate the typical characteristics of an "underdeveloped" country.

In agriculture laborious hand methods largely prevail; there is little mechanization, except on some plantations and foreign-owned agricultural enterprises; even the better and cheaper, readily available hand tools and animal-powered machines and appliances are scarcely used. Accessible land readily capable of agricultural development with disease and pest control, transportation facilities, soil surveys, water control and water supply, and cultivation techniques is not being utilized. Modern fertilizers and plant and animal genetic practices are not used. Some of the countries have almost no manufacturing industry; the rest are mainly in the incipient stage, though in some instances a few industries may be well started, as in the case of steel production in India.

In most instances their own readily available physical and biological resources and raw materials are either inadequately exploited or not utilized or processed at all, even for the home market. Per-capita energy consumption (from coal, petroleum, water power) is low even where available.

A preponderant proportion of the labor force, in notable instances over 80 per cent, is concentrated in peasant subsistence agriculture. Davis has pointed out that the peasant agricultural regions have an average of 113 male agriculturalists per square mile of agricultural land, while the modernized countries have only 32.[2] This means also a definite underdevelopment of industry and commerce. While there is high productivity per acre in some areas due to a most intensive application of labor on the part of an agriculturally redundant labor supply, there is a tremendously high ratio of men per unit of land and a low net output per worker and per man-hour. The vast agricultural population is underemployed

---

[2] 1952, p. 15.

much of the time. The manpower, whether in agriculture or in industry, is ineffectively employed. It is not using available knowledge, skills, and techniques; it is handicapped by deficiencies in mechanical power assistance and in capital equipment, such as working quarters, tools, and machinery. Most of the labor force, as well as the general population, is not utilizing its full potentialities because of the low level of consumption, evidenced especially in undernourishment and malnutrition, and because of poor health, the result of a lack of basic health facilities and programs. The average life span is short, thus reducing the per-person and total productivity of the population. Both physical and human resources are underused or going to waste; both could be turned to useful purposes by an expansion of technique and technical equipment.

There is low capitalization and a shortage of capital equipment. Capital equipment—tools, machines, and labor-enhancing and labor-saving devices generally—are lacking in both agriculture and industry. With the poverty of the people there is practically no surplus that can be saved for capital investment. In some instances there are sizable investable surpluses among the small, privileged upper classes, but often these are not mobilized for national productive purposes, being either hoarded in the form of precious stones, gold, and silver, or sent abroad as funds for investment in industrialized countries. In some instances, also, the peasant produces a small investment surplus over and above his narrow margin of consumption, but ". . . it is wrung from him through various gimmicks in the price system, by inflation, by land taxes, by duties, and by the use of physical services."[3] The very growth of a population very near the bare subsistence level impinges continually on feeble national financial resources and makes first demands on the national income simply for the maintenance of the additional population.

Transportation of all kinds is underdeveloped, thus impairing internal supply and exchange and reducing the possibility of developing and utilizing resources.

Many of these peoples are dependent upon the outside world for the great bulk of their industrial products, for the production of many of which they have both natural and labor resources. They

---

[3] Bekker, p. 239.

are not contributing to the markets of the world what they are potentially capable of under modern conditions, what the world needs, and what they need to export in order to acquire various imports. In general, the economic underdevelopment of these peoples applies not to agriculture alone, to urban industry alone, to internal or international commerce alone, but to the whole economy.

These countries are also characterized by a very limited development of commercial, financial, credit, professional, research, organizational, and humane services. The mass of the people are underdeveloped educationally, both as to general education and as to the great array of practical aptitudes and skills.

Economic advancement, both in the development of indigenous resources and facilities and in the acquisition of the means of life through international exchange, is lagging behind population growth. The great masses of the underdeveloped peoples are "poor" in the economic sense—grindingly poor. Not only is their plane, or level, of living, that is, the economic level upon which they are enabled to live, very low as compared with the more advanced countries; even their standard of living—the minimum of consumption goods and services that are considered indispensable— is low, because of their retarded condition and limited economic perspectives. In some instances, the impoverished condition seems to be growing worse, as will be noted in the next chapter.

While underdevelopment is mainly a matter of lagging development in physical technology and industry-commerce, it unavoidably has inherent in it other elements. It is also a matter of intellectual climate, spirit, and ideology. These are affected by physical and cultural isolation, by illiteracy and social ignorance. They in turn affect the degree of ability and of willingness to borrow technology and use existing know-how. A related aspect of underdevelopment is the persistence of religio-magical attitudes toward the world and a tendency to accept the world apathetically instead of resolutely experimenting, coping with it, and attacking it. Related also is a lack of discipline and of reliability for modern industrial and commercial activity and organization.

Underdevelopment also implies poor social organization, considering the great areas inhabited in some cases, the great and dense populations, the needs for communication, cooperation and integration. This social organization is quite inadequate in the light of what we know about requirements, principles, and available efficient social instrumentalities. These countries are still retarded by archaic institutions suited only to an agrarian subsistence economy. The associations and large-scale formal organizations so essential in carrying on the multiple tasks of modern complex societies—educational, research, and health services, all manner of industrial, commercial, financial, communication, transportation, and other economic activities—are inadequate, though transferable "patterns" exist.

Underdevelopment among these peoples is also evidenced in an underdeveloped state apparatus. The state is not yet developed to the point where it can provide the multiple requisite controls and services or realize with fair effectiveness the political or the social-economic aspirations of the people.

OPTIMUM POPULATION AND OVERPOPULATION

It has been evident in Chapter IV that the technology, economy, and general social state of a people or country bear a very close reciprocal relation to their demographic condition. It has also been hinted in the present chapter that underdevelopment and redundant population have reciprocal influence. The frequently occurring concepts regarding the population aspect of the population-resources equation—namely, underpopulation, optimum population, and overpopulation, and the conditions involved in each—need brief examination.

OPTIMUM POPULATION

The very terms "underpopulation" and "overpopulation" imply that some sort of bench mark is being used to determine whether there are too few or too many people in the country. The concept "optimum population," though still widely criticized, though still subject to much controversy as to specific content and interpretation of components by its users, and though still lacking in ready and precise practical applicability, comes nearest to providing us with a standard. A key concept, even though not yet fully developed, is fruitful for analytical purposes. Adumbrations of the idea, at the hands of such men as Sismondi and Cantillon, are found in the eighteenth century; indeed, it goes back much earlier, for when Plato set up the ideal number of citizens for his city-state in the

Laws he was skirting the edges of the idea. The main development, however, has come during the present century, especially since World War I. The distinctive name was given the concept by the economists Edward Cannan and Knut Wicksell.[4]

In very general terms, the concept is concerned with what is theoretically the "right" or the "best" or the "most desirable" or "ideal" relationship of population to existing resources, technology, and institutional conditions among the people of an area. Such an ideal relationship of the various pertinent factors, deliberately established, serves as a standard in the light of which the actual relationships may be evaluated. When a society has the most appropriate number of people utilizing its resources and its technical and organizational facilities, it can be likened to a "smooth-running motor," to use Wolfe's phrase.[5] Or, as Fairchild points out, a society can be compared to the great ship *Queen Mary*, which should have the right-sized crew to operate most efficiently; with too few crew members it is undermanned, and when there are too many, some are definitely superfluous.

The concept, in its present state, has been most specifically and comprehensively formulated by the economists, and mainly in terms of economic components. This does not mean, however, that there is general agreement among these economists as to how the components, quantitatively and qualitatively, and their peculiar existence in the particular area or society at a given time, are to be weighted and tested in order to provide the elements of a valid and workable standard. Other social scientists and some philosophers have added what are deemed to be essential considerations. We will examine the concept of optimum population mainly with respect to the social-economic considerations and objectives with which the great bulk of the most scientific theoretical discussions have been mainly concerned.[6]

[4] For treatments of optimum population see Bowen, Carr-Saunders, Dalton, Fairchild, Ferenczi, Hobson, Hoover and Duncan, Leibenstein, Mukerjee (1933), Penrose, Reuter, Robbins, Thompson (1953), United Nations, and both Wolfe references.

[5] 1934, p. 588.

[6] Fairchild has called attention to considerations, other than social-economic, that historically have entered into the concept of optimum population, such as the *militaristic* argument, current where and when "group or national prestige, power, even survival, demanded the maintenance and increase of the body of

The cautious report of the Population Division of the United Nations, by way of summarizing the ideas of the economists, defines the "economic optimum population" as ". . . that size of population which, given the technical and economic conditions existing in a given country, allows maximum *per capita* output."[7] This provides us with a point of departure. A brief and rough synthesis of the ideas reveals the minimal array of variables, each, of course, implying important subvariables, which are involved in determining the optimum. The task in determining the optimum is one of proportioning the productive resources and other factors, of securing the most efficient quantitative relation of the factors, all of which in actual life are variable, but to different degrees. A very brief presentation of the economic variables follows.

The *population* aspect of the elements in the equilibrium, as developed by most students, concerns not only total numbers, but also the composition of the population from the point of view of labor force, especially its age and sex distribtuion, its literacy and technical proficiency, occasionally its quality. Some also call attention to economic attitudes and habits of the people, and the degree to which these promote or hinder maximum output.

The *resources,* at any given time, consist of the land and all that it provides in the way of materials that can be processed into further producers' and into consumers' goods. Usually resources available through interareal and international exchange are also included.

The *technology,* in this connection, includes the total organization of techniques and instruments for manipulating, controlling, and utilizing the available resources—the "state of the arts" of production. Of the technological elements, the kind, amount, and effective quality of the capital, or capital equipment, is a strategic factor in developing the maximum productivity per capita. There

---

fighting men"; the *religious* argument, based upon the expansion and maximum size of the number of true believers; the *dynastic* argument, relating to the enhancement of the power, prestige, and wealth of the group, in part at least, by means of a sizable and growing population; the *ethnic egoism* argument, based on pride of race, nationality, language, etc., and involving the size of the select and superior as against the "lesser breeds without the law"; and several other arguments. Pp. 153-157.

[7] P. 233.

is also the occasional implication that the arts of consumption, the degree of efficiency in the technical utilization of consumers' goods by the people, are also involved.

The *organization of production,* as a variable, refers to the way the factors of production—labor, resources, capital equipment—are quantitatively combined (for example, as to whether the productive system, in both its agricultural and industrial aspects, uses a vast amount of labor in relation to the other factors, as among underdeveloped countries), the system of distribution of the proceeds of production among the factors, the ways in which technology is utilized, the degree of functional specialization and the level of complexity of the organization, the nature and level of technical organization and administrative management, the degree of large-scale formal organization, the wage system, the system of communication and transportation, the financial (monetary and credit) system, the marketing system, the tax system, the property system, and the way in which, and the degree to which, international trade is involved in the particular productive system. Very few students use all of these items as pertinent in their conception of organization of production as an element in the optimum. There is occasional reference to other major social institutions, such as the governmental, the legal, the educational, the scientific, even the familial, as having direct or indirect, but nevertheless significant, effects on the way the production of particular peoples is conducted, and hence as influencing the "maximum productivity per capita."

The *distribution of income,* though a phase of the organization of production, is sometimes given separate treatment as a variable. Here attention is called to the fact that it is not only the total amount of income produced in a given country in relation to total numbers which is important, but also the degree to which it is fairly equitably distributed among the whole population, as compared with a disproportionate part of it being consumed by a small minority in the form of luxurious goods and services. The adequacy of income per head is an important factor in the proficiency of the labor force, as also is the way in which income as distributed affects consumer demand.

[8] Cf., the treatment by Leibenstein.

Most of the economists and practically all of the other social scientists are agreed that the ultimate objective in the establishment of the optimum population is the maximization of social-economic welfare and of human happiness. But, lacking objective standards of welfare and happiness, the economists tend to strive for fairly concrete objectives, the realization of which depends upon definite items and variables which can to some extent be quantitatively expressed.[8] The economists also bear down on economic welfare as the touchstone, meaning the welfare which results from the production, distribution, and consumption of economic goods and services. Hence, almost all are agreed on "maximum per-capita output of goods and services" as the main objective. This is translated into maximum per-capita *real* income in the way of actually available and supplied goods and services per head, and this, in turn, is reflected in the "average" economic level of living. The population that most efficiently produces this "best" per-capita economic level of living is the optimum population.

Some of the economists, however, maintain that certain less tangible and not exclusively economic elements or variables should also enter into the concept of the optimum. For example, in some of the writings[9] it is suggested that the subjective, or human, costs of producing the real income, and the distribution of costs between persons, be considered, that is, whether the productive processes are arduous or light, painful or enjoyable for the producers, whether the employment is regular, whether the work is more galling and burdensome for some portions of the population than for others.

Beyond the economists, other social scientists and philosophers present quite an array of relatively intangible elements involving the values of various cultures relating to the Good Life broadly conceived, over and above economic welfare. In this connection we find reference to health and other physical well-being, plenty of elbow room and privacy, the enjoyment of natural features even though some of them might be utilized for strictly economic purposes, liberty, abundance of personal opportunity and security and a "wide margin of safety," leisure for intellectual, aesthetic, and spiritual satisfaction and expression, and other possibilities of ex-

---

[9] Cf. Dalton, pp. 30-32.

panding the human spirit. The optimum is thus extended beyond material income to *humane* income. Such broader conceptions of optimum population rest upon the reigning values as to what is good and desirable. These are translated into standards which, in their very nature, are less precise and more controversial than those governing economic criteria. Needless to say, though items such as these are less tangible, they are, nonetheless, very real. Many people in all cultures prefer fewer material consumption goods in order to have more elbow room, or more freedom, or greater opportunity for recreational, aesthetic, or religious satisfactions.

One very important aspect of the optimum population, thus far not considered, is time. Regardless of the number and tangibility or intangibility of factors taken into consideration, they are always involved in the effective proportioning or equilibrium of elements only as of the particular time (even moment) of assessment. There can be no definite unchanging optimum over a period of time. The setting and all of the ingredients and factors are continually changing, though not at the same rate. There are fluctuations in birth rates and death rates, changes in sex and age and other compositional aspects of the population as well as emigration and immigration, changes in literacy, technical skills, and other proficiencies of the people. Technologically significant inventions and improvements may occur, and there may be importations of technological elements which change the techniques of production and consumption. Even changes in the organization of production may be brought about. The physical resources, available and utilizable, change with new discoveries of internal sources, with deterioration or exhaustion, with new access or curtailment of access to those from without the borders of the country. There may be shifts in the institutionalized habits of the people (as along educational lines). Every alteration of values brings about modified standards regarding material, political, aesthetic, spiritual and other welfare ends. There may be changes in political conditions and configurations, for example, as they affect international cooperation. Changes outside the country, the discovery of abundant raw materials, or the development of new, lucrative markets may change the optimum. Change in any one of the variables affects the position of the optimum. Hence, the optimum has to be a moving figure, a flowing affair, changing as the conditions, techniques, and perspectives alter.

It is obvious that the determination of the optimum population presents a host of diffcult problems. In the theoretical development of the concept there is the task of selecting the minimal number of relevant component elements, of deciding whether, logically or realistically, noneconomic as well as economic factors in well-being should be included, of setting the optimum point or range for the population of a given country under existing conditions as the factors are proportioned, and so on. Hence, the task of establishing a concrete composite index as of a given moment is a most complicated matter. It is difficult at present even if only the economic factors in the equation are included, in spite of the fact that they are now being subjected to quantitative measurement that has been fairly well standardized. When we note the necessity of its being a flowing index, its practical development and applicability are further complicated. Thus, the theory is still not precisely formulated, and the task of working it out as an actual practical instrument for determining overpopulation or underpopulation is still something that lies ahead for the social engineers. Therefore, there are some who would discard the estimate of the optimum as of little practical value and consider as more useful the advantages or disadvantages to the country of alternative rates of population change.

Nevertheless, the devising of such a composite index in terms of the quantified relevant ingredients in the near future is not an altogether hopeless matter. Sampling techniques are being improved very rapidly. The ability to quantify not only economic but also noneconomic variables through their behavioral expressions is proceeding apace, notably for instance, the expression of attitudes and values. To cope with the necessarily flowing nature of standards, we have had, for example, some fairly respectable results. In a more limited area, to be sure, the "sliding wage scale" as found in certain American agreements between unions and corporations or industries is based on an arbitrarily selected set of standard-of-living items as developed by the Bureau of Labor Statistics. Nor is it altogether utopian to consider the use of electronic computing machines in the compilation of an index from the complex data of variables involved.

The upshot of the whole matter is that the students of population do have some sort of vague but neverthless working concept of a right or optimum population when they think of overpopulation or underpopulation. It is a sort of composite image based on a rough consensus and consists of cautious guessing as to items—demographic, economic, social, valuational—and as to their weighting and interplay in the whole. The task ahead seems to be to make the optimum a scientifically selective, valid, and workable index or formula. The need for it is undeniable for both analytical and practical purposes. Needless to say, if conceived of in its social-economic well-being aspects, it can be a primary feature of national and international population policy.

OVERPOPULATION

Historically, underpopulation has been a common situation as newly discovered and nuwly opened lands suitable for easy human habitation and ready economic utilization have become available. It was notable in most of Europe and the Mediterranean area in the days of Hellenic and Roman expansion and in the Western Hemisphere from the sixteenth to the twentieth centuries. Even at present some areas and countries, not only in the Western Hemisphere, but also in Europe and possibly elsewhere, occupied by the more technologically-economically advanced peoples, can, on the basis of the concept of optimum population, be considered underpopulated. By underpopulation, as already implied, we simply mean that there are too few people in relation to available and developed resources, economic and social know-how, and technical and organizational means to achieve the level of living that would be possible. The underpopulated peoples, however, are decidedly a minority in the present world, as might be surmised from previously discussed population trends and comparative demographic data. Furthermore, underpopulation is an ephemeral phenomenon that usually rights itself in a surprisingly short historical time. From time immemorial overpopulation has tended to be the chronic state of many human societies. Today it is a major problem for the greater proportion of the peoples of the world.

The notion is still current that overpopulation is a matter of large numbers of people per square mile of land. When peoples were, or are, mainly dependent upon hunting, grazing, or simple agriculture, then density is an important factor. But the development of technology, especially in industry and transportation, has changed this. According to 1950 densities,[10] Norway with 26 people per square mile, the United Kingdom with 536, Belgium with 733, and the state of Nebraska with 17 were all on about the same level of well-being, and all were infinitely better off than the pre-Columbian inhabitants of the area of the United States with possibly less than one-tenth person per square mile. Today, overpopulation, by consensus of authorities generally, is not a matter of man-area ratio, or standing room, but a situation in which the population at the given time and in the given area is too large in proportion to the available resources and all of the pertient productive and distributive means of effectively utilizing these resources; hence, there is low per-capita output and low per-capita real income. The number of people has increased beyond the optimum point and various penalties in well-being exist.[11] A people who are not overpopulated are fairly safe and comfortable with their means of existence; their life conditions permit a sense of security and adequacy with respect to the actualities of production and consumption in the present and the continued possibility of these in the foreseeable future; they have a ratio of population to available resources and the facilities for production and distribution that make possible an expansive individual, social, and cultural life; they are not ground down by the race to keep supplies merely up to the subsistence point for an ever-increasing number of human beings.[12]

---

[10] United Nations, *Demographic Yearbook, 1951,* for national data.

[11] Note the following definitions of overpopulation. "Population pressure (tantamount to overpopulation) exists, not when the population per square mile surpasses a certain figure, but when the population of that square mile does not have sufficient economic resources, natural resources, industrial production, services to support itself." N. Doman, *The Coming Age of World Control* (New York: Harpers, 1942), pp. 258-259. "Theoretically, any region might be described as overpopulated in which a higher level of living and more rapid economic progress could be expected if there were fewer people, with the present capital equipment, social organization, and personal characteristics." F. Lorimer, "Issues of Population Policy," *Annals Am. Acad. Pol. & Soc. Sci.,* 237 (Jan., 1945): 193-203, esp. pp. 196-197.

On overpopulation see also Davis (1951); Fairchild; Hofstee; Ross; Thompson (1947); and D. R. Taft and R. Robbins, *International Migration: The Immigrant in the Modern World* (New York: Ronald Press, 1955), pp. 60-64.

[12] Overpopulated people usually show certain characteristic signs. Some of these have been mentioned, though with a different analytical objective, in

MALTHUSIAN CONSIDERATIONS

There is always the search for the fundamental principles and factors involved in human situations. For more than a century and a half the thinking about the relationship between population, resources, and well-being has recurrently concerned itself with the so-called Malthusian Doctrine. In fact, it is no exaggeration to say that Thomas Robert Malthus not only posed one of mankind's most demanding problems, but probably did more than anyone else to found modern population theory. During the last decade there has been a new and acute interest in this body of thought, precipitated, no doubt, by the critical post-war social, economic, and political conditions and the unprecedented increase in the population of the world. We will present its core principles in barest outline, merely state the more outstanding offsets and limitations, and indicate briefly its acceptable residues.[13]

In 1798 Malthus published the first edition of his *Essay on the Principles of Population as its affects the Future Improvement of Society, with Remarks on the Speculations of Mr. Godwin, M. Condorcet, and other Writers.* A substantial revision followed in 1803 with a change in sub-title, and further editions appeared in 1806, 1807, 1817, and 1826, each in response to criticisms, refutations, and "replies." The several editions through which his work went attest to the pointedness of the ideas and the tremendous interest aroused by them. Some of the doctrines which he promulgated, or at any rate some aspects of them, had already been promulgated by Machiavelli and various other writers, especially during the eighteenth century. But he elaborated, focused, epitomized, and synthesized these ideas, added features and interpretations of his own, supported his contentions with a vast amount of historical data, and gave them universal application. While there are in Malthus' work dogmatisms, contradictions, oversights, limitations of perspective, and impracticalities, there is a set of central and essential principles that seem to have stood the tests of time and circumstance.

the examination of Group III people in the previous chapter, and others will be pointed out in the treatment of obstacles to modernization in the next chapter.

[13] On the Malthusian Doctrine see the treatments by Bennett, Bonar, Boner, Clark, Coyle, Darwin, Fairchild, Field, Flugel (1947), Glass, Penrose, Reuter, Smith, Spengler (1945, 1949), Thompson (1953), and Vance.

THE ESSENCE OF THE MALTHUSIAN DOCTRINE

In essence Malthus asserted that human reproduction—like that of other species—is governed by a powerful and "necessary" biological urge—"the passion between the sexes"—to increase; this urge "will remain nearly in its present state"; therefore, the potential increase, all other things being favorable, is unlimited. Nature, on the other hand, "has been comparatively sparing in the room and nourishment" (the "niggardliness of nature"), in "the means of subsistence," "the supply of food"—those things "necessary to the existence of man." Furthermore, man is indolent and torpid by nature, "inert, sluggish, and averse from labor, unless impelled by necessity." Thus, population (1) has the capacity to increase faster than the means of existence; (2) has a constant tendency to increase beyond the means of existence; (3) tends continually to increase into and keep pace with any additions to the food supply, and (4) tends, in general and in the long run, "to press upon the food supply."

These postulates are based on two fundamental "laws" with respect to ratios of population increase and the food supply. First, population, unchecked, increases by a geometrical ratio; and, second, food increases only by an arithmetical ratio. By geometrical rate, or geometrical progression, Malthus means, to use his own figures, that "the human species would increase as the numbers 1, 2, 4, 8, 16, 32, 64, 128, 256." Subsistence, increasing at an arithmetic rate or progression, would be "as 1, 2, 3, 4, 5, 6, 7, 8, 9." If the two rates were permitted to work themselves out, and assuming, as he did, a possible doubling of population every twenty-five years, "in two centuries the population would be to the means of subsistence as 256 to 9; in three centuries as 4,096 to 13, and in two thousand years the difference would be almost incalculable."

However, such a progressive distortion in the respective rates of increase of population and subsistence has not occured, and cannot occur, because numbers of population *have* to be confined to the existing limits of the food supply; it is truistic that there must be sufficient food for the subsistence of any existing population at any given time. Hence, the third fundamental feature of his doctrine, namely, that the conflict between population and subsistence is resolved by subjecting population to an array of *checks*, which renders it compatible with subsistence. These checks fall into two broad categories: the *positive,* which increase the death rate; and the *preventive,* which restrict births. "The positive checks to population include . . . all unwholesome occupations, severe labor and exposure to the seasons, extreme poverty, bad nursing of children, great towns, excesses of all kinds, the whole train of common diseases and epidemics, wars, plague and famine . . ." The "ultimate check . . . appears . . . to be a want of food. . . . But this ultimate check is never the immediate check, except in cases of actual famine. . . . The immediate check may be stated to consist of all those customs, and all those diseases, which seem to be generated by a scarcity of the means of subsistence; and all those causes, independent of this scarcity, whether of a moral or physical nature, which tend prematurely to weaken and destroy the human frame."

The preventive checks are peculiar to man. There are the involuntary ones making for sterility, such as prostitution and other forms of sexual vice. But with the second edition of the *Essay* Malthus stresses the voluntary preventive check, his prudential consideration, "moral restraint," namely "restraint from marriage," or deferred marriage, which is preceded by continence and "which is not followed by irregular gratifications." Thep ositive checks restore the balance between numbers of human beings and subsistence, which has been temporarily upset, by reducing the number of mouths to be fed; they trim population to fit subsistence. The voluntary preventive checks enable man to keep his numbers within subsistence, and to "get on top of the other checks."[14] To sum up, in Malthus' own words again:

1. Population is necessarily limited by the means of subsistence.
2. Population invariably increases where the means of subsistence increase, unless prevented by some very powerful and obvious checks.
3. These checks, and the checks which repress the superior power of population, and keep its effects on a level with the means of subsistence, are all resolvable into moral restraint, vice, and misery.

Here are the elements of the Malthusian Doctrine. Let us now attempt some evaluation of its validity and applicablity.

[14] Field, pp. 25, 26.

OFFSETS AND LIMITATIONS

There were certain conditions and developments of the period which were either in such an incipient stage that Malthus failed to notice them or were misinterpreted or inadequately appreciated by him. At least for a time these seemed to discredit some of his tenets, or suggested a partial emancipation from the dilemma which he posed.

Among the most important offsets must be mentioned the fact that improvements in transportation during the nineteenth century gave access to vast, rich agricultural lands, especially in the Americas, South Africa, and Oceania—an extension of land the like of which had never occurred before. For a time the extensiveness and the possibilities of this new land created a labor shortage. Also, for several generations, both available land and food supply increased faster than population, and there were increasing returns per unit of input.

The nineteenth and early twentieth centuries were also a period of unprecedented expansion of the scientific and technological frontiers. In agriculture great advances in tools and machines, the use of mechanical power, more efficient techniques in cultivation and in the management of water, the use of fertilizers, and the genetic improvement of plants and animals greatly increased the productivity of some parts of the world. Improvements in manufacturing improved the processing and utilization of materials, and those in transportation and exchange gave access to heretofore unavailable food sources and other essential and desirable materials. The increasing political, social, and economic democratization facilitated and encouraged vertical social mobility, which in turn had a restraining effect on birth rates.

Certain pertinent limitations of theory and perspective should be mentioned. Malthus seemed to be concerned with what might be referred to as the *power* of population to increase in connection with his "geometrical ratio," that is, maximum physiological capacity to reproduce. This power to reproduce has seldom been exerted, however, and has only rarely been achieved. Malthus also did not seem to be aware of the fact that among most primitives as well as known civilized peoples reproduction has always, in some measure, been controlled.

While Malthus paid some attention to "luxury," mainly as a stimulant to production and exchange, he gave inadequate weight to the standard-of-living factor and the aspiration for ever-higher levels of living as important variables in reproductive performance. He also underestimated the possibility of inventions and improvements in techniques of expanding the production of food and other necessities for an indefinite future time. Nor did he adequately assess the possibilities inherent in medical science for reducing death rates and misery.

While shortage of food is the ultimate check upon population increase, Malthus seemed to think of it as the sole check at any given time and place, and to consider vice and misery, and rebellion and war, primarily as functions or effects of the deficiencies in the food supply. Needless to say, there are many other checks to population increase—physical, biological, economic, and institutional.

His "moral restraint"—"restraint from marriage from prudential motives, with a conduct strictly moral during this period of restraint"—has been very exceptional historically and is undesirable for a considerable number of economic, social, psychological, and moral reasons.

Finally, he failed to appreciate or advocate birth control as a salutary voluntary means of avoiding some of the effects of his dilemma. It consisted of an ancient set of procedures that he must have been aware of when writing his earlier editions. Furthermore, it had developed as the central issue of a social movement in northwestern Europe during the last two decades of his life. In the fifth edition he 'reprobates" it.

THE PRINCIPLE OF DIMINISHING RETURNS

Before taking up the acceptable and all-important "residues" of the Malthusian Doctrine, it is desirable that brief attention be given to the principle, or "law," of diminishing returns, which had its inception in Malthus' day, and which is of central significance in any examination of demographic-economic equilibrium. Malthus' *Essay* is not based on the law of diminishing returns as it applies to land, but he had an inkling of it; it is what he was groping for in the arithmetic ratio. It remained for David Ricardo, John Stuart

Mill, and other economists of the nineteenth century to give the principle its full theoretical stature.

The law, in its early and essential form, arises out of the peculiarity of land from the economic standpoint. Land, unlike capital and labor, at any given time is fixed in quantity and quality. As population increases, the demand for the produce of the land increases, and men are obliged to study the ways by which they can bring new and presumably inferior land into cultivation, or avoid deterioration of the existing land and obtain an increasing quantity of produce from it. "There are two ways in which this can be done. The first is by discovering and applying improved methods of production. The second is by using increasing quantities of the other agents of production: capital and labor." When improvements are made in the methods of cultivation and/or when successive doses of labor and capital are applied to land, there are usually increasing returns, but after a certain point has been reached, diminishing returns follow: a less than proportionate increase per unit of input occurs.[15]

The limitations of Malthus' conception of the law of diminishing returns is brought out by Field.

> Of the three angles to the problem of diminishing returns—the historical taking up of poorer land, the exhaustion of the soil, and the failure of added doses of other factors applied to land to increase the output proportionately—Malthus seems to be consciously aware of only the first two. . . . In his mind resort to inferior soils is the dominating idea; exhaustion of older land comes second. The third aspect of the idea of diminishing returns, that of the lack of proportionality in the returns to added applications of labor and capital, is there only by implication. Malthus probably did not appreciate the significance of this idea, although he used it to good advantage.[16]

The law of diminishing returns is not a principle which asserts itself suddenly with catastrophic effects; there are always developments which postpone its operation. There may be increasing returns for a while under all three major conditions: as technology

---

[15] The quotation and most of the analyses of this paragraph are from H. Wright, pp. 29-31.

[16] P. 16.

improves, as heretofore uncultivated lands and other (such as oceanic) sources of food are exploited, and as increased amounts of labor and capital are applied. But eventually the point of increasing costs and diminishing returns is reached.

There are three—and only three—possibilities of increasing the food supply *when population increases*. In each case, however, the law of diminishing returns operates eventually.

A fixed supply of land under cultivation and no change in the efficiency of labor or capital. Here the increased population would imply an increased labor supply; we can also imply an expansion of the supply of capital proportionate to the labor increase. By increasing units of labor and capital per unit of land (the total quantity being fixed at a given time), we might for a while get increasing returns with each successive increment of the same quality of labor and capital. There may have been a less-than-optimal use of both labor and capital. But, since the productivity of the land is not unlimited, because of the limited and expendable nature of its component elements we eventually get diminishing returns in produce per additional unit of labor and capital.

A fixed supply of land, with labor and capital not only increasing but improving in productive efficiency. Here the output per unit of labor and capital applied to a given amount of land may increase very considerably for a time; but the use of continually more efficient labor and capital on the unit of land simply postpones the beginning of diminishing returns.

Bringing new land under cultivation. The unavoidable assumption is that the new land is inferior to the land under cultivation. Otherwise, with the increase of people to be fed and with a given state of the arts, it would already have been under cultivation. It is almost certain that it is poorer land in any or all of several respects: as to soil, moisture (too much or too little), temperature (for both man and productive crops and/or livestock), climate, terrain, and accessibility (for settlers and to markets). With the same efficiency of labor and capital we immediately have increasing costs to get the same returns per acre. By improving efficiency we simply postpone diminishing returns somewhat longer.

We people of the Western lands, with our vast and still accelerating technological advances, our great quantity and high quality of capital equipment, our efficient labor supply, and—among some of us—stores of investment funds and surpluses of food, cannot allow the highly advantageous conditions we are enjoying to distract our attention from the ultimate eventuality of diminishing returns among us. In fact, we already note them in certain aspects of our economy. And, as will be noted more particularly in Chapter VII, even with an indefinite improvement of the arts, diminishing returns are inevitable in the end because of the very finiteness of the earth, and of the fact that all of its resources are eventually available only at increasing cost. We run into the law of diminishing returns, not because of labor limitations, but because of limitations of capital—capital which men must everlastingly create and improve. Capital equipment itself derives originally from natural resources, and the very materials from which it is produced are subject to the law of diminishing returns. The source materials for the development of atomic energy are fund resources, and the capital equipment necessary to utilize such an eternally given and unlimited supply of energy as that of the sun must be made from materials limited in amount and usable quality, and hence subject to this law.

APPLICABILITY OF THE MALTHUSIAN DOCTRINE

Even when we grant the various limitations of some of Malthus' theory, the errors as to details introduced because of his time-bound perspective, his occasional misrepresentation of what is incontrovertible, and the effects of his own idiosyncratic prejudices, there is still a sturdy residue. Population theorists cannot afford a pedantic preoccupation with his details or even with many of his historical examples; nor is a strictly "literal" interpretation of his doctrine in order at present. Our concern must be with the residues that have survived and are pointedly demonstrable today, and with the general principles of his doctrine and the signal overtones that emanate from it.

There are certain small particular residues that stand out. (1) Malthus' theoretical possibility of great human increase has not been disproved, even though it does not necessarily occur at a geometric rate. Population increase and even population pressure are always a potentiality, and the imminence of overpopulation continues to be a vital problem. The offsets simply mean that the possibilities of overpopulation become operative more gradually. (2) While the food supply is not the only or always the immediate

factor, it is the *ultimate* limiting factor in population increase.[17]
(3) The operation of the positive checks, including their presence among most of the peoples of the earth at the present moment, is too obvious to be denied. The fact of death through want is likewise incontrovertible. Throughout history, malnutrition and starvation, endemic and pandemic diseases, intertribal and interracial warfare, famines, physical catastrophes, and widespread resort to infanticide and abortion seem to have been the outstanding causes of death, and indicate that it was high death rates, not low birth rates, which held back the increase of population. Furthermore, this general contention is amply supported by the very burgeoning of population when the main positive checks on natural increase are diminished in effect by improvement of the means of existence through gains in land extension, by improved cultivation, by better distribution and importation of necessities, and by medical advances and improved hygiene and sanitation. (4) Malthus did rightly stress the need for and the possibility of some voluntary control of numbers, though the particular means he suggested were doubtless rather futile. Man, by the exercise of intelligence and prudence, could, in a humane manner, keep his numbers in check.

Over and above these residues are the broad, fundamental principles of Malthus and the over-all general demonstration of them. In fact, in the light of all experience, this doctrine today has the universality, validity, and applicability of a scientific postulate. In realizing this, it is necessary to avoid certain misunderstandings and confusions, which Flugel has well stated. Malthus was not concerned with the number of people that the earth may be able to support at some future time as compared with the number it now supports. He was not concerned with the fact that countries and peoples are not making the fullest and best use of their present or even future productive potentialities. He was not concerned with the indubitable fact that during the last 150 years many countries have shown themselves capable of supporting not only much larger populations, but of supporting them in greater comfort than that enjoyed by their smaller population of the past. It is con-

---

[17] It should be pointed out in connection with both (1) and (2) that it is axiomatic in biology that no species can multiply without limit, and there is no reason for believing that man is an exception.

ceivable that under certain conditions we might—for a while—have the operation of the "law of increasing returns" for much or all of the earth, because of the vast improvements in extractive industry and in secondary industry (thus obtaining more utility from raw materials), because of the extension at home of fertile lands, and because of advances in transportation that would give cheap and ready access to excellent new land. It is possible, as Darwin points out, that the food production of the world could be increased a thousand times above its present level (through the development of synthetic food, the discovery of and ability to use the food supplies of the depths of the oceans, etc.) without invalidating the fundamental principle.[18]

The fundamental proposition of Malthus is that population always has the potentiality or the tendency to press upon the supporting power of the land (the subsistence supply) at any given time, with a given stage of the arts and a given standard of living. This is a threat everywhere; and the recurrent operation of the positive checks throughout history, including the present, attests to its frequency.

There are related considerations. There is a pointed relation between population and the means of subsistence *at any given time and place,* irrespective of the ultimate population or food supply, or whether the population or the food supply is at the moment increasing or decreasing. In this connection, there is always the possibility that though the food supply may be increasing, the population may be increasing at an even faster rate.

There is also the unavoidable fact that improvements in the production and distribution of food and other essentials take time and involve costs. Furthermore, anticipated improvements cannot abolish any shortages that exist now.

Finally, though there may here and there be phenomenal increases of food for a while, amounting to increase in world supply greater than the world's population increase, this supply cannot be increased at the same rate and with the same ease forever. The earth is finite, and none of its resources are indefinitely extendable in use without eventually greater difficulty and expense. As its *fund* or nonreproducible resources—our "geological capital"—are

[18] Pp. 34-35.

used, its inhabitants must resort to ever poorer grades or more inaccessible supplies, or transfer to substitutes often more difficult and expensive to acquire. Its *flow*, or naturally reproducible resources (such as water power, much plant and animal life, etc.), is never limitless at any given time, and even with anticipated technological advances the *means* essential to their development (fund materials, capital, etc.) are not indefinitely extendable. In fact, diminishing returns are *ultimately* probable—even inevitable—for any given area, and for the world as a whole.

We have noted in Chapter III the tendency of population during the long span of the life of man on the earth eventually to expand into every technical, ecological, and economic gain. This fact has been elaborately demonstrated in the stupendous increase of population during the last three centuries, and especially among the rapidly advancing European peoples. "When goods increase, they are increased that eat them."[19] Such calm and objective analysts of the world's food supply, past and present, as Pearson and Harper state: "Man's history has always been a race between food supplies and mouths to be fed."[20]

In spite of the wish on the part of millions with various complexions of interest and thought that it were not so, the unhappy fact is that to avoid Malthusian Determinism or the Malthusian Dilemma and to effect a displacement of the "Malthusian Equilibrium"[21] we must have either an increase of subsistence at an ever accelerated rate, or an increase of deaths, or a decrease of births. "Nature in the raw" can be modified by man's intelligence and restraint, but it is always in the background ready to take over.

Malthus was thinking mainly in terms of a given country. Today we have to think of the implications of this dilemma on a global scale; a "planetary ecology" prevails. Even with a most conscientious devotion to the highly successful application of science and technology in the increase of the means of existence, unrestrained optimism is silly and profligate. Man seems to be caught in the wheels of a Juggernaut: find more food to supply more people, ad infinitum, in a limited world. Like Alice's Red Queen, we

[19] *Ecclesiastes* V: 11.

[20] F. A. Pearson and F. A. Harper, *The World's Hunger* (Ithaca: Cornell Univ. Press, 1945) , p. 1.

[21] For the use of this term see Leibenstein, pp. 3-33.

"have to run ever faster to stand still" and have to run even harder to get ahead. The question is whether the world can afford to go on increasing its population.

It may be pointed out, in the light of world experience to date, that population will continue to grow into every gain made, and that improvements in all techniques and increased prosperity will accelerate this growth, unless rationally checked. Furthermore, the modern world really hastens the operation of the Malthusian principles by drawing *all* productive lands and people into the *want and exchange* orbits. The actual and potential "good" land is worked and used up so much the faster. One need only recall the extent to which Europe and Asia are drawing upon the lands and food supplies of North America north of the Rio Grande, the temperate zone of South America, and Australia. Finally, there is the fact, to be examined more extensively in Chapter VII, that every increase in population requires more standing room, more residential space, more space for industrial and commercial enterprises, more space for highways and military installations, and so on, and that this space is mostly on "good earth" and must be continually subtracted from the good and even the best agricultural land of the earth. It must be recalled that, at the present rate of growth of world population, additional standing room is required every year for nearly the equivalent of one-fifth of the population of the United States. There are well-grounded reasons for prudence.

POPULATION AND WAR

Overpopulation or population pressure *within* nations, in the sense of an adverse ration of population to usable resources and techniques and hence the existence of a low level of living, and marked population and socio-economic differentials *between* nations suggest the relationship between these and such international disturbances as migration and war. Both of these create crucial problems which are a matter of great international concern. Migration in the modern world will be dealt with in Chapter VIII. Our present task is to examine briefly the problem of war from the point of view of population pressure as a presumptive "cause" of war.[22]

[22] For references see Brown; Davis (1954); Fairchild, pp. 211-226; Flugel (1947, pp. 21-25), (1952); Hankins; Kirk; Mukerjee (1941, pp. 429-458); Penrose, pp. 306-336; Ross, pp. 165-176; Staley (1939); Thompson (1946), pp. 18-21,

Historically there has been much evidence of at least a close relationship between population pressure and wars of expansion and conquest. As Homer put it in the *Iliad*:

> It is impossible to conceal the belly's eagerness—a ruinous thing, that brings many evils to men; for the sake of it well-benched ships are fitted out and bear mischief to foemen over the unvintaged sea.

The recurrent raids and wars of preliterate peoples, the mass migrations, the aggressive invasions and wars of the Huns, Celts, and Goths in the Dark Ages, the spectacular outbursts of the great raiders and conquerors, Genghis Khan, Kubla Khan, and Tamerlane, in the thirteenth and fourteenth centuries, the expansions, conquests and wars of Spain, Portugal, Holland, France, and Britain beginning with the sixteenth century, and of Germany, Italy, Japan and other nations in the nineteenth and twentieth centuries, as well as innumerable other instances, doubtless had some degree of population pressure as an incitive factor. It is probable that economic distress is still one of the underlying and predisposing factors in most international wars.

The situation is one of differential rates of population increase and differential man-land ratios as between countries and peoples; of a world limited in area all the time and limited in *available* resources at any given time; and of great inequalities in the distribution and ownership of resources and/or access to resources, in the technical use of resources, and in the levels of consumption. Some people always have more and some have less. As all worthwhile areas, with their resources, are occupied and controlled, certain peoples have frequently felt that the only way in which they could obtain additional land was to take it away from somebody else; or, in more highly involved relations where war itself was not feasible, there has been a struggle for trade routes, for relatively exclusive markets, for some kind of control over undeveloped areas, and various other kinds of rivalry and exercise of power which in the last analysis have reflected stringent home conditions in the aggressive nations.

338-343; Thompson and Whelpton; Walter H. Wright, pp. 130-140; and both Q. Wright references.

There are few events which are wholly dissociated from economic factors, and war is certainly one of these, but the economic factors are rarely the only ones. It is only realistic to call attention to numerous other interrelated contributory situations, such as autocratic sovereigns using people to fight out their quarrels, ambitious dynasties seeking to extend their power and domain (Napoleon, Hitler), chip-on-the-shoulder nationalism, militarists and the military spirit (Bismarck and William II of Germany), imperialism and imperialists (Britain, Spain, Germany, Japan), armed religious expansion (Islam and Christianity), the spread of social-economic and political creeds, entangling alliances, balance-of-power manipulations, and the combatting of threats to power and security.

While incompatibility between the differential growth of population and the differential ownership, utilization, and enjoyment of the world's resources is a potent background factor, it would be highly unrealistic to assume that this population pressure (and economic stringency) is necessarily an initiating cause of disturbance, or that in itself it necessarily and automatically creates the possibility of warlike activity among a given people. Until recently at least, India, China, the densely populated Malay States, and Indonesia, for example, with their high birth rates, dense populations per square mile, and vast numbers of mouths to feed, have not greatly endangered the peace of the world. The population factor taken alone and considered merely in its biological and economic aspects is not a satisfactory explanation for aggression or war.

A host of socio-cultural factors of a traditional, evaluational, technological, social-psychological, education, and social-organizational nature are also involved before pressure can become effective as military activity. Both Thompson and Quincy Wright have made important contributions to our understanding of these elements. Thompson points out that it is not absolute poverty which measures the degree of population pressure as a danger to peace, "but the *felt* lacks, the *felt* pressures on resources, the *felt* discriminations in access to the resources of the world."[23] "Extremely poor peoples are too feeble to wage war with any hope of success against the great powers already entrenched in the desirable areas. . . . The greatest degree of *felt* population pressure is generally found

[23] 1946, p. 19.

among peoples who have already passed from the direst poverty, who have tasted some of the good things of life, and who believe that they are being deprived of their deserts by those who have arrived ahead of them."[24]

On the other hand, we usually find among a "backward" people, in spite of "absolute" pressure, a vast ignorance, a profound apathy, physical and political incompetence, submissive suffering of their "fate," and no consciousness, or even existence, of means.

A people must be "kinetic" instead of "static" to wage war in the present world. Quincy Wright[25] has called attention to some of the conditions under which overpopulation is likely to suggest war as a policy. Among others, the distressed peoples must know of other areas that seem to be underpopulated; there must be means of mobility; the physical (geographic) obstacles and the social and moral barriers must not be too formidable; a host of subjective conditions must exisit, such as a willingness to sacrifice an accustomed way of life in order to achieve sometimes vaguely perceived and uncertain advantages.

To these may be added others. A developed psychological situation of tension and "touchiness," of anxiety, and a feeling of inferiority must exist. There must be the development of knowledge, of relatively clear concepts of economic welfare, and an appreciation of alternatives to their present state. Arousal and expansive visions and hopes are essential. There is invariably a developing political consciousness, a strongly developing sense of nationality and concepts of nationhood. There must be developing industrial techniques and growing economic power, the development of military potential and organization, and the development of an effective political organization. There must be a growing sense of self-confidence, a sense of urgency, the development of various kinds of leaders with know-how and with initiative and energy. Finally, there must be the belief on the part of the potential wagers of war that they have the essential technical, military, and general social-organizational advantage over those whom they seek to conquer, and often there is the belief that they are superior racially and culturally and better adapted than the present possessors to develop

---

[24] 1947, p. 106.
[25] In both cited references.

the available areas. In general, they have come to be a people ready
to enter upon the "swarming stage of development," to use Thompson's term, and are prepared to take a calculated risk. As one of
the world's best recent examples of these hypotheses, one need only
recall the Japan of the Tokukawa Shogunate and Japan since the
turn of the century.

THE DANGER SPOTS

What is the significance of the discussions of this chapter up
to this point? It is apparent that there are vast areas of underdevelopment, areas which are below the optimum and, hence,
which according to fairly standard criteria are overpopulated, areas
where the Malthusian Equilibrium prevails. As two world wars
have attested, in these days of international contact and inter-
dependence the problems of well-being and peace are no longer
local or even regional or continental. Areas of relative wretchedness
and hardship which are likely to disturb peace anywhere are now
a world danger.[26]

In the light of our discussion of Groups I, II, and III, it is evident
that the countries of high population pressure and of potentially
high pressure due to the early demographic effects of modernization are the hazardous areas; and the peoples of these areas constitute more than 60 per cent of the world's population. Of course,
not all are equally dangerous. The lesser danger spots consist
mainly of much of southern and eastern Europe. The major danger
spots consist of most of Africa, especially and immediately Egypt;
most of the Caribbean region, especially Mexico, Puerto Rico and
Haiti; and most of the rest of Latin America. But worst of the
danger spots is Asia, with over half of the population of the earth
living far below the accepted standards of the modern world.

Why are they danger spots? A considerable number of demographic reasons are already apparent. Several others might be
mentioned. While their inhabitants are waking up and emerging
into the "swarming stage," where will they swarm to in the present
world, and how? Many of them have made signal political and
military contributions during and since World War II. The rest
of the world cannot take back what has been given to these people

[26] Cf. his *Danger Spots in World Population* (New York: Knopf, 1929).

in new perspectives and objectives, nor can it obliterate the keen notion they have developed of their vast importance in the present world.

They are developing economic and political leaders of international as well as national importance. With mechanization and industrialization and growing political organization and strength comes the possibility of military power. Furthermore, they realize that there is an eastward movement of world power into the Pacific area.

Japan has been symptomatic of the situation for more than half a century, and during the last decade China, India, all of southeastern Asia, Egypt, Central and South Africa, and many other parts of Asia and Africa, as well as much of Latin America, have shown that among them are all the ingredients for periodic and devastating explosions.[27] The problem of eliminating international disturbances and that of eliminating hunger, deprivation, misery, and tension cannot be divorced from each other.

OBJECTIVES FOR THE UNDERDEVELOPED COUNTRIES

In general, the major objectives of the people interested in peace, security, good will, and well-being in the world today are concerned with bridging the great gaps between the rich, modernized countries and the poor, underdeveloped, overpopulated, peasant-agrarian peoples comprising three-fifths of the world's population. These peoples are problems, even hazards, for all of the countries of the world as areas of endemic and epidemic diseases, as areas of economic dependency, as explosive centers of unrest and rebellion, and as possible disturbers of world peace if and when they should attempt the age-old nostrum of alleviating their population pressure by aggressive action against presumably more favorably situated peoples. It is desirable, in fact essential, that they be extricated from their adverse state at the earliest possible moment.

Prosperity among the peoples of the earth is a very important element in well-being and peace. Prosperity means not only economic prosperity, but also social, political, spiritual, and psychological well-being. All the peoples of this shrinking world have to have these and enjoy them together. Two major, reciprocally related objectives standout.

[27] Cf. Flugel, 1947, pp. 23-25, 93; Thompson, 1947, pp. 100-105.

The first objective is to raise the level of living and to develop, according to modern standards, a state of physical adequacy for these peoples. This is an immediate humane consideration. These are *poor* peoples, ill fed, ill housed, ill clothed; they are in ill health and shortlived; they are ill educated; they are overcrowded and many of them live in squalor; they are otherwise bereft of the decencies, amenities, and material conditions and satisfactions deemed standard and essential among the more advanced peoples of the world. Raising the level of living of these peoples is a vast concerted enterprise consisting, among many efforts, of providing an adequate and balanced food supply for each people and country and increasing by all possible means the world's food supply, of increasing the production of and accessibility to the other individual and group material essentials of life, of satisfactorily protecting the people against the rigors and hazards of the physical and biological environment, of effectively controlling disease and improving health, and thus improving the physical quality of life, energy, and working efficiency and correspondingly lengthening the period of life expectancy. It is obvious that this physical adequacy and well-being should be enjoyed by all countries and by the total population of each country, and not only by certain small segments of the world or of national populations, for nowadays the welfare of those best off is tied up, unavoidably, with those badly off.

The other related objective is that of getting population increase under control, especially by reducing fertility. While this too has its ultimate humanitarian overtones as an important factor in producing a *quality* of life, it is mainly a pressing utilitarian consideration, since upon it depends in large measure the effective operation of most of the means of achieving the first objective. Not only need both birth rates and death rates be reduced for the sake of the physiological and economic savings that accrue, but they need to be brought into a more economical and rational balance with each other. The possible technological-economic improvements essential to the realization of the first objective simply cannot forever compensate for the constant and accelerated increase of population. Furthermore, as will be noted later, every population increase among underdeveloped peoples seems to impede their economic development. Therefore, it is somewhat unrealistic to try to do something on the technological-economic side and nothing on the population side.

These objectives, as noted, are reciprocally related, and both imply modernization. Yet they are antagonistic in one very important respect. If the first objective is effectively carried out by means of modernization procedures, the first, most noticeable effect is that of a marked decline in the death rate, possibly a slight temporary increase in the birth rate, and, most certainly, a rapidly accelerating natural increase rate—which is precisely what the second objective seeks to avoid. Yet the first objective can only be brought about by modernization. The reduction and control of morbidity and mortality, as involved in both objectives, can only come from modernization. Similarly, wherever modernization has run its full course, it has tended, indirectly and ultimately, to provide both the motivation for fertility reduction and control, and the means—in the form of secularized and rationalized values and attitudes, modified institutions, and essential knowledge and techniques. The ultimate objective therefore, in order to avoid loss of net gains under the first objective through a crushing increase in population, is to obtain the most rapid and effective modernization possible in order to hasten, indirectly, the reduction of fertility. The crucial problem among the underdeveloped countries is that of maintaining a rate of technological, economic, and educational growth in excess of the rate of population growth. Among many of them at present added productivity is swallowed up by further increases in numbers, and its proceeds are not available for education, for capital formation, for plant extension and so on. The desired social, economic, and demographic effects of modernization can, because of delay in developing it, easily be "too little and too late."

In the remainder of this study we will attempt to spell out, constructively though also critically, the major means and procedures, with the inextricably related problems, for coping with the world population situation. In subsequent chapters we will examine (1) the promotion of modernization of the underdeveloped countries in terms of principles, internal possibilities and problems, and considerations regarding the use of external assistance; (2) the possibilities of extending the cultivable land of the earth, of increasing the productivity of the present cultivated land, and of otherwise increasing the supply of food and other essentials for fair existence; (3) the questionable possibilities of migration from overpopulated countries—one of the age-old remedies—in the world as it is. Since time is lacking, however, for full dependence upon the automatic and gradual operation of modernization as a fertility reducer among the underdeveloped peoples, a final chapter will treat briefly certain population policies and programs, especially those concerned with more direct and immediate means of bringing birth control before the people.

BIBLIOGRAPHY

BATES, MARSTON. *The Prevalence of People.* New York: Scribners, 1955. Pp. 62-79, 126-141.

BEKKER, KONRAD. "The Point IV Program of the United States," in Hoselitz, pp. 230-247.

BENNETT, M. K. *The World's Food: A Study of the Interrelations of World Populations, National Diets, and Food Potentials.* New York: Harpers, 1954. Pp. 43-58.

BONAR, JAMES. *Malthus and His Work.* London: Macmillan, 1885.

BONER, H. A. *Hungry Generations: The Nineteenth Century Case Against Malthusianism.* New York: Kings Crown Press, Columbia Univ., 1955.

BOWEN, H. "Capital in Relation to Optimum Population." *Soc. Forces,* 15 (March, 1937): 346-350.

BROWN, HARRISON. *The Challenge of Man's Future.* New York: Viking, 1954. Pp. 228-235.

BUCHANAN, N. S., and H. S. ELLIS. *Approaches to Economic Development.* New York: Twentieth Century Fund, 1955. Pp. 3-22.

CARR-SAUNDERS, A. M. *The Population Problem.* Oxford: Clarendon Press, 1922.

CLARK, F. LE GROS, and N. W. Pirie (eds.). *Four Thousand Million Mouths: Scientific Humanism and the Shadow of World Hunger.* London: Oxford Univ. Press, 1951. Pp. 6-29.

COYLE, D. C. *Day of Judgment: The Economic and Political Challenge to the West.* New York: Harpers, 1949 Pp. 55-62.

DALTON, HUGH. "The Theory of Population." *Economica,* 8 (March, 1928) : 28-50.

DARWIN, SIR CHARLES G. *The Next Million Years.* New York: Doubleday, 1953. Pp. 29-38, 170-178.

DAVIS, KINGSLEY. "The Controversial Future of the Underdeveloped Areas," in P. K. Hatt (ed.), *World Population and Future Resources.* New York: American Book, 1952. Pp. 14-24.

————. "The Demographic Foundations of National Power" in Meyer Berger, Theodore Abel, and C. H. Page (eds.) *Freedom and Control in Modern Society.* New York: Van Nostrand, 1954. Pp. 206-242.

————. *The Population of India and Pakistan.* Princeton Univ. Press, 1951. Pp. 204-212.

FAIRCHILD, H. P. *People.* New York: Holt, 1939. Pp. 61-108, 152-179.

FERENCZI, IMRE. *The Synthetic Optimum of Population: An Outline of an International Demographic Policy.* Paris: International Institute of Intellectual Co-operation, 1938.

FIELD, J. A. *Essays in Population and Other Papers.* Chicago: Univ. of Chicago Press, 1931. Pp. 1-86, 249-268.

FLUGEL, J. C. "Population Policies and International Tensions." *Sociological Rev.* (Brit.), 44 (1952): Sec. 1.

————. *Population, Psychology and Peace.* London: Watts, 1947. Pp. 1-90.

GERSCHENKRON, ALEXANDER. "Economic Backwardness in Historical Perpective," in Hoselitz, pp. 3-29.

GLASS, D. V. (ed.) *Introduction to Malthus.* New York: Wiley, 1953.

HANKINS, F. H. "Pressure of Population as a Cause of War." *Annals Am. Acad. Pol. & Soc. Sci.,* 198 (July, 1938): 100-108.

HENSHAW, P. S. *Adaptive Human Fertility.* New York: McGraw-Hill, 1955. Pp. 56-65.

HOBSON, J. A. *Economics and Ethics.* New York: Heath, 1929. Pp. 340-371.

HOFSTEE, E. W. "Population Pressure and the Future of Western Civilization." *Am. Jour. Soc.,* 55 (May, 1950): 523-532.

HOOVER, G. E., and K. DUNCAN. "The Quantitative Optimum of Population." *Annals Am. Acad. Pol. & Soc. Sci.,* 162 (July, 1932) : 198-205.

HOSELITZ, B. F. (ed.) . *The Progress of the Underveloped Areas.* Chicago: Univ. of Chicago Press, 1952. Preface, pp. v-viii.

KIRK, DUDLEY. "Population Changes and the Postwar World." *Am. Soc. Rev.,* 9 (Feb., 1944): 30-35.

LEIBENSTEIN, HARVEY. *A Theory of Economic-Demographic Development.* Princeton: Princeton Univ. Press, 1954. Pp. 171-191.

MALTHUS, T. R. *An Essay on the Principles of Population.* (Various editions from various publishers.)

MUKERJEE, RADHAKAMAL. "The Criterion of Optimum Population." *Am. Jour. Soc.,* 38 (March, 1933): 688-698.

————. *The Political Economy of Population.* London and New Lork: Longmans Green, 1941. Pp. 160-308, 429-458.

NOTESTEIN, F. W. "Summary of the Demographic Background of Problems of Undeveloped Areas," in *International Approaches to Problems of Undeveloped Areas.* New York: Milbank Memorial Fund, 1948. Pp. 9-15.

PENROSE, E. F. *Population Theories and Their Application, with Special Reference to Japan.* Stanford, Calif.: Food Research Institute, 1934. Pp. 3-91, 306-336.

PIQUET, H. S. "Point Four and World Production." *Annals Am. Acad. Pol. & Soc. Sci.,* 268 (March, 1950): 148-159.

REUTER, E. B. *Population Problems.* Philadelphia: Lippincott, 1937. Pp. 277-283.

ROBBINS, LIONEL. "The Optimum Theory of Population," in T. E. Gregory and Hugh Dalton (eds.), *London Essays in Economics: in Honour of Edwin Cannan.* London: Routledge, 1927. Pp. 103-137.

Ross, E. A. *Standing Room Only?* New York: Century, 1927. Pp. 127-141.

Sax, Karl. *Standing Room Only.* Boston: Beacon Press, 1955.

Smith, Kenneth. *The Malthusian Controversy.* London: Routledge & Kegan Paul, 1951.

Spengler, J. J. "Economic Factors in the Development of Densely Populated Areas." *Proc. Am. Phil. Soc.,* 95 (Feb., 1951) : 20-53.

―――――. "Malthus's Total Population Theory: A Restatement and Reappraisal." *Canadian Jour. Econ. & Pol. Sci.,* 11 (Feb., 1945): 83-110; 11 (May, 1945): 234-264.

―――――. "The World Hunger—Malthus, 1948." *Proc. Acad. Pol. Sci.,* 23 (Jan., 1949): 53-71.

Staley, Eugene. *The Future of Underdeveloped Countries: Political Implications of Economic Development.* New York: Harpers, 1954.

―――――. *World Economy in Transition.* New York: Council on Foreign Relations, 1939. Pp. 100-121.

Stamp, L. Dudley. *Land for Tomorrow: The Underdeveloped World.* Bloomington: Indiana Univ. Press, 1952. Pp. 15-19.

Thompson, W. S. *Plenty of People.* Lancaster, Pa.: Jacques Cattell Press, 1947. Pp. 99-107.

―――――. *Population and Peace in the Pacific.* Chicago: Univ. of Chicago Press, 1946. Pp. 18-21, 338-343.

―――――. *Population Problems* (4th ed.). New York: McGraw-Hill, 1953. Pp. 20-32, 447-456.

―――――― and P. K. Whelpton. "Levels of Living and Population Pressure." *Annals Am. Acad. Pol. & Soc. Sci.,* 198 (July, 1938): 93-100.

United Nations, Population Division, Department of Social Affairs. *The Determinants and Consequences of Population Trends: A Summary of the Findings of Studies on the Relationships between Population Changes and Economic and Social Conditions* (Population Studies, No. 17). New York, 1953. Pp. 233-235.

Vance, Rupert B. "Malthus and the Principle of Population." *Foreign Affairs,* 26 (July, 1948): 682-692.

Waller, Willard (ed.). *War in the Twentieth Century.* New York: Dryden, 1940. Pp. 3-35.

Wolfe, A. B. "On the Criterion of Optimum Population." *Am. Jour. Soc.,* 29 (March, 1934) : 585-599.

―――――. "The Theory of Optimum Population." *Annals Ab. Acad. Pol. & Soc. Sci.,* 188 (Nov., 1936): 243-149.

Wright, Harold. *Population.* New York: Harcourt Brace, 1923. Pp. 20-58, 130-140.

Wright, Quincy. "Population and International Tensions." *Annals Am. Acad. Pol. & Soc. Sci.,* 188 (Nov., 1936): 318-328.

―――――. *A Study of War.* Chicago: Univ. of Chicago Press, 1942. Vol. II, pp. 1118-1145.

6

*The Modernization of
the Underdeveloped Countries*

THE NEED FOR MODERNIZATION

The great advances in socio-economic and political well-being
that characterize the advanced nations of the modern era have
been due to that complex of processes that we have called modernization. The great demographic achievements, both with respect to
morbidity and mortality reduction and control, and such fertility
reduction and control as has occurred, have in part at least been
effects of modernization. Where and when demographic balance
has been achieved thus far, it has been associated with, if not
entirely due to, modernization. Modernization certainly is involved as an important factor if such a balance is to occur among
the overpopulated countries of the world.

Any improvements in agriculture, any extension of cultivable
land whether for present occupants or immigrants, any utilization
of heretofore unused sources of food or means of increasing the
food supply, any other extension of primary production, and any
development of secondary and tertiary production in the underdeveloped countries of the world seem to be a matter of modernization.
It appears to be the key pattern of procedure, though by no means
a panacea or an unmixed blessing.

The urgency of modernization is great if the world is to make
gains in the realization of the major objectives presented in the

preceding chapter. Not only is it necessary to bring the under-developed three-fifths of the world's people economically abreast of the most favored fifth and to achieve a demographic-economic balance among an even greater portion; but also there is the pressing, herculean, and ever-growing task of developing additional facilities to take care of the annual world population increase of 30 or more million.

As will be noted in later chapters, modernization is necessary for a variety of specific reasons, such as the provision of an alternative field of employment for the burgeoning agricultural labor force in most of the underdeveloped countries; raising the average per-capita income and the general level of living; the development of agriculture, and hence the increase and the qualitative improvement of the food supply; the production of manufactured goods both to enrich the consumption at home and for market exchange for additional food supply, for needed raw materials, for various kinds of lacking capital equipment, and for funds to provide various important facilities and services—health, education, and so on.

As indicated in Chapter IV, there is no part of the earth wholly untouched by modernization and its consequences. There is great variation in the degree to which the different sectors of the globe have been affected by it, but there are no known people, however physically or culturally isolated, who have not, directly or in-directly, by exploitation or through contact with its products, been influenced by it. Nevertheless, the greater part of the people of the earth are still largely in the infant, childhood, or adolescent stage of this development.

In spite of some features of their contact with it, most of the underdeveloped areas are anxious to modernize for economic, political, and military reasons,[1] and along all lines which do not necessitate too many changes in their established behavior patterns and cultural and social organization, and do not controvert too many of their precious values. Their governments and their edu-cated people realize that it is the only means to a higher level of living and proficiency, which, in turn, is essential if they are to take their place among the nations of the world. In some degree all have

---

[1] Cf. Leighton, and Theodorson.

". . . started the fateful 'forward' march, under foreign or local impetus, and the pace will certainly accelerate rather than slacken."[2]

FITTING THE PATTERN TO THE UNDERDEVELOPED PEOPLES

The fact that all of the major features of modernization originated among the Western nations, which are made up mainly of peoples of European stock, and that it has had its development and "patterning" among them raises the questions: Is it Western? Is it racial? Is it related to particular natural conditions or a part of particular socio-cultural contexts? As noted, no people have been completely immune to at least some of its features. It is quite apparent that technical skills are not confined to peoples of a particular culture or race. During World War II many of the aboriginal people of the islands of the Pacific not only learned how to operate, but also how to service and repair, complicated modern machines. The long-isolated people of the Middle East easily develop into dependable, intelligent, skilled workers, as the great petroleum corporations have discovered. Says Linton,

> There is abundant evidence that the members of any society can be taught to use mechanical and even scientific techniques. Many of these techniques can be learned without any understanding of the principles involved. They do not even entail surrender of established beliefs in magic.
> We have abundant evidence that, as far as intelligence and learning is concerned, there is no group in the world which cannot be mechanized.[3]

It has also been pointed out that ". . . no new technological level that has emerged in human culture has failed to diffuse widely over the world, and of all the levels that have thus far emerged, industrialism has diffused more rapidly than any other."[4] Neither rurality nor low educational level has effectively insulated particular peoples from *some* participation in the ways of modern industrial society. Modern technology apparently can be transferred to any corner of the world.

The supreme example of the modernization of a non-Western country is, of course, Oriental and mongoloid Japan. Though

---

[2] Moore, "Primitives and Peasants in Industry," p. 44.
[3] Pp. 77, 78.
[4] Davis, *Population of India and Pakistan*, p. 219.

having very few of the raw materials essential to industrial development (such as iron ore, coking coal, and petroleum) and a very limited amount of cultivable land for producing an agricultural surplus, and being in an area of the earth whose poverty has limited the markets for industrial products, this country since 1870 has emerged from feudalism and agrarianism and reached a high degree of industrialization and political-military power—sufficient to challenge, successfully for a while, the combined countries of the West. Elsewhere—in the more accessible portions of semitropical areas, in "caste-ridden" India, in the supposedly "static" and impervious cultures of many primitive and peasant peoples— some of the features of modernization have been eagerly accepted, but selectively incorporated. The accumulated evidence indicates that it is somewhat independent of natural conditions, racial and ethnic backgrounds, and particular institutional contexts. Furthermore, its expansive strength and penetrative ability seem to be tremendous. It is inevitable that no underdeveloped culture will be left untouched, since complete insularity is no longer possible, and also since its boons, once known, are eagerly sought. However, the particular forms it will take, the amount of it accepted, and the tempo with which it is developed will vary greatly among the various peoples and territories.

What is significant for the present study is that even incipient modernization seems to produce some degree of fertility restriction. In India, in Puerto Rico, even in China, not to mention Japan— in fact, wherever and whenever there has been industrial development, a rising level of income and consumption, an improvement in the level of education, urbanization, employment of females outside the family, increased physical mobility and the possibility of social mobility, any secularization of values and institutions, any influence of Western social, economic, and political democracy— there has been, among the limited segments of the population so affected, a noticeable corresponding decline in their fertility.[5]

[5] Davis, *Population of India and Pakistan*, throughout Part VI; P. K. Hatt, *Backgrounds of Human Fertility in Puerto Rico: A Sociological Survey* (Princeton: Princeton Univ. Press, 1952), pp. 83-86, 185-190, 294-334, 463-466; Shu-Ching Lee, "China's Traditional Family, Its Characteristics and Disintegration," *Am. Soc. Rev.*, 18 (June, 1953) : 272-280; see also Irene B. Taeuber, "Migration and the Population Potential of Monsoon Asia," in *Postwar Problems of Migration* (New York: Milbank Memorial Fund, 1947) , pp. 7-29, esp. pp. 15-17.

The process of adopting the essential features of modernization is fraught with vast and complicated problems, since great and crucial differences in conditions exist between the West when it developed modernization and the present Group II countries. However it is to be explained, the Western peoples "swarmed" first. During the nineteenth and twentieth centuries the countries of the West had access to vast, rich, relatively undeveloped and climatically favorable areas of the earth, both for their resources and as areas of settlement—lands which could be made productive quickly, cheaply, and with small capital outlay. National wealth and levels and standards of living improved rapidly. The people had already developed a considerable degree of individualism and institutionalized competitiveness and many democratic traditions and institutions. For several centuries, among most of them, social action had come to be oriented typically toward self-interest. Mainly hedonistic values prevailed; interpersonal relations had usually been regulated by contract rather than custom and according to a means-end pattern of thought. They were not greatly embarrassed by conditions of overpopulation—in fact, as they spread over the open spaces of the earth they were often in short labor supply. For centuries they had been developing machines and complicated handicrafts. They already had populations preponderantly literate. They had had centuries of experience in innovation, nonconformism, reformation, experimentalism, in self-motivated action, and secularization along various lines. They had had centuries of experience in self-government. Finally, time was not pressing, and the development occurred at its own spontaneous, evolutionary pace.

The present underdeveloped people, by contrast, have few of these favoring conditions. Their societies are mainly of the "solidaristic" type, with social action oriented toward the preservation of the long-standing structures and ways and the whole group conceived as a "community of fate." They live in a possessed world where all lands and resources are closely controlled; they are mostly very poor, grossly overpopulated, and largely illiterate; most of them are only in the early stages of emergence from feudalism and agrarian peasantary; some are still subject peoples and many have only very recently freed themselves from colonial status; they have been somewhat cautious and slow in tempo; they have had very limited self-governing experience; many have extremely rigid stratification systems. With all of them time is crucial in their modernization—both for their own and the world's sakes. Every decade of delay means simply a greater population, lower levels of living, and greater requirements of assistance—technological, financial, supervisory, educational, possibly even military—from the rest of the world. Finally, it will largely be an *induced* development under the auspices of their own governments and/or with the assistance of outsiders; and this situation is a new one.

Every complex culture pattern, not to mention a whole sociocultural way of life, has certain subtle but nevertheless essential and characteristic features which are not so easily comprehensible, learnable, or applicable in other historical cultures.

Suffice it to say at this point that the modernization of these underdeveloped peoples means not only certain economic and technological changes, but it also involves a host of political, social, evaluational, and psychological factors, and it means stupendous substitutions, transformations, and reorganizations, and not a few dislocations in almost every department of their individual and collective lives. It may, in many instances, bring about such a profoundly new orientation in most of their ways of life as to amount, in ultimate effect, to social revolution.

In view of these conditions, we must be concerned with the social and cultural dynamics of modernization. How transferable is it? What does its effective establishment in an area require and mean? What economic, demographic, attitudinal and evaluational, social-organizational, and cultural obstacles are involved? What social-scientific principles should be observed by outside instructors and technicians in aiding in its development?

THE REQUISITES AND ACCOMPANIMENTS OF MODERNIZATION

In Chapter III we indicated very briefly and very generally some of the major characteristics of modernized as against non-machine, folk-agrarian societies. At this point of our discussion, in order to understand an array of problems that will be discussed later, we will point out briefly what the basic requisites are for the modernization of an underdeveloped country and what some of the likely accompaniments in the way of changed situations and ways are likely to be.

The basic essential is physical resources, local and/or readily accessible at a fair price, both as raw materials (agricultural, mineral, etc.,) to be machine processed, and as sources of power (coal, water power, petroleum) to provide energy for the processing. The utilization of the productive potentialities in the way of un-exploited or inadequately exploited natural resources is a primary developmental objective. Beyond this and related to it are a host of concomitant requisites.

In the modern world all primary and secondary production, almost all engineering construction, and almost all other social services (medical, public healtfh, social engineering) are largely a matter of technology. There must be available, or made available, physical equipment in the form of tools, machines, and appropriate buildings (plant) for machine industry; and tools, machines, better livestock and plants, and chemical fertilizers for agriculture. There must be the necessary know-how in the form of theoretical knowledge and technical skills for both physical and social engineering; there must be both theoretical and engineering research; there must be planning and execution of all manner of programs and procedures; finally there must be the implementing organizations and the over-all regional or national organization.

An essential aspect of this technological development is the expansion of expensive capital equipment, since such development means building railways, highways, and often water transportation; extending and improving communication facilities, power and other public utilities; constructing and equipping steel mills, cotton mills, jute mills, grain mills, plants for the construction of machinery and the manufacture of appliances and chemicals, and hundreds of other types of factories; operating mines and building smelters; developing irrigation and drainage projects; extending the arable land by clearing and levelling and by control of pests. But all this necessitates a huge capital supply and large-scale investment in these production facilities. In general, production must be sufficiently efficient to produce a surplus—a portion that can be withheld from consumption and diverted to capital formation. There must be adequate financial and credit facilities—private and public—for agriculture, manufacturing, and commerce.

In order to entice investment capital, investors must be reasonably certain that the principal and interest will be paid on schedule.

This depends upon competent planning and efficient and economical management of the undertakings, upon the certainty that profitable markets for the products and essential exchange facilities exist, and finally upon internal political stability.

The misconception that industrialization is the one and only goal must be avoided. This does not mean that the importance of industrialization is underestimated; it remains perhaps the central and most crucial aspect of modernization. It is the main way of accelerating the increase of wealth, of raising the levels and standards of living, of satisfying the distinctive and increasingly ubiquitous wants of the modern age, of meeting the requirements of national standing among nations. Specifically, among many of the underdeveloped peoples, it is the only method of achieving a significant increase in the national production by utilizing the surplus labor that can be withdrawn from agriculture without reduction in agricultural output. It is also the only way of providing employment for the growing and pressing population in those countries where the possibility of extending cultivation to new land or of emigrating is extremely limited. Industrialization is a long-term solution of the economic problems of these impoverished and malnourished rural folk. However, no people can afford to resort to it exclusively.[6] There must be an effective interplay of industrialization and agriculture.

In most of these countries the development of agriculture is a matter of immediate urgency. For a number of reasons the protection and improvement of the agricultural base are essential to all else. (1) Unless there is the assurance of an adequate and long-continuing resource supply for home processing, the industrialization of a country is bound to end in failure. Agriculture is always a main source of materials, and it is preferable for countries to have as many of their own sources as possible. (2) In order to increase and diversify the home base of food agriculture needs to be developed in these countries, most of which are on a bare subsistence diet. No underdeveloped people can advance if they are victims of malnutrition, low vitality, and ill health. (3) Efficient and productive agriculture is necessary to produce a supply of products

---

[6] Fairfield Osborn, in fact, has pointed out the critical consequences of overindustrialization, especially in Australia and Argentina.

for export, which, in turn, will enable the people to import needed raw materials, manufactured products, capital equipment, cultural and other materials from other countries. In brief, it enables them, without a vast change in skills, techniques, values, and ways of life, to produce materials for exchange in the markets of the world. This, of course, also means that they will have to produce kinds and qualities of agricultural products that will find outlets in the competitive markets of the world. (4) Though unimportant in some of the underdeveloped countries of the world since agricultural unemployment or underemployment already exists, agriculture must be improved to some extent through mechanization where it can be done without reduction of per-acre or per-man-hour output, in order to release agricultural labor for urban manufacturing and commercial and service pursuits. Most of the underdeveloped peoples, because of their vast rurality, have a very limited urban population as labor supply for secondary and tertiary production. (5) Finally, and just as a matter of expediency, people cannot be moved into urbanized industry too fast; approximately two-thirds of the underdeveloped peoples as a whole, and in some instances more than 80 per cent of them, are agricultural peasants and have been for millennia.[7]

However, a level of economic achievement sufficiently high to enable a country to compete adequately with other nations cannot be realized by agriculture alone, as Lengyel has pointed out with respect to the Middle East.[8] In general, agriculture *and* machine industry and modern commerce have to develop together. Urban machine industry must be developed in all of its diverse forms to produce such items as tools, implements, chemical fertilizers, processed animal feeds, and insecticides, and to provide the outlet for the often underemployed and surplus rural population. Also, with industries using the tremendous productivity of the machine, a country can improve its maintenance, increase its national and per-capita income, improve its purchasing power, and raise its level of living even though lacking in basic raw materials, as Switzerland and Japan have demonstrated.

[7] See, for example, Beckett; United Nations, *Determinants and Consequences,* pp. 275-276.

[8] Emil Lengyel, *World Without End: The Middle East* (New York: John Day, 1953), pp. 297-298.

In connection with the above it must be pointed out, as a stern and unavoidable requisite, that the increases in production and net savings and the advances in quantity and quality of capital equipment must be at a greater rate than the increases in population. Otherwise the efforts and achievements are of no avail. There will simply be *more* people as badly or worse off than they were before. There are a host of other requisites which we can little more than mention.

The countries need a proficient population as labor supply, physically healthy, and at least semi-literate, and with adequate knowledge and technical skills, to enable them to compete efficiently and productively with the workers in the more advanced nations. For this are needed a vast improvement and expansion of general education, since illiteracy rates are very high. There must be extensive vocational training, especially in industrial, commercial, and professional specialized skills and proficiencies.

If the programs to raise productivity by means of progressive industrialization are to be effective, the workers will have to develop new work attitudes, become amenable to work incentives, and acquire many new habits, all associated with machine productivity and concomitant urban life. The rural-agrarian mode of life is characterized by self-discipline, a go-at-your-own-pace tempo, and frequent seasonal vacations and holidays. Urban machine industry and commerce present a very different way of life and create requirements which are not readily met. The workers will have to yield to Western incentives to engage in factory and office work, to have individual aspirations to occupational proficiency and upward socio-economic movement. They must submit to the discipline of the job and the formal organization, to the job's never-ending routines and fixed hours of work, to the daily rhythm of work and leisure fixed by the clock and the calendar and not by the task. They must continuously and persistently apply themselves to the task during fixed work hours, day after day, and abide by a great array of imposed standards and rigidly enforced specifications and rules. Many of them will have to work away from their families and even their home communities. Needless to say, such changes represent a marked departure in the ways of life of these people.

Needed also will be mobility in the population, both physical and social. The complex division of labor and the selective assignment of individuals to jobs and positions in the industrial system require a great deal of flexibility and mobility on their part. The essential and unavoidable physical mobility will consist mainly of the movement of the labor force from rural to urban areas; and from places of redundant to places of short labor supply. Likewise, social mobility of a horizontal nature is necessary as people shift from occupation to occupation until they have found the most compatible one. Because of the special kind of individual competition of industrial societies, which is oriented toward the achievement of higher positions and graded rewards, and hence of new prestige scales, ther will be much new vertical social mobility. These mobilities will produce some tearing apart of the web of customary relations and positions.

There will be notable and unavoidable ecological reorganization as technological development occurs. Among many such changes, much population subjected to various kinds of selective influences will shift from the rural to the urban areas. Regional changes in population density, population location, and land use will come about. In the cities there will be great changes due to industrialization—the development of factory areas, the location of workers' residential areas closer to the factories, and the various processes of ecological succession that have characterized the cities of the West.[9]

A final basic requisite is a well-developed and well-organized government. Internal peace and order must be maintained. Sound monetary and credit systems are essential. Governments must take the lead in capital formation and acquisition. Government is necessary, for example, to raise investment funds by taxation or by borrowing from ts own people, or by borrowing or otherwise obtaining funds from outside sources. Among most of these people, governments actually have to plan, initiate, finance, construct, and operate (or make arrangements for the construction and operation of) essential public works, such as telephone and telegraph systems, highways and railways, irrigation and drainage projects, power projects, extension of cultivable lands, and housing. Much of the agricultural and industrial development and the facilitation of trade among them depends upon governmental action. Govern-

---

[9] For an interesting study along this line see F. and L. O. Dotson. "Ecological Trends in the City of Guadalajara, Mexico," *Soc. Forces*, 32 (May, 1954): 367-374.

ments must provide for both general and special education if it is to be sufficiently widespread. Governments will have to conduct resource surveys, land reforms, land-use programs, and carry on a variety of other study, research, and organizational undertakings. They will have to provide many varieties of experts and leaders, both from within and without. Governments will have to be the main medium, not only for acquiring funds and equipment from abroad, but also for obtaining the benefits of planning, guidance, and assistance from outside semi-public organizations, other governments, or the United Nations. Governments will have to supervise and regulate labor and facilitate mobility and relocation of labor.

There will also be various accompaniments of the modernization process. A new set of social incentives will be created; through individual initiative and through elevation of their level and standard of living people will seek to better their lot—a relatively unknown endeavor for most of these peoples. Corresponding to this will be the increasing flexibility of their stratification system and a weakening of the traditional status arrangements. New bases of esteem, prestige, and power will appear. Occupational competition and widespread conspicuous or social rated consumption are likely to be strange and new experiences. Many features of the reward system will change. A middle class, almost non-existent at present among some peoples, is likely to develop.

With the increased division of labor, specialization and proliferation of many functions, urbanization, and the weakening of caste or rigid stratification systems, there will be a decline of many old roles and a great increase in new ones accompanied by a multiplication of roles to be performed by the individual. Most of these will be confusing and at first difficult to execute.

There will very likely be a marked modification in the way of secularization ("rationalization") of many features of their historical value systems, along social, economic, ethical, and religious lines.

There will also be a tendency toward individualization, especially a weakening of the hold of the kin-group and the local community. Their social organization inevitably will undergo great change. The economic, political, educational, and religious institutions will be greatly revised; the family, particularly the extended or joint family which is quite common among them, will be weakened. There will be a shifting of the relative power of different groups. New types of groups and organizations, such as corporations, labor unions, and cooperatives, will come into being. There will be new elites and new types of leaders, for example, a shifting from elders, tribal leaders, and village head men to politicians, technical experts and supervisors, labor union leaders, and business executives.

There will be the change from rural community to urban life, and with it increasing urbanization, involving the imposition upon the whole population of urban values, attitudes, material products, and ways of life. The growing cities among them—as has been the case with cities in the past—will very likely be the chief loci for the introduction of new ideas and methods and accelerate adjustment to new technologies, new consumption and production patterns, new or greatly revised social institutions, and many other social, political, intellectual, and cultural innovations.[10]

The individuals themselves will undergo great modifications of their behavior, such as changed habits of work, changes in the length of time devoted to doing things, the use of new equipment and resources, new work and recreational routines. They are likely to develop changed habits of consumption, saving, and investment. They will live increasingly anonymous and impersonal lives. Demographic changes will occur with respect to numbers, location, mortality and fertility rates and differentials, age composition, sex composition, occupational and socio-economic structure, and number and size of households and families.[11]

OBSTACLES TO MODERNIZATION

The culture of any group that has long endured is not a mere congeries of behavior traits, knowledge, beliefs, institutions and organizations; it is an interlocking, systematic, and rigidly organized whole.[12] All significant aspects of it—its forms of economic production and consumption, its political system, the family and com-

---

[10] See the excellent article by B. F. Hoselitz, "The Role of Cities in the Economic Growth of Underdeveloped Countries," *Jour. Pol. Econ.*, 6 (Feb., 1953): 195-208. See also G. Sjoberg, "The Preindustrial City," *Am. Jour. Soc.*, 60 (March, 1955): 438-445; N. S. Ginsberg, "The Great City in Southeast Asia," *Am. Jour. Soc.*, 60 (March, 1955): 455-462; R. L. Crane, "Urbanism in India," *Am. Jour. Soc.*, 60 (March, 1955) : 463-470.

[11] For a comprehensive treatment of some of the points raised in this discussion and many other requisites and accompaniments of the modernization process, see Moore, 1951, pp. 166-177, and Buchanan and Ellis, pp. 23-73, 237-454.

[12] Cf. Goldschmidt.

munity organization, its body of religious and ethical values, attitudes, beliefs, and practices, even its underlying world orientation—are relatively consistent and integrated, and all together constitute an effective functional whole. These underdeveloped near-primitive and peasant peoples have long-established and, until recently, closely knit agrarian cultures with, in later times, the marks of colonial status. Modernization is still a culture complex that has developed mainly in the Western world—a unique and complex bundle of techniques, ideologies, social-institutional features, and objectives. While there may be no general antipathy, and while many segments of the population of the underdeveloped peoples are eager to take over certain aspects of modernization, especially the fruits of a modernized economy and political state, it is for them still an alien affair, external in origin and in many respects uncongenial in nature.

As the underdeveloped peoples modernize, they emerge from "folk" society to technological, highly organized and rationalized "state" society; they undergo transition from the folkways and mores and the organizational forms of a "sacred" (traditional) society to the technicways, stateways, and large-scale formal organizations of "secular" society. In effect, they move from primitivism or medievalism to modernism. As it is, vast gaps exist between folk-agrarian society and industrialized-urbanized-rationalized-democratized society. Many underdeveloped peoples are not interested in some quite crucial features of modernization; they misunderstand or completely miss others; they are disturbed by what is for them the inherent "alienness" of still others and seek to avoid them. Modernization involves a large-scale transformation of the whole way of life of these peoples.

When cultures *meet* they meet as systems, and one system is never taken over *in toto* by the other. Furthermore, any durable culture protects itself and its adherents, consciously or unconsciously, lest dislocations and loss or distortion of precious elements occur. Hence, the transference of culture elements between highly dissimilar cultures is always complicated and problematical: various kinds of resistance and conflicts are encountered; recipients often fail to comprehend the underlying meanings and the nature and purpose of foreign elements; certain isolated elements are often adopted out of their context and hence have peculiar repercussions;

the adoption is always piecemeal, and inconsistent new and old elements may be combined; selective modifications of the items borrowed occur with distorted and diminished effects; the new developments may be arrested at peculiar and unforeseen stages. In general, as Moore states, "The greater the dissimilarity of cultures, or the more unsuitable the prevailing social and psychological attributes for the new development, the more difficult the transition and the greater the change necessary . . . if the transfer is actually completed."[13]

Because of this general situation, there are a variety of obstacles to the modernization of the underdeveloped countries, even where it is accepted willingly and enthusiastically.

Most of these peoples suffer an initial handicap in that they are newcomers and tyros competing with the established economic and political power of highly developed predecessors. At the same time, as newcomers, they have certain distinct advantages in their modernization processes which Europeans, at home and overseas, did not have at the beginning of their development. The Population Commission of the United Nations has put it as follows:

(1) The newcomers have at their disposal a wealth of scientific and technical knowledge which has been developed since the beginning of the Industrial Revolution in the West, and which can contribute enormously to their efficiency in almost every branch of economic activity. (2) They also have before them the record of economic, social, and political development of their predecessors, which should help them to avoid some of the blunders that delayed and in many cases still seriously impede the progress of the latter. They can systematically chart their course so as to take the fullest advantage of this knowledge; for economic development in the twentieth century, unlike that of Europe and America in the last two hundred years, is more and more a matter of national planning. (3) Besides, the underdeveloped countries can look forward to receiving help from abroad, including assistance from the United Nations and its specialized agencies, in both the planning and execution of their development programmes.[14]

[13] 1951, p. 197.
[14] *Findings of Studies on the Relationship between Population Trends and Economic and Social Factors. Part Three: Summary of Principle Findings Relevant to the Economic Development of Under-Developed Countries* (E/CN.9/55. Add.2, 2 May 1950), p. 2.

Nevertheless, there are certain crucial obstacles inherent in the situation. Some of the more typical ones will be briefly examined.[15]

THE ECONOMIC EFFECTS OF POPULATION PRESSURE

The underdeveloped countries are overpopulated in relation to already developed resources and productive capacity. Certainly the populations currently existing in southern, southeastern, and eastern Asia, the Middle East, and most of Africa approach the maximum that can be supported by the present type of economy; and, as we have repeatedly noted, the great majority of the people exist at a bare subsistence level. It has been the almost universal experience among these peoples that any technological-economic improvement which is effected is almost immediately canceled out in additional population. Thus there is a continuous and persistent pressure of numbers upon physical resources and productive procedures. Some of the ways in which this unrelenting population pressure operates to obstruct or retard the betterment of the peoples' material conditions will be briefly examined.

The population pressure focuses economic effort on consumption, rather than on production. As the growth continues, if the bare necessities are to be met, their supply must be constantly expanded merely to maintain the new population at the old poverty level. New gains in production thus tend to be converted into immediate subsistence consumption. This is alarming when food production and per-capita diet at best are so inadequate. A crucial aspect of this situation is that it prevents or makes difficult any appreciable

[15] This cannot be even an effort at a complete inventory of obstacles and difficulties. Nor can we make specific reference to specific qualifications for the different areas and countries. This in itself would be a work of encyclopedic proportions. At best only some of the more universal obstacles can be indicated. The obstacles are stated with a positiveness that is not entirely justifiable; but space does not permit a whole array of qualifications. At best, we are obtaining only a very general working knowledge. It should be pointed out also that in many instances, efforts are being made, at least in some small degree, to alleviate these and other obstacles by the peoples themselves.

For works, most of which the writer depended upon in preparing this section, and for a more extensive development of the obstacles treated here, see: Buchanan and Ellis, pp. 74-91; both Davis references; Dobby; Herskovits; Lorimer *et al*, pp. 58-90, 151-203; McGranahan; Mead, pp. 194-278; the last four references to Moore, especially *Industrialization and Labor*, pp. 14-55, 106-139; all four references to Spengler; United Nations, *Determinants and Consequences*, pp. 194-223, 262-286; and Zinkin, pp. 208-237.

improvement in family levels of living, or even the development of any interest in higher standards of living.

This need for devoting production so largely to immediate necessities of existence makes difficult, even unlikely, any personal or private saving for investment purposes. On a national scale it vastly hinders the accumulation of surpluses and the utilization of energies essential to capital increase, and consequently hinders the improvement and augmentation of production facilities. In brief, possible future advantage, both in the way of improved production and greater volume of consumption goods, is sacrificed to present necessity. Highly important internal investment capital is small in amount and hard to increase.

The pressure of numbers increases the strain upon the nation's land as of any given time. The chief instrument of production—land—becomes ever more scarce and expensive to acquire. The amount of land per cultivator and per family declines. Even production for subsistence purposes becomes more strained. What is equally significant is the fact that much of the land is devoted to food crops for local sustenance rather than to export crops for exchange in the world market, the proceeds from which would be available for investment and expansion.[16] Related to this is the fact—due to various conditions and having various obstructive effects—that per-capita national income and real wages are low.

The population growth tends to bring about the strained use of most of the known resources, especially by accelerating the rate at which the store of exhaustible and non-replaceable natural resources is being used up and by increasing the costs of their use.

---

[16] It is only fair to point out that almost all of these peoples have *some* crops which they produce for export. Products of primary production—agriculture produce, timber products, minerals, etc.—are in fact, in most instances, the only export items they have. In southeastern Asia there is some commercial rice farming, which incidentally has supplemented the inadequate rice supply of India, China, and Japan. Most of this is carried on, however, by rather primitive methods. Copra, tea, coffee, rubber, sugar, bananas, sisal, and rice are well-known export crops. Some of these are produced under the plantation system, and often the plantations are foreign-owned and the profits go outside the country. The actual cultivators supplement their wage incomes by what amounts to part-time subsistence farming. In other instances, the production is according to a sharecropper system. The small independent agriculturist who produces some small surplus for sale usually does so under tremendous difficulties created by the landlord, the usurer, and the factor who purchases his crop.

Due to intense population pressure in these agrarian economies, labor is immediately cheaper than machinery. Hence, abundant and cheap labor is employed instead of expensive machinery, and future advance is sacrificed to present expediency. Furthermore, the rate at which the mechanical and other equipment of the labor force can be increased is reduced.

OTHER ECONOMIC PRODUCTION OBSTACLES

The agriculture of the underdeveloped peoples, which is the base of any socio-economic advance, is in the main archaic according to modern standards. Tolley calls attention to certain obstacles and inadequacies in carrying on production on the land now under cultivation among them; many of these have existed for centuries and in some cases have worsened.

> Found alone or in combination, they [archaic practices] are responsible for low yields, in spite of the great amount of labor applied to each acre; often the same soil-depleting crop is produced year after year; erosion has taken its toll and the fertile topsoil disappeared long ago. Little or no natural or commercial fertilizer is used. Pesticides to combat insects and fungi, and vaccines for the prevention or cure of livestock diseases are practically unknown. Pastures are unimproved and overgrazed. Where water is used for irrigation, the supply is often undependable, and may be used wastefully. Only poor seed of unimproved varieties is available to the farmer for most of his crops. Improved breeding of livestock for increased production is needed. Feed for the livestock, especially grain, is usually so limited that the productivity of the livestock is far below the physical potential. Food for the people is so scarce that most of the cereals and other grains are used directly as food. Farm implements are primitive —often the cultivator has only a hoe and other hand tools; and the largest power-unit in a community is a single bullock or at best a pair of bullocks. Forms of land tenure in many areas are still substantially the same as they were in ancient times.[17]

There is an actual shortage of land in some of the densely populated underdeveloped countries. This results in a small product per unit of labor employed, and also means unemployment or underemployment of agricultural workers.

---

[17] Tolley, pp. 56-57.

It may also be pointed out that in some countries the parcels of land per cultivator are very small and becoming smaller because of population increase, and often, under certain modes of inheritance, the subdivision among the offspring generation after generation results in tiny land fragments. In addition, there is the contrast between the small farms and the large estates.[18]

The agriculture is often wasteful, even destructive, leading to the depletion of a basic natural resource. For example, there is the practice (under various names) in Indo-China, the Philippines, and parts of Latin America of cultivating patches of land cleared by burning the forest on them, farming the patches for several years until worn out, then abandoning them and shifting to new ones, with destruction of the soil of patch after patch.

The obstacles to the development of urban machine industrial production are obvious. Raw materials are often lacking, or what is just as important, tradable products with which to acquire raw materials in the markets of the world. The lack of surpluses to be converted into essential capital equipment has already been alluded to. Monetary and credit facilities are often inadequate, as are also the sufficiently widespread knowledge and use of them.

The productive labor force is low grade—not what it should be if it is to compete successfully with that of the more advanced countries. It suffers ill health and low vitality and hence has a low level of working efficiency. There is still much ignorance and superstition. The poverty is great, and the people suffer from malnutrition and poor housing. The chronic diseases, such as malaria, hookworm, typhoid, dysentery, trachoma, tuberculosis, bilharzia, sleeping sickness, and venereal diseases are a continual drain on vitality and efficiency. The great plagues like typhus, cholera, influenza, and smallpox interrupt all important social processes. These conditions hold down the physical efficiency of the workers, lead to lassitude, reduce the proportionate number of workers available and the number of working days per year. In general, the productivity of workers is low in relation to that of the advanced countries.

The labor force is also somewhat lacking in appropriate conditioning and training. As noted above, the great majority of the

[18] See, for example, I. Samkalden, "Land Tenure and Land Reform," in Ruopp, pp. 153-170.

workers have been self-employed in family agriculture or simple handicrafts, working at their own pace and without much sense of competition with others. By the very nature of their work they have enjoyed frequent holidays and if dependent have been cared for by the clan or extended family. The people of many of the underdeveloped areas have been dependent upon subsistence-agriculture for centuries. Dobby points out that in southeast Asia, for example, it is more a mode of living than an economic means of production; it is a long-standing, interwoven way of life. The daily individual routines, the family and village life, and a whole array of folkways, customs, beliefs, and values are part of it. The people know it and understand it; all of their past securities and survival values are related to it; they are not easily weaned from it.[19]

The potential wage earners are not ambitious, and they are not very concerned with money or the standard of living. The average peasant of southeast Asia, for example, has long been content with a small plot of ground, a tiny hut, his one wife and several children, possibly sharing with others a bullock and cart, and having a pair of dice and a fighting cock. Such people lack a ready ability to submit to plant discipline and they are without a sense of the importance and urgency of time; routines are abhorrent to them; absenteeism is high (the workers frequently return to their native village when they have accumulated a small "stake," and ceremonials and festivals absorb days and even weeks of their time); labor turn-over is high; there exists little or no interest in "rational efficiency."

UNFAVORABLE AGE STRUCTURE

Most of the underdeveloped countries have rapidly growing populations, and such populations are typically "young," that is, they have a large proportion of children, and a relatively smaller proportion of people in the adult, productive period of life. The more advanced nations, with whom these peoples must compete, because of lower birth rates, have a larger proportion of their populations in the productive years of life, a condition making for a favorable ratio of producers to dependents.[20] This age-structure situation among the underdeveloped peoples produces several

---

[19] Dobby, pp. 125-139, esp. p. 135.
[20] For specific comparative data see United Nations, *Determinants and Consequences*, pp. 143, 265-266.

untoward conditions. Children are nonproducers, or low producers where they are used as part of the labor supply. Usually they are nonproductive dependents, and if they are a disproportionate part of the population, they create a condition which aggravates the difficulties of economic development since it reduces the proportion of the population likely to be in the labor force. "A relatively young population, whether it is growing rapidly or not, will spend a larger share of its income on food than an older population with the same *per capita* income."[21] In many cases, energy, food, and supplies are wasted in producing children who eventually die before reaching productive age, thus creating an additional drain on the economy. A young population increases the need for educational facilities and teaching personnel. This is especially difficult in poor countries, where education is needed most. It creates what has been referred to as the "drag of excessive fertility on educational progress."

The burden of childhood dependency in the underdeveloped countries is usually lightened by the practice of putting the children to work at an early age, especially within the agricultural population. It is for this reason that large families are frequently viewed as an economic advantage to the parents. However, the contribution of an employed child is much less than that of an adult. Moreover, the extensive employment of children interferes with the improvement of the labor force and the elevation of the standard of living, particularly since employment is possible only at the expense of a neglect of education. In this connection, the United Nations report concludes:

> Thus the people of the under-developed countries continually resort to wasteful exploitation of the oncoming generations of workers in their efforts to achieve a more nearly adequate current standard of consumption. Their position is rather like that of peasants compelled by hunger to harvest their wheat every year before it has ripened.[22]

ILLITERACY AND LACK OF SKILLS

An industrial and self-governing society is almost unthinkable without a population which is highly literate, possessed of in-

[21] *Ibid.*, p. 213.
[22] P. 265. See also pp. 194-200, 213-214, 217-219, 222-223.

dustrial, commercial, and political know-how and diverse occupational skills, and adequate educational facilities for continually acquiring them. Anywhere in the world today even small farmers must, to be efficient, have a certain minimal technical knowledge and skill; for example, they must be familiar with the operation and repair of machines, the use of chemical fertilizers, insecticides, the principles of genetics, and the principles of land management. In fact, the technical knowledge and skill required by farmers is probably greater and more varied than that required by urban assembly-line or commercial workers.

In general there is a shortage of properly qualified manpower. The lack of appropriate vocational skills and aptitudes, both in agriculture and for factory and commercial activities, is one of the major reasons for the low productivity in underdeveloped countries. A skilled labor force is necessary not only for the effective operation of complex equipment, but also for its continuous maintenance and repair. It is commonly observed that workers acquire the superficials of technology but are not widely proficient in the underlying principles. The facilities for providing such training are still lacking in large measure. There is also the need for formal education for the population generally, and for research facilities.[23]

Most of the people of the underdeveloped countries are illiterate, the rates in some instances running above 80 per cent. Efforts are being made by the governments concerned and by outsiders to correct the situation. However, funds are lacking to provide the buildings, equipment, and staff.

There is also the need for adjusting education to the probable future careers of the students and for modifying attitudes toward personal educational objectives. As it is, because of ancient values related to the stratification systems, the education process frequently founders. For example, as noted, the countries need large numbers of people trained in many technical skills, both for agriculture and urban industry and commerce. Not only do they not have these people; they do not have nearly enough native experts to teach them. But the upper classes, who are the only ones who can afford to give their sons a higher education at home or abroad, prefer to have them trained in white-collar occupations, especially in the

[23] Cf. Graham.

higher professions. Says Linton, "Even when they do go into such fields as engineering, they prefer theory to practice, and feel that any sort of manual work, even as a part of training, is socially degrading."[24] In so many instances, however, where elementary educational opportunity is available, the native folk seem to believe that by learning to read, write, and do simple sums they acquire the right to sit in an office chair.

In the Mohammedan world of the Middle East, caste divisions, while existent, are not so hard and fast. Here, as Lengyel puts it, "university credentials open the door to the fellah offspring into the exalted company of the effendis. . . . Very often graduates believe that by spending a few years at a school of higher learning they have bought themselves immunity from work for the rest of their lives. . . . After graduation many of them appear to be only too ready to accept the higher government positions and other 'glamorous' occupations."[25] In fact, in many of these countries government service has become the hallmark of high prestige and the epitome of social advancement, with the result that these services are overweighted, but not necessarily with the kind of public servants the countries need, such as county agents and home demonstrators. On the other hand, skilled technical jobs, research and survey jobs, engineering and supervisory jobs go unmanned.

In brief, the limited educational procedures of most of these peoples do not yield sufficient general education to enable the population to live intelligently in the modern world; they do not provide the necessary technical knowledge and training or a sufficient number of teachers and trainers.

ORGANIZATIONAL FEATURES

Non-Western societies, as compared with those of the West, are to a great extent "closed societies"; they are, in the main, ancient and have a greater fixity of existence; their aim is to maintain this pre-established pattern of social and cultural life.[26] Certain features of these somewhat archaic and rigid social structures militate against modernization. While the stratification systems are by no means alike, most of them are inflexible as compared with those of the

[24] P. 85.
[25] *Op. cit.*, pp. 39-40.
[26] Van Nieuwenhuijze, esp. p. 70.

West at the present time. Statuses are relatively fixed, especially by convention, religion, and long-standing economic conditions; both levels of consumption and family occupations are established; the lower strata are not accustomed to emulating those higher up in the social scale; each stratum has its long-established, sanctioned social functions. In some areas, such as the Middle East, there are deeply entrenched ruling classes with special privileges, such as land holding, voting, and office holding, and vested interests and power which make them strongly resistant to almost any kind of change unless it is to their own distinct advantage. Much absolutism still prevails.[27] In many of the areas, the middle class— the class of change and adaptability—is small or nonexistent.

Recently Moore has pointed out that there is a lack of appreciation of the new status system that industrialism would impose upon them. Referring to a specific aspect of such status, he states:

> New occupations simply do not fit traditional standards of prestige, or are valued negatively because they involve manual labor and merit placement irrespective of age, kinship position, caste, or other forms of "ascribed" status.[28]

The "extended" or "joint" family system, which prevails among most of these peoples, and especially in India and China, is a serious obstacle. Through its emphasis upon offspring as agents of ancestor worship, it gives a tremendous religious stimulus to high fertility. The common ownership or use of land tends, generation after generation, to parcelization of holdings to the point where they are almost microscopic. The individual amounts to little by himself; he is continually identified with his family and bound to its traditions and values, its community status, its occupation, its land and place, and the forms of authority of the elders over the younger generations. In times of unemployment or other catastrophe it functions as the social security agent for its members. At such times they will return to it to live upon it. At the same time the members of the wider kinship group hold it a right to descend upon any temporarily advantaged member and share what he earns or what he has acquired; he must support them even though it

---

[27] Cf. Haskins, pp. 88-90.
[28] 1955, p. 159.

dissipates all his personal gains, which he might otherwise have invested productively. Consequently, very often the joint family strongly limits both physical and social mobiilty, retards the assumption of independence, and reduces labor incentive.[29]

The great majority of the people of south, southeast and east Asia and many of those of Africa and Latin America live in tiny medieval agrarian villages. These villages are to a considerable extent economically self-sufficient (on their low economic plane) and seek to remain so. The villagers have relatively limited contacts with the surrounding world because of their limited purchasing power, their language or dialect differences, and their satisfaction with their life. Ancient roles, skills, routines, and methods of work prevail. The social positions are relatively fixed and sanctioned by the ancient values, and the mainly archaic social controls are understood and revered. Their frequent ceremonies, holidays, and seasonal times of leisure are precious to them. Here they can live an understood, close-knit, and secure way of life. These villages, in spite of partial industrialization and urbanization for many individuals, are looked upon as the "true home" and permanent place of abode. Members who have gone to the cities or other regions return to them whenever they can. Needless to say, by virtue of the village way of life the perspectives and the aspirations of the people are greatly limited.

The various prevailing land ownership and land cultivation systems are not generally conducive to local economic development. Under the plantation system, whether the plantations are individually owned estates or owned and operated by commercial companies (corporations), they are usually foreign-owned, and the profits do not remain where they are obtained. Most of them are mono-crop farms (rubber, tea, fiber, sugar) and do not provide much incidental instruction in diversified agriculture, though they do provide examples of highly scientific and technically efficient modern agriculture procedures. Frequently workers divide their time and labor between their personal holdings and nearby plantations, thus supplementing their incomes.

Another even more widely found land system is that of the semi-feudal or feudal estate owned by long entrenched, wealthy aristo-

---

[29] Cf. Lorimer *et al.*, pp. 58-90.

cratic native landlords—as, for example, in China (at least prior to 1946), the so-called "native states" of India, and much of southeast Asia. Here the situation of the agricultural workers on their allotted plots is at worst little better than that of serfs and at best that of sharecroppers.

A third common form is that of native production by the indigenous population on its own holdings. These holdings, as we have indicated, because of populaton increase and parcelization are usually small. Smallness of holdings and lack of capital in most instances limit production to subsistence crops and make commercial agricultural production for national and international markets negligible, if not almost impossible. Many of these small cultivators are the perpetual victims of the moneylenders.

The governments, in many instances, are as yet inadequately prepared to assume the tremendous burdens falling upon them.[30] In many of these countries the masses are chronically hungry and poor and illiterate; and where poverty is great and enlightenment low, political stability is hard to maintain, and unrest and revolts tend to thrive.

Many of the countries where such conditions obtain have been colonies until after World War II, and some still have a subject or dependent political status. The populations lack recent experience in self-government. Those who have achieved independence are still working out their constitutions; their national electoral processes and representation principles have not been clearly defined or tested (or even applied); their "power forces" are still unbalanced with respect to each other. The leaders sometimes lack experience; some of them have overpromised regarding social reforms and have been unable to eliminate basic evils besetting their people and to deliver Utopia. Vast gaps exist at all levels and in all departments of governmental, technical, administrative, and educational personnel.

In the underdeveloped countries, because of the poverty of the masses and the limited national income from the few industrial and commercial enterprises, tax resources of otherwise available funds for public uses are scarce, hence the necessity for foreign or international borrowing or soliciting. But when governments are

[30] See p. 127.

indecisive and inexperienced, the risks and uncertainties respecting the security of property, the return (repatriation) of invested capital, and the earning and receiving of profits are great. Investors both private and public, internal and external, become increasingly cautious about investing in the country.[31]

Furthermore, while probably desirable from the point of view of national survival, several of these countries have allocated a vast portion of their public funds to military ends (recently some 60 per cent in the case of India and Pakistan). This, of course, blocks the very developments which give a people a manpower and material development essential to national strength and prosperity.

UNFAVORABLE VALUES, ATTITUDES, AND BELIEFS

There seem to be certain values, attitudes, and beliefs that stand in the way of effective economic and social development through technological means. Some of these are intimately bound up with a static, land-based economy. McGranahan points out that in such societies most of the people have very little to risk and are not inclined to risk that little in new propositions; savings tend to be

---

[31] The problem of acquiring capital from foreign governments or private investors is itself an obstacle to the modernization of underdeveloped countries. The UN report referred to above calls attention to the viewpoints of many economists who maintain that the bulk of the nation's additions to its stock of capital must be produced at home. The reasons advanced are: "First, a large proportion of a nation's capital equipment is immobile. Second, because of the complementary relationships existing between different kinds of capital at different stages of a country's development, a nation's internal rate of capital formation determines in part the amount of capital from abroad which can be economically absorbed at any time, even though such capital can be obtained on relatively easy terms. Third, the foreign exchange required to service past foreign borrowings and to provide such requisites of industrialization as are only to be had from abroad imposes a financial limit (as distinguished from a technical one) upon the amount of capital that can be obtained outside a country. Finally, foreign capital can usually be obtained in large amounts only if a nation's internal economic conditions are propitious, and such is not likely to be the case if low *per capita* income is creating social disorganization and political instability." (pp. 281-282). An earlier report, preparatory to the 1953 report, adds another factor, namely that foreign investors prefer to invest in government securities, public utilities, banks, plantations, mines, and other industries working for export, and are not attracted by typical manufacturing industries working chiefly for the domestic market. UN Population Commission, *Findings of Studies on the Relationships between Population Trends and Social and Economic Factors. Part Two: Effects of Population Changes on Economic Conditions,* (E/CN.9/55/Add.1, 1 May 1950), pp. 68-69. It is quite obvious that most of the underdeveloped countries reveal all of the weaknesses implied. See also Nurkse.

hoarded rather than invested. Changes proposed by any out-group are regarded with suspicion.[32]

Doubtless, partly due to the illiteracy, the essential "sacredness" of their way of life, and the ancient secluded village life, there is a hesitancy to innovate and to experiment. Related to this is the fact that probably as a result of the centuries-old struggles for existence, the demands of their conquering or ruling elements, and their religious philosophies many of the peoples have a fatalistic attitude that is difficult to change. ("Allah wills it!") There is a resignation to conditions that is incompatible with the striving and reconstructing so essential to modernization.

Ancient religions dominate these people and permeate every phase of their existence; in fact, most means as well as ends are viewed in a religious light. Superstition and belief in and resort to magic are rife; beliefs and procedures are rigid. The effect is that the essential scientific, empirical, naturalistic, experimental, pragmatic approach to the world is neither understood nor practiced. Consciously or unconsciously, this creates a strong resistance to technological and democratic change.

The case of Hinduism (or Brahmanism) in India may be taken as an illustration. The religion supports the caste system with its definite restrictions on types of labor that can be performed by caste members. It is bound up with the joint family and sanctifies progeny. A series of dietary taboos prevents a diversification of diets and the addition of what are now essentials to adequate nutrition. All animal life is sacred; hence animal pests and marauders cannot be destroyed, nor can animals be used as food. The cow is especially venerated as a sacred creature: it can go where it pleases and breed without let or hindrance, and consequently it consumes food that is desperately needed by humans, overgrazes, and produces eroded lands.

Hinduism, Buddhism, Islam, and some of the other religions prevailing among these peoples also create a wholly different philosophy and outlook on life and the world than have developed in the West, especially under Protestant Christianity. In effect, the religions often actually discourage ambition or the acquisition of a better material life. The people may be convinced that life here

[32] P. 15.

is expected to be poor and sorrowful and that poverty and suffering are natural. Under the sway of their religions they have no inclination to secure a better earthly life, no inclination, for example, to organize in labor movements in order to gain better pay and enjoy more and greater satisfactions. Theirs is a philosophy of resignation and not of "progress."[33]

The underdeveloped peoples desire the social, economic, and political gains to be derived from carrying into effect many of the features of modernization, which is a combination of mainly Western innovations. They know that they must, in the last analysis, depend on the West for scientific and technological knowledge and skills, for funds and capital equipment, for consultants, advisers, instructors, and supervisors, and, by no means least of all, for markets, both as sources of materials they need and as exchange outlets for their own resources and products. Yet, in spite of all this, they retain lurking and sometimes very positive attitudes of opposition to the West. Though unfortunate, this is quite understandable. Many of these peoples have been colonial subjects of Western powers and have only recently achieved independence; some are still colonies or mandate areas. Though not always seriously exploited, they were always manipulated—sometimes benevolently as in the case of the United States in the Philippines. Notwithstanding, these people are often suspicious of and somewhat resistant to Western intentions, ideas, and practices, however honorable they may seem. Their hostility expresses itself, variously among the different peoples, in a series of "anti" attitudes and movements —anticolonialism, anti-West nationalistic movements, anti-Westernism generally, anti-white-race-ism, and anti-capitalism.[34]

[33] See the chapter on "Creeds" in Charles G. Darwin, *The Next Million Years* (New York: Doubleday, 1953), pp. 100-114.

[34] With respect particularly to attitudinal barriers to industrialization Moore points out that these underdeveloped peoples try to avoid the sacrifice of "freedom" as independent artisans and agricultural peasants; they resent the submission to the authority, routine, and discipline of the industrial way of life. They avoid the "loss of workmanship" associated with mechanization and the division of labor and are reluctant to learn new techniques. They resent the loss of markets for the products of their handicraft skills, as evidenced in home and village industries. 1951, pp. 44-47, 55-58, 119-126; On the role of attitudes and values see also Buchanan and Ellis, pp. 74-80.

THE GREAT DIVIDES

Finally, there are a variety of cross-cultural blocks which might appropriately be called "Great Divides." These exist both within the larger bodies of underdeveloped peoples and between the various interdependent nations of the world. They consist of vast and sometimes almost insurmountable differences in religion and *Weltanschauung,* differences in levels of literacy and cultural background and sophistication between classes, ethnic and racial groups, regions, and nations. Within peoples there are a multiplicity of languages, nationalistic cleavages, racial and "color" bars and conflicts, class and caste divisions, and other majority-minority oppositions.[35]

For example, with respect to internal "divides," the Indian subcontinent alone has four major contending religions—Hinduism, Islam, Sikhism, and Jainism—as well as innumerable tribal religions, which interfere with every other kind of social and cultural activity.[36] The different "racial" stocks are in part arrayed on different caste levels. More than 200 separate languages, with only thirteen among them having nine million or more speakers, and 40 different forms of writing make communication beyond the village an arduous and complicated procedure[37] and will continue to do so until Hindi is firmly established as the universal national language. In Burma 18,500,000 people speak 126 different languages and dialects. More than 800 different languages are said to be spoken in Africa. In Abyssinia alone some 70 languages are spoken among the different racial stocks. In general, the greater the illiteracy and immobility of a people, the less uniformity of language there is among them.

In addition to the various international "divides" already mentioned, attention must be called to the "curtain" barriers that exist in the world today—the Iron, Bamboo, and Dollar curtains—and especially the sinister uncertainties and cleavages produced by the

---

[35] For a trenchant sociological analysis of the relationships between racial and ethnic situations and industrialization, and of some of the major problems and effects, see Hughes.

[36] Says Davis, "The adherents of different faiths become peoples set apart. Each group tends to have its own folkways and mores, its own outlook, and its own allegiance superior to all others. Each faith thus becomes a nation within a nation." *Population of India and Pakistan,* p. 177.

[37] *Ibid.,* p. 157.

tug-of-war between the Communist and the capitalist, free enterprise, democratic countries.

The world is still bedeviled also by economic "divides" such as tariff walls and international cartels.

CONCLUSION

In view of the vastly different conditions under which modernization is developing and will continue to develop among the underdeveloped peoples, including in our purview the obstacles just discussed, it is quite certain that it will be a different affair in many respects from what it has been among Western peoples (present Group I). Some of the features and stages of the pattern of development that Western countries have had cannot be repeated. Some do not need to be repeated or duplicated. In fact, as noted earlier in this section, the underdeveloped countries of the world have a signal advantage over the Western countries: namely, they need not go through the troublesome, time-consuming, and expensive stages of experimental development in modernization, especially in its technological aspects. They need only borrow and adapt a ready-made pattern of organization and operation. At the outset, they have at their disposal efficient machines and techniques for land clearance, power development, and the exploitation of minerals. In transportation they can have the airplane before the railway or the engineered, hard-surface highway; in communication they can have the radio before the newspaper and other printed matter. They have at their disposal the end-products of scientific knowledge and proven technical procedures for the organization of modern industry, commerce, and government—prizes representing centuries of expensive experience in the West.

SOCIAL-SCIENTIFIC PRINCIPLES OF INDUCED
MODERNIZATION

We have seen that the modernization of the underdeveloped peoples is an urgent matter, both for their own well-being and for the peace, stability, and prosperity of the world as a whole. The people themselves, while resisting some of its features, at the same time wish for many of its gains. They all need aid in establishing the essential features of the process. The nations with the important implementing facilities are in considerable part able and willing to render such assistance.

The aiding and developmental process is, however, an induced and directed rather than a spontaneous, evolutionary process of change; new equipment and techniques are deliberately introduced, and systematic efforts are made to obtain their widespread, effective operation. While technical change is as old as civilization, this purposively initiated change on an international scale is new. Where ever this deliberate introduction occurs very different cultures are thrown together; cross-cultural situations of grave complexity and implication come about, and a very considerable cultural reorientation, especially of the receiving peoples, is certain to take place. A unique value system, a complicated set of technologies, peculiar ways of life, and special patterning of societal organization go with the machines and the techniques and the ends of the West. Some of these elements are now being infused into the lives and societies of the world's village dwellers.

As pointed out at the beginning of the preceding section, the various elements of all cultures are rather closely integrated and have a "toughness" that makes them resistant to changes and highly selective in what they admit from without. The principle of "cultural relativity" is directly related to these facts and has vast importance for the subject matter of the present section. Cultural relativity means that the various parts of a culture have a direct relevance to each other; all of the parts—the ideas, practices, techniques, and so on—are functionally interrelated and must be comprehended in their established evaluational and institutional context and in relation to the cultural whole. Furthermore, as Mead points out, "change in any one part of the culture will be accompanied by changes in other parts, and only by relating any planned detail to the central values of the culture is it possible to provide for the repercussions which will occur in other aspects of life."[38]

At best, modernization of the underdeveloped peoples, including the rendering of technical assistance, will mean considerable and irretrievable modification, even disruption, of relevantly combined and equilibrated patterns of living and will produce serious social, economic, and social-psychological stresses which reach into every aspect of the people's life. Some of these changes will be unantic-

[38] Mead, p. 10.

ipated on the part of both donors and recipients. In general, however, the adoption of any new element is likely to represent something more than an isolated addition, for it has reverberations among many other cultural characteristics.

Therefore, new items and activities should be fitted in a way that is appropriate to the existing cultural and social system; for they unavoidably become structural and functional parts of it. The less distortion produced, the more likely they are to become part of a meaningful and viable pattern of social existence. If they are not smoothly introduced they are likely to be ineffective or to miscarry.

Technical assistance, then, is vastly more than the mere introduction of techniques derived from the biological and physical sciences for the solution of material problems involving, for example, enginering, industry, agriculture, and public health. The technology must be assimilated to the established behavior patterns and social organizations of the various peoples. This makes such assistance a most delicate and complicated task of "social engineering," a crucial phase of the "strategy of induced change," imposing a heavy responsibility on the experts and policy-makers involved.

The anthropologists and sociologists have developed a scattered body of principles that have a direct bearing on this situation. Some of the more pertinent ones will be briefly presented under two main headings: (1) those involved in avoiding serious dislocations in the indigenous culture as technological, economic, and related innovations are introduced; and (2) those involved in bringing about the quickest, most intelligible, most effective acceptance and utilization of the essential scientific, technological, and social agents and techniques.

AVOIDING SOCIO-CULTURAL UPHEAVAL

As far as possible the innovations should be related to existing or developed felt needs of the people. In general, people resist changes that threaten something known or something which has been related to a feeling of security and well-being, or at least something which has been a part of a known way of life. People ordinarily do not vary their traditional attitudes or customary behavior unless they are keenly aware of some need which the existing ways do not satisfy. The new thing or technique, therefore, should be related as closely as possible to existing, long-felt needs of the people. The people, however, may be relatively unaware of many of their own most crucial contemporary needs. Therefore, ways of establishing a sense of need must be resorted to before proceeding with the change. The change must point to recognizable advantages—advantages sufficient to outweigh the losses to the people.[39]

The people should not feel that the changes are being forced upon them. In general, people resist forced changes. To be sure, a highly authoritarian imposition of new ways will produce *some* measure of conformity, but the adjustments and adaptations of the people are grudgingly made and largely confined to external forms. In general, ways adopted under coercion, especially direct coercion, are not effectively carried out. Ordering people to adopt a new thing or new way may focus their attention and energies on resisting the command and on studious efforts to circumvent it, rather than on the advantages of the required change.

Closely related to this is the fact that people also resist changes advocated or promoted by those toward whom they have feelings of suspicion, fear, and/or antagonism. If the innovators are so regarded by the people, the resistance may not be due to the nature or even the possible effects of the innovation (there may even be a secret longing for it), but rather to the innovators. The innovation may thus become a symbol of the opposition to the feared or hated ones. The aiders and innovators and the means they use, therefore, are very important factors in the situation.

In general, at least in the initial stages, it is good social strategy to introduce new ideas and practices as far as possible in the guise of what is already familiar and acceptable.

Very important also is the fact that the economic and technical advice be given without creating a sense of inferiority in the recipient country or engendering any suspicions about the motives and objectives of such programs. Assistance should be given with the object of furthering the socio-economic development of the peoples and not with political intentions, as, for example, an instrument of the Cold War.

The introduction of "foreign" elements should upset or undermine the existing value system and social organization as little as

---

[39] Cf. Spicer, pp. 13-20, 285-296; Goldschmidt.

possible. Both the value system and social organization are the basic "capital" of any social mechanism upon which its stability and effective operation depend. At best, the introduction of "foreign" elements produces some dislocation.

Any loss of nonmaterial values that reside in the traditional system and community life and are not absolutely antagonistic to the essential new views and values should be avoided. Where values have to be modified an oblique procedure should be followed. The existing social organization—established groups, organizations, institutions—is the societal machinery that has to be used at any given time. The new techniques and developments can be most effectively introduced into the societies if they are fused with and/or made an extension of comparable or similar structural and functional counterparts of the indigenous culture.[40]

This does not mean that all existing societal forms can be used, or that some strategic ones will not have to be altered. It does mean, however, that if attitudes favorable to innovation in the crucial technological and institutional areas do not exist, they have to be developed. In general, the new technology ought to become part of the economic and social life of the people of the underdeveloped peoples.[41]

All of the essential contextual features of a culture complex must be taken over by the borrowers if it is to be effective in the long run. The abstract and intangible, as well as the external, readily perceptible and applicable, features have to enter the conceptualizations and actions of the people. This holds also for the complementary and supplementary structures and functions. With special reference to the industrial aspect of modernization, Moore states:

> A complicated machine may be transported quite successfully, and may even be satisfactorily operated with a few simple instructions. But its successful maintenance and its fulfilment of its function depend on a vast array of other interrelated factors, such as mechanical knowledge, available parts and supplies, a market for the output, transportation and communicative facilities, some measure of literacy if only for the purpose of reading directions.

[40] McGranahan, p. 14; Goldschmidt, p. 150; Batten.
[41] Cf. Hakim.

Industry comes wrapped in a bundle. In the beginning it may enter a culture in the form of a few isolated strands, but its substantial development depends upon the roughly parallel or collateral development of the whole complex.[42]

The representative, respected, prestigeful elements of the community should be persuaded to appreciate, approve, and, if possible, promote the essential ideas and techniques. Any kind of change, great or small, material or non-material, requires a human agency. In final analysis, the problem probably hinges on the question of leadership. Also, certain types of persons or "officers" are more effective as culture bearers and cultural representatives than others; some influence public opinion in the necessary direction in accepting innovations more than others. In these primitive and peasant societies the sanctions for actions are usually derived from persons of traditional authority, that is, such "natural" leaders as chiefs, village headmen, the council of elders, or the leaders of religious cults. Under some circumstances it might be a missionary teacher, an agriculturalist, a doctor, or a native government clerk. Always it must be a person who is respected and influential, though the particular situation will likely determine the person or persons who assume the leadership roles. In general, there seems to be a rough proportionality between the prestige of the innovators within the receiving culture and the acceptability of the innovation by other members of the society.

The essential reorganization and construction should, as far as possible, be in the hands of the people themselves. Foreign aid, however essential it may be at the moment, is a stopgap, a form of relief. It does not *solve* any of the world's ills either quickly, cheaply, or effectively. It cannot be carried on indefinitely; the resources essential to it, even in the United States, and the willingness to devote the resources to foreign aid, are not unlimited. Outside assistance is always "hand-me-down," however fine spirited and skillfully given it may be; long-continued dependency has a debilitating effect; actual parasitism may be the result. Furthermore, technological and economic proficiency cannot be handed to people on a platter. Foreign aid, however valuable and highly appreciated, must be viewed as marginal and supplementary to the

[42] "The Theoretical Aspects of Industrialization," pp. 298-299.

efforts of the peoples themselves. The development programs, where desirable or necessary, need to be formulated by the peoples themselves in consultation with the experts and technicians from abroad. The upward climb must be made by the peoples themselves under their own initiative and with agencies of their own devising All aid should be given and administered with this in mind. The peoples, as soon as possible, should assume the primary responsibility for all the essential changes. In the end, they have to initiate and carry through their own technological, industrial, political, and ideational revolutions and purge their own governments of inefficiency, misdirection, extravagance, and corruption. They should manage their own financing, develop their own capital equipment, and operate their agriculture and other industry efficiently under modern competitive world conditions. In general, it is necessary for them to find their own ways of adapting and transforming their cultural patterns and social-reorganizational forms to the requirements of modern economic, social, and political progress. If not, they continue to be, or they become, dependents of other national or international bodies.

The benefits of aid should accrue to the masses of the people. The aid should not be for the profit of some particular class, faction, party, group, region, or totalitarian leader. The assistance miscarries if it remains in the form of reports, recommendations, programs, and blueprints of development. It is only worth while, to the receiver and the giver, if it is translated into new, or revised and extended, productive techniques that increase the wealth, greatly elevate the level of general well-being, and inspire aspirations for higher standards of living. If it does not do this, it falls far short of its purpose, amounts to a waste of effort and resources, and leads to frustration and disillusionment.

Changes should be effected gradually. As noted, the changes involved in the modernization of these peoples imply virtually an entire reorganization of their individual and social life. The technical assisters need to be particularly aware of one signal aspect of such change. If the changes are too drastic and too rapid, the whole social edifice is endangered. All advance needs a stable basis in the masses of the people and in the cultural and social organization of the society. The people need to be psychologically acclimatized. New or greatly revised attitudes and habits have to be substituted for old ones. For the society as a whole it means greatly revised structures and functions.

Long social experience throws much light on the rate at which sound advance can occur and the strategy to be pursued. That advance is best, in general, which comes through the accumulation of many consistent fractional improvements effected as far as possible at the logical moment. This means that it is a step-by-step process, with each step coordinated with and developing out of the preceding stages, each step a matter of judicious temporary adjustments, compromises with the necessities of the situation, and the careful application of established principles. The people must be educated and prepared for the next step and intelligently fitted to participate in it willingly. The social structure must be built or rebuilt with tested material. All sudden leaps and bounds and all violent and arbitrary forcing should be avoided. Whatever else its tactics may be, the constructive movement should not out-distance the masses of its supporters, but march just far enough ahead to be able to lead. Often the best development comes by occasional flank movements, instead of head-on attacks.

Modernization as rapidly as possible is imperative for many reasons. The above considerations do not mean that the snail should be taken as mentor; they do not mean that the processes of reorganization cannot be hastened. Rather, advantage should be taken of every chance that comes. Alert promoters should be ready to tack with the wind.

SPECIFIC TECHNIQUES FOR TECHNOLOGICAL INNOVATION

The Western technologists and inaugurators and supervisors of foreign aid programs have delicate and difficult tasks to perform. They come from societies in which a high degree of literacy prevails, where people are used to all manner of formal *and* informal instructional procedures and depend upon these as they take up some new tool or way; they come from societies in which modern rationality governs, that is, where practical ends are highly regarded and efficient means respected and utilized, even though this means abandonment of reigning ends and practices; they come from societies where almost everyone has some rudimentary scientific knowledge and in which the entire population is conditioned to machines and technical operations from childhood on. These

Western aiders have ways of talking, acting, and thinking which are sharply different from those of the people among whom they are working. When native peoples, on the other hand, have carried on most of their life operations on the basis of superstition, magic, and customary rule-of-thumb, and have little or no "scientific" knowledge of cause-and-effect in the biological, chemical, physical, or social realms, the task of getting the essential new techniques accepted and put quickly and effectively into practice is not an easy one.

Social scientists, on the basis both of careful study and successful experience, are able to suggest certain principles of procedure. These will be briefly presented.[43]

Preliminary and fundamental to all else is a careful culture analysis. Each culture is different. The outsider coming into a culture to introduce innovations and to modify it must have a knowledge of the elements of the indigenous culture, both to enable him to be effective in his own work and to avoid doing harm to the culture and social organization by ill-advised action. He needs to know how the elements, especially the outstanding and determining ones such as the economic, domestic, and religious, are related and integrated. He must know and understand the value system and the social organization—the nature of the community organization, the forms of leadership and administration that prevail, the existing organizations and the standard forms of acting in cooperative undertakings. He needs to know the existing channels of communication and the sources of influence. He needs to know about the existing biases, prejudices, and preconceptions, the deep-seated attitudes and habits, the traditions and customs, the taboos and imperatives. This knowledge, carefully acquired, is essential if he is to be aware of what obstacles need to be overcome, what favorable conditions exist, what the effects of the innovation are likely to be, and what type of strategy should be employed in the processes of introduction, instruction, and supervision. As Spicer states, such an analysis of the culture and social organization provides the teams of assisters with "maps of the terrain" in

---

[43] They have, in the main, been suggested by procedures examined in connection with the *special cases* presented in Spicer.

which they are working.[44] But this is merely *groundwork* for the fundamental task.

Rather than subject the people broadside and on an area-wide scale to any scheme, the plans and possible procedures should first be tried out by means of an exploratory model, or pilot project, on a small scale. The effects of such experiments should be meticulously observed. Such projects enable demonstrators to note the physical as well as the social difficulties involved and to examine the progressive effects upon the existing cultural life and its social patterns. Attention can be given to the possibility of new social groups and new roles of leadership being developed out of the changed situation. Consideration should be given to the relationship of the scheme's administrative and technical personnel to the local people. These observations can be used as the basis for necessary modifications of the original plan. Such a procedure enables those charged with making the innovation to learn what they themselves are trying to do; their own behavior is "fed back" to them and becomes part of the planning process and of actual procedure.[45]

The processes of introduction and development in the use of the innovations will be the work of policy-makers, experts, and specialists—technical investigators, engineers of all sorts, extension agents in agriculture and nutrition, private and public health advisers, specialists in vocational guidance and training and in child and adult education, supervisors and administrators, members of ministries of health, education, agriculture, and commercial and industrial development. Many of these will be advisers from Western countries, even though, in some instances, they will be acting under the auspices of special agencies of the local governments and/or the United Nations. The character of the people who make the contacts and who function as the cultural representatives is exceedingly significant. The wrong kind of men and women can produce most unfortunate consequences by creating stresses and antagonisms. As important as their knowledge and special skills will be their personality. Their effectiveness will depend in considerable part on their own attitudes and behavior and the kind

[44] P. 290. See also Mead, pp. 291-299.
[45] See Little, pp. 94-96; Mead, pp. 316-317.

of attitudes the indigenous population has toward them, which, in turn, will depend upon the understanding and sensitiveness of the foreign agents to the people and the situation.

They should not be dominating, overbearing persons, with arrogant self-assurance, who try to force their methods on the people; not exercisers of "superiority" attitudes; not overzealous scientific missionaries who confuse the people with their highly technical knowledge and thereby invite apathy. Needed are people of goodwill and humility; people who accord the local culture dignity and value, and know and respect the regnant traditions and ways; people who are sensitive and patient in their suggestion of and application of techniques and devices; people who can graciously yield and compromise but also quickly and diplomatically use an opening; people, in short, who are warmly human. Obvious of course is the ability to instruct and demonstrate the nature, operation, and effects of the innovation, and to establish it successfully as a working part of the social system. Finally, they should be people who can work on teams.[46]

The eventual ability to utilize competently any innovation introduced from without is fundamentally a process of learning about it and of developing incentives to use it in place of (an unlearning process) or in addition to an existing practice. Adequate learning, if it is to be timely, is a matter of deliberate and appropriate instruction. The instructional procedures will vary greatly, depending upon the general nature of the culture, the particular levels and segments of the population being dealt with, and the nature of the instructional task.

In the course of the instruction, in order to make possible the acceptance of the necessary knowledge and the development of technical proficiency, it is essential, in many instances, that a favorable attitude be developed toward the innovation. This involves, among other things, subtly neutralizing retarding or antagonistic beliefs and actions, highlighting the pertinence and urgency of the needs it is to meet, and creating positive convictions in its behalf.

In the actual process of instruction, both oral and written means will have to be used, but there are distinct limitations to the use of each. There are limitations as to vocabulary in the languages

---

[46] See the excellent study by Dickson.

of the indigenous populations, and the foreign experts themselves often do not have great facility in the language of the people. Translators and interpreters are at best a complication. Since large portions of the indigenous populations are illiterate, written instructional aids cannot be widely used.

Therefore demonstration comes to be one of the most important instructional procedures. People can see and understand demonstrations. Many things can be put across in spite of language difficulties and of deficiencies in cultural background. The demonstrator does not have to argue; often seeing is believing. By means of the demonstration the observers directly acquire know-how, see the actions and sequences involved in the procedure, see its effects, and are quite likely to acquire experimental interests and convictions favorable to its use.

The decisive procedure in obtaining high favor for and high proficiency in the operation of new cultural features—whether technological, economic, or political—is to go beyond demonstration by providing opportunity for active participation in the new or revised procedures. This is learning (and being convinced) by doing.

In its more adequate form participation means that: (1) the people are confronted with the task of thinking through their problems themselves and seeing the need for change; (2) they are acquiring knowledge and skill "on the job"; (3) they are taking part in the planning and enjoying the advantages to be derived; (4) they are part of the procedure for introducing and executing the innovation; (5) they learn how to use the essential principles, techniques, and facilities; (6) they devise and voluntarily make the necessary changes in the values and institutions involved and thus work out in their own way their adjustment of the new form to their way of life. Participation is also one of the better-tested ways of preventing or breaking down resistance to the needed way of acting and of developing a sense of responsibility for its effective operation.

BIBLIOGRAPHY

ALLEN, H. B. *Rural Reconstruction in Action: Experience in the Near and Middle East.* Ithaca: Cornell Univ. Press, 1953.

BANKS, A. LESLIE (ed.). *The Development of Tropical and Sub-Tropical Countries, with Particular Reference to Africa.* New York: St. Martin's Press, 1955.

BATTEN, T. R. "Social Values and Community Development," in Ruopp, pp. 80-86.

BARCLAY, GEORGE W. *Colonial Development and Population in Taiwan.* Princeton: Princeton Univ. Press, 1954.

BEALS, RALPH L. "Urbanism, Urbanization, and Acculturation." *Am. Anthrop.* 53 (Jan.-March, 1951): 1-10.

BECKETT, W. H. "The Development of Peasant Agriculture," in Ruopp, pp. 132-152.

BELSHAW, C. S. *Changing Melanesia: Social Economics of Culture Change.* Melbourne: Oxford Univ. Press, 1954.

BOECKE, J. H. *Economics and Economic Policy in Dual Societies as Exemplified in Indonesia.* New York: Institute of Pacific Affairs, 1953.

BOWLES, GORDON T. "Point Four and Improved Standards of Living." *Annals Am. Acad. Pol. & Soc. Sci.,* 268 (March, 1950) : 140-147.

BROWN, HARRISON. *The Challenge of Man's Future.* New York: Viking, 1954. Pp. 225-233, 243-253.

BROZEN, YALE. "Determinants of the Direction of Technological Change." *Am. Econ. Rev.,* 43 (May, 1953): 288-302, and comments by I. H. Siegel, pp. 308-309.

————. "Determinants of Enterpreneurial Ability." *Soc. Research,* 21 (Autumn, 1954): 339-364.

BUCHANAN, N. S., and H. S. ELLIS. *Approaches to Economic Development.* New York: Twentieth Century Fund, 1955.

CALDER, RITCHIE. *Men Against the Jungle.* London: Allen & Unwin, 1954.

DAVIDSON, BASIL. "Enlightened Colonialism: The Belgian Congo." *Reporter,* 12 (Jan. 27, 1955): 34-39.

DAVIS, KINGSLEY. "Population and the Further Spread of Industrial Society." *Proc. Am. Phil. Soc.,* 95 (Feb., 1951) : 8-19.

————. *The Population of India and Pakistan.* Princeton: Princeton Univ. Press, 1951. Pp. 127-176, 204-220.

———— and HILDA HERTZ. *Pattern of World Urbanization.* New York: Macmillan, 1954.

DECKER, C. R. "Southeast Asia: Proposals for the Future," in Thayer, pp. 259-267.

DE SCHWEINITZ, K., and K. W. THOMSON. *Man and Modern Society: Conflict and Choice in the Industrial Era.* New York: Holt, 1953.

DICKSON, A. G. "The Concept of Team" in Ruopp, pp. 227-244.

DOBBY, E. H. G. "Food and the Changing Function of Southeast Asia," in Thayer, pp. 126-139.

FRANKEL, S. H. *The Economic Impact on Under-Developed Societies.* Cambridge: Harvard Univ. Press, 1953.

GARD, R. A. "Ideological Problems in Southeast Asia," in Thayer, pp. 147-165.

GERSCHENKRON, ALEXANDER. "Economic Backwardness in Historical Perspective," in Hoselitz, *The Progress of Underdeveloped Areas,* pp. 3-29.

GHOSH, D. *Pressure of Population and Economic Efficiency in India.* London: Oxford Univ. Press, 1946.

GILFILLAN, S. C. "The Prediction of Technical Change." *Rev. of Econ. & Stat.,* 34 (Nov., 1952) : 371-383.

GIST, N. P. "Occupational Differentiation in South India." *Soc. Forces,* 33 (Dec., 1954): 129-138.

GOLDSCHMIDT, W. R. "The Interrelations between Cultural Factors and the Acquisition of New Technical Skills," in Hoselitz, *The Progress of Underveloped Areas,* pp. 135-151.

GOODRICH, CARTER. "Bolivia: Test of Technical Assistance." *Foreign Affairs,* 32 (April, 1954): 473-481.

GRAHAM, A. B. "Some Aims and Methods of Fundamental Education," in Ruopp, pp. 209-217.

HAKIM, GEORGE. "Technical Aid from the Viewpoint of the Aid-Receiving Countries," in Hoselitz, *The Progress of Underveloped Areas,* pp. 259-269.

HASKINS, HALFORD L. "Point Four with Reference to the Middle East." *Annals Am. Acad. Pol. & Soc. Sci.,* 268 (March, 1950): 85-95.

HAYES, S. P., JR. "Personality and Culture Problems of Point IV," in Hoselitz, *The Progress of Underdeveloped Areas,* pp. 203-247.

HAZELWOOD, ARTHUR. "The Economic Background," in Ruopp, pp. 123-131.

————. *The Economics of "Underdeveloped" Areas: An Annotated Reading List of Books, Articles, and Official Publications.* New York: Oxford Univ. Press, 1954.

HERSKOVITS, M. J. "The Problem of Adapting Societies to New Tasks," in Hoselitz, *The Progress of Underdeveloped Areas,* pp. 89-112.

HOSELITZ, B. F. (ed.) *The Progress of Underdeveloped Areas.* Chicago: Univ. of Chicago Press, 1952.

————. "The Role of Cities in the Economci Growth of Underdeveloped Countries." *Jour. Pol. Econ.,* 61 (Feb., 1953): 195-208.

HOSKINS, H. L. "Point Four with Reference to the Middle East." *Annals Am. Acad. Pol. & Soc. Sci.,* 268 (March, 1950): 85-95.

HUGHES, E. C. and H. M. *Where Peoples Meet: Racial and Ethnic Frontiers.* Glencoe, Ill.: Free Press, 1952. Pp. 61-82.

HUNT, C. L. "Cultural Barriers to Point Four." *Antioch Rev.,* Summer, 1954: 159-167.

JAFFE, A. J. "Technological Innovations and the Changing Socio-Economic Structure." *Scientific Monthly,* 67 (Aug., 1948): 93-102.

LA MACCHIA, F. R. "African Economics: Basic Characteristics and Prospects." *Annals Am. Acad. Pol. & Soc. Sci.,* 298 (March, 1955) : 39-51.

LAMBERT, R. D., and M. BRESSLER. "A Sensitive-Area Complex: A Contribution to the Theory of Guided Culture Contact." *Am. Jour. Soc.,* 60 (May, 1955) : 583-592.

LEAKE, H. M. *Unity: National and Imperial.* London: Allen & Unwin, 1935. Pp. Pp. 9-10, 15-16, 23-24, 105-123, 134-175, 204-207.

LEIBENSTEIN, HENRY. *A Theory of Economic-Demographic Development.* Princeton: Princeton Univ. Press, 1954.

LEIGHTON, A. H. Foreword in Spicer, pp. 9-11.

LE TOURNEAU, ROGER. "Social Change in the Muslim Cities of North Africa." *Am. Jour. Soc.,* 60 (May, 1955): 527-535.

LINTON, RALPH. "Cultural and Personality Factors Affecting Economic Growth," in Hoselitz, *The Progress of Underdeveloped Areas.* Pp. 73-88.

LITTLE, K. L. "Social Change in a Non-Literate Community," in Ruopp, pp. 87-96.

LOOMIS, C. P., J. O. MORALES, R. A. CLIFFORD, and O. E. LEONARD (eds.). *Turrialba: Social Systems and the Introduction of Change.* Glencoe, Ill.: Free Press, 1953.

LORIMER, FRANK, et al. *Culture and Human Fertility: A Study of the Relations of Cultural Conditions to Fertility in Non-industrial and Transitional Societies.* Paris: UNESCO (New York: Columbia Univ. Press), 1955. Pp. 58-90, 151-203.

MADAN, B. K. (ed.) . *Economic Problems of Underdeveloped Countries in Asia.* New York: Oxford Univ. Press, 1953.

MALINOWSKI, BRONISLAW. *The Dynamics of Cultural Change: An Inquiry into Race Relations in Africa.* New Haven: Yale Univ. Press, 1945.

MANDELBAUM, K. *The Industrialization of Backward Areas.* London: Oxford Univ. Press, 1945.

MAY, STACY. "Folklore and Fact about Underdeveloped Areas." *Foreign Affairs,* 33 (Jan., 1955): 212-224.

McGRANAHAN, D. V. "Some Remarks on the Human Implications of Technological Change in Underveloped Areas." *Soc. Problems,* 1 (June, 1953): 13-16.

MEAD, MARGARET (ed.). *Cultural Patterns and Technical Change.* New York: UNESCO (Columbia Univ. Press) , 1953.

METRAUX, ALFRED. "Applied Anthropology in Government: United Nations," in A. L. Kroeber (ed.) , *Anthropology Today: An Encyclopedic Inventory.* Chicago: Univ. of Chicago Press, 1953. Pp. 880-894.

MOORE, W. E. *Economic Demography in Eastern and Southeastern Europe.* Geneva: League of Nations, 1945.

————. *Industrialization and Labor: Social Aspects of Economic Development.* Published for the Institute of World Affairs, New School for Social Research. Ithaca: Cornell Univ. Press, 1951.

————. "Labor Attitudes Toward Industrialization in Underdeveloped Countries." *Am. Econ. Rev.,* 45 (May, 1955): 156-165.

————. "Primitives and Peasants in Industry." *Soc. Research,* 15 (March, 1948): 44-81.

————. "Theoretical Aspects of Industrialization." *Soc. Research,* 15 (Sept., 1948): 277-303.

MOSK, S. A. *Industrial Revolution in Mexico.* Berkeley: Univ. of California Press, 1950.

NIEUWENHUIJZE, C. A. O. VAN. "Implications" (of community development in underdeveloped ocuntries) , in Ruopp, pp. 61-79.

NURKSE, RAGNAR. *Problems of Capital Formation in Underdeveloped Countries.* New York: Oxford Univ. Press, 1954.

ODUM, H. W. "Folk Sociology as a Subject Field for the Historical Study of Total Human Society and the Empirical Study of Group Behavior." *Soc. Forces,* 31 (March, 1953): 193-223.

OPLER, M. E. "The Problem of Selective Cultural Change," in Hoselitz, *The Progress of Underdeveloped Areas,* pp. 126-134.

OSBORN, FAIRFIELD. *The Limits of the Earth.* Boston: Little, Brown, 1953. Pp. 29-30, 41-42, 52-57, 66-69.

REDFIELD, ROBERT. "The Folk Society and Culture." *Am. Jour. Soc.,* 45 (March, 1940): 731-742.

ROSTOW, W. W. *The Process of Economic Growth.* New York: Norton, 1952.

RUOPP, PHILLIPS (ed.). *Approaches to Community Development: A Symposium Introductory to Problems and Methods of Village Welfare in Underdeveloped Areas.* The Hague: W. van Hoeve, 1953. "Approaches to Community Development," pp. 1-20.

SHARP, W. R. *International Technical Assistance: Programs and Organization.* Chicago: Public Administration Service, 1952.

SIEGEL, I. H. "Technological Change and Long-Run Forecasting." *Jour. of Business of Univ. of Chicago.* 26 (July, 1953) : 141-156.

SINGER, H. W. "Economic Progress in Underdeveloped Countries." *Soc. Research,* 16 (March, 1949) : 1-11.

—————. "Obstacles to Economic Development." *Soci Research,* 20 (Spring, 1953). 19-31.

"Social Implications of Technical Change." *Int. Soc. Sci. Bull.,* Vol. 4, No. 2 (Summer, 1952).

SPENCER, D. L. "Mixed Enterprise as a Tool of Economic Development: India's Contribution." *Am. Jour. Econ. & Soc.,* 14 (Jan., 1955): 139-158.

SPENGLER, J. J. "Aspects of the Economics of Population Growth." *Southern Econ. Jour.,* 14 (Jan., 1948) : 233-266.

—————. "Economic Factors in the Development of Densely Populated Areas." *Proc. Am. Phil. Soc.,* 95 (Feb., 1951): 20-53.

—————. "The Population Obstacle to Economic Betterment." *Papers & Proceedings of the 63rd Annual Meeting.* Ann. Econ. Assoc., Vol. 41, No. 2 (May, 1951): 343-354. See also discussion by P. A. Baran, pp. 355-358.

—————. "Theories of Socio-Economic Growth." in National Bureau of Economic Research, *Problems in the Study of Economic Growth.* New York, 1949. Pp. 46-115.

SPICER, E. H. (ed.). *Human Problems in Technological Change: A Case Book.* New York: Russell Sage Foundation, 1952. Introduction, pp. 13-20; "Conceptual Tools for Solving Human Problems," pp. 285-296.

STALEY, EUGENE. *The Future of Underdeveloped Countries: Political Implications of Economic Development.* New York: Harpers, 1954.

STAMP, L. DUDLEY. *Our Underdeveloped World.* London: Faber, 1953.

STEEL, R. W. "Africa: The Environmental Setting." *Annals Am. Acad. Pol. & Soc. Sci.,* 298 (March, 1955) : 1-10.

TAEUBER, IRENE B. "The Future of Transitional Areas," in P. K. Hatt (ed.), *World Population and Future Resources.* New York: American Book, 1952. Pp. 25-38.

THAYER, P. W. (ed.). *Southeast Asia in the Coming World.* Baltimore: Johns Hopkins Press, 1953.

THEODORSON, G. A. "Acceptance of Industrialization and Its Attendant Consequences for the Social Patterns of Non-Western Societies." *Am. Soc. Rev.,* 18 (Oct., 1953): 477-484.

TOLLEY, H. R. "Farmers in a Hungry World." *Proc. Am. Phil. Soc.,* 95 (Feb., 1951): 54-61.

UNITED NATIONS. *Measures for the Economic Development of Underdeveloped Countries.* New York, 1951.

UNESCO. *Education in a Technological Society: A Preliminary Survey of the Nature and Efficacy of Technical Education.* Washington: UNESCO Relations Staff, 1953.

————. *Technical Assistance for Economic Development: A Human Approach* ("UNESCO and Its Programme," No. 5). Paris: UNESCO, 1951.

UNITED NATIONS, Population Commission, Department of Social Affairs. *The Determinants and Consequences of Population Trends: A Summary of the Findings of Studies on the Relationships between Population Changes and Economic and Social Conditions* (Population Studies, No. 17). New York, 1953. Chap. XI, "Population and Labour Supply," pp. 194-209; Chap. XII, "Population and Consumption," pp. 210-219; Chap. XIII, "Effects of Population Growth on Per Capita Consumption," pp. 220-238; Chap. XV, "Implications of Population Trends in Underdeveloped Countries," pp. 262-286.

ZINKIN, MAURICE. *Asia and the West.* London: Chatto & Windus, 1951. Pp. 18-56, 199-202, 208-237.

For more extensive bibliographies on the subject of this chapter see: Margaret Mead (ed.), *Cultural Patterns and Technical Change,* pp. 321-336; W. E. Moore, *Industrialization and Labor,* pp. 365-390; United Nations, *The Determinants and Consequences of Population Trends,* pp. 319-369, whose bibliography contains more than 2,500 diversified items with pertinent references in English, German, French, Spanish, Dutch, Italian, Swedish, Norwegian, Finnish, Russian, and several other languages.

7

Increasing The World's Food Supply

THE IMPORTANCE OF FOOD IN THE WORLD SITUATION

For several reasons the problem of the world food supply is of elemental importance in any study of world population. In the first place, food, adequate both as to quantity and quality, is a basic essential in the general physical well-being of the world's peoples, and well-being is one of the most urgent of humane objectives. As noted in our discussion of the three groups, approximately three-fourths of the world's people are undernourished in that they fall short quantitatively of that tolerable level of subsistence indicated by the scientifically established bench mark of 2750 calories per person per day. While all people are lacking somewhat in the variety and quality of the food elements in their diets from the point of view of scientifically developed standards, the great bulk of the population of the world—the underdeveloped peoples—are so dependent upon starches, and so lacking in proteins and fats (especially animal proteins and fats), in essential acids, minerals, and vitamins as to to be in a continual state of malnourishment. They are suffering from the treacherous "hidden hungers." Deficiencies in both quantity and quality of food mean inefficiency and lethargy due to low vitality and energy, organic and other physiological impairment, certain widely prevalent food-caused diseases, as well as susceptibility to many other diseases, and inability to recuperate from them. The hungry people of the world are below normal with respect to their per-capita and national economic productivity, a certain general level of which is essential to individual, national, and world well-being. These hungry peoples are centers of incubation for endemic diseases, and epidemic diseases cut their tragic swaths among them.

In the second place, food for all is a crucial factor in world peace. Hunger is a root-cause of misery, dissatisfaction, frustration, and unrest and functions as a powerful motivator to aberrant thinking, rebellion, and war.

And in the third place, the food supply and the size of a population are directly related, as Malthus and others before and since his time have pointed out. This is the most important aspect of what Osborn has recently called the "eternal equation."[1] He states:

> We are under the power of a timeless principle, exerting its influence relentlessly on a global scale. This principle is closely related to the law of supply and demand. It finds expression in a simple ratio wherein the numerator can be defined as "resources of the earth," and the denominator as "numbers of people."[2]

Within rather narrow limits, food resources especially must be equilibrated with the number of people; that is, the food supply must be increasing correspondingly with the increase of population. Food in minimal amount and kind is always the primary determinant of existence and the ultimate determinant of numbers. This holds whether the food supply of a given people is produced within the national limits or supplemented by exchange or gift from without. The eternal problem is: adequate food *or* famine, malnourishment, disease, starvation, and death.

WORLD FOOD IN RELATION TO POPULATION INCREASE

As through all of human history, the production of food is still the major preoccupation and occupation of the bulk of the world's population. Two striking facts were brought out at the international food conference held at Hot Springs, Virginia, in May, 1943: first, that even now, long after the start of the Industrial Revolution, two-thirds of the people of the world are still engaged in producing food; and, second, that two-thirds of the people of

[1] 1953, p. 58.
[2] *Ibid.*, p. 207.

the world normally do not have enough to eat. Moreover, there is fairly reliable evidence indicating that the present race between food and population has been a close one, with population the winner in most of the critical areas.

The recent reports of the Food and Agricultural Organization of the United Nations present us with most sobering data. The report of the *Second* World Food Survey (November, 1952) pointed out that while world food production from 1945 to 1951 was about 9 per cent greater than the period from 1934 to 1938, the number of the world's people increased by 12 per cent.[3] The FAO's most recent report, The State of Food and Agriculture, 1955 (September, 1955), shows some improvement since the immediate post-war period, but it still provides no grounds for optimism. With respect to population, it shows that, taking the 1934-1938 average as 100, by 1946 it had increased to 111, and by 1954 to 124. The 1954 figures for certain critical areas were as follows: Latin America, 147; Africa, 131; the Near East, 130; and the Far East, 127.[4] With "pre-war" as 100, total world agricultural production was 92 for 1946-1947 and rose to 120 for 1954-1955; food production slumped to 92 for 1946-1947 and also rose to 120 for 1954-1955.[5] However, the world per-capita total agricultural production was 85 for 1946-1947 and 100 for 1954-1955, and the per-capita food production was 85 and 101. The different major regions, however, showed considerable variation: for example, the 1954-1955 per-capita food production for Latin America was down to 94 and for the Far East down to 86, while for the Near East it had risen to 106 and for Africa to 109.[6] The study shows that the average annual increase in world production, 1946 to 1954, was 2.9 per cent for food, 3.8 per cent for non-food, and 6.6 per cent for manufactures.[7]

The situation with respect to average calorie and protein intake shows that the critical areas of the world just before World War II were all far below the bench marks. By 1947-1948 their condition

[3] See, e.g., pp. 3-20.
[4] Table II-4, p. 21.
[5] Annex Table 1, p. 233. See also Tables II-1 and II-2, p. 15.
[6] Annex Table 2, p. 223.
[7] Table V-9, p. 101.

had further deteriorated in a most alarming manner. Since then conditions have improved only very slightly.[8]

While some of the food-short areas have made advances, the sinister fact is that there is still an appalling deficiency of food among all of the underdeveloped countries, both in quantity and quality. A disproportionate part of the increase of food has been produced in those parts of the world which were already food-surplus areas. Only five countries of the world are capable at the present time of producing more food than their people need: Australia, New Zealand, Canada, Argentina, and the United States. Furthermore, while the prospects for newer developments and increased production are fairly good among some of the underdeveloped countries, the greatest likelihood of substantial increases exists among those regions which are already more economically advanced.

The food-population ratio in the future presents even more acute conditions and problems when we note the possible population trends. With a doubling of world population in around 60 years at the present rate of growth, and a world in which a large part of the people at present are underfed, the problem of increasing the food supply is a crucial one. On the basis of the present average quality of land under cultivation, the present agricultural techniques, and the present average level of subsistence, 2 to $2\frac{1}{2}$ acres of land are required to produce the annual per-capita ration. If the increase of the number of human beings in the future is no greater than the present approximate 30 million per year, the world will need as a minimum an additional 60 million equally good acres each year just to feed the additional population at the present average standard;[9] or it will need a corresponding increase in output by means of more intensive cultivation from the already cultivated land. If, at the same time, the balanced calorie bench mark is to be achieved for all of the world's people, the task is still more enormous.[10] Can we feed, at present standards, a popula-

[8] Cf. Figures V-11, p. 95, and V-12, p. 96, and Annex Tables 3 and 4, pp. 224-226.

[9] At the same time it is estimated that about 14,600,000 acres are lost to cultivation annually for various reasons.

[10] In 1946 the FAO calculated that if this were to be achieved for the prospective population of 1960, the following percentage increases in food production would be necessary: sugar, 12%; cereals, 21%; roots and tubers, 27%; fats, 34%;

tion which can well have grown to 4 billion or even more by the end of the present century, not to mention the 50 per cent increase in food supply necessary to provide the quantitatively and qualitatively adequate ration for the entire world population? The task is both to catch up as far as present quantitative and qualitative deficiencies are concerned, and to keep up with one ever-expanding world population. What this means is indicated by Brown when he states:

> In the one-half of the world which is badly undernourished, an increase, in food production of approximately 50 per cent is necessary if the people are to have adequate nutrition. Thus, for the world as a whole at the existing population level, an increase in food production of approximately 25 per cent is necessary. But we have seen that in the years to come the population of the world probably will increase considerably above the existing level —possibly reading 4.8 billion in another 50 years and 6.7 billion in another century. Thus in another 50 years food production might have to be two and one-half times greater than it is today, and by the year 2050, production might have to be multiplied three and one-half times.[11]

The Second World Food Survey of the FAO points out that the large increases in food should occur in the areas where the need is greatest, especially the Far East, Near East, and Africa. The reason for this is that

> . . . Increased production in the surplus regions cannot possibly furnish the expansion required in food supplies for the world as a whole. At best . . . the surplus areas can provide only a small fraction of the needs of the major deficit regions.[12]

As will be noted shortly, however, these deficit regions are in most instances the very areas where the food-producing land has for centuries and even millennia been utilized under conditions of continuous population pressure with maximum intensity.

Possible mortality and/or fertility changes might affect the situation greatly. This aspect of the problem and what might be done

---

meat, 46%; pulses, 80%; milk, 100%; and fruits and vegetables, 163%—an average of nearly 50%. *World Food Survey*, p. 18.

[11] Pp. 145-146.

[12] P. 26.

about it will be given further consideration in later chapters. Here we will briefly examine especially the food aspect of the numerator, the resources of the earth.[13] What, by way of a very general survey, are the possibilities and the implications of increasing the world's food supply? The examination of such possibilities, on the basis of recent investigations and evaluations, falls into three general categories, namely: (1) the possibilities of profitably extending the production of food to land not now used for such purposes; (2) the possibilities of increasing the food yields on lands now cultivated; (3) the other possible ways of increasing the food supply, such as incorporating in diets available but now now used nutritive elements, resort to unused and undeveloped sources of food in the waters of the earth, synthetic foods, hydroponics, and so on.

THE AGRICULTURAL LANDS OF THE WORLD

Before taking up each of these categories it is desirable that we have some idea of the situation regarding the approximate amount of land at present used for agricultural purposes and that additional amount estimated to be potentially available. Man still gets nearly all his food from the soil, only about three per cent coming from the sea. We may in time greatly augment the world food supply from the food resources of the waters of the earth and from the widely discussed artificial foods; but in the main, for the immediate and pressing future at least, we must rely on agriculture, and agriculture means land on which crops, vegetable and animal, can be raised. Land, therefore, is a crucial consideration in determining the world's population-carrying capacity.

However, it is only one of the major determinants in the food supply. It does set the absolute natural or outer limits. But the other inextricably related major determinant is what man does with this nature-given instrument. In other words, the relative limits are set by man's culture—by the attitudes, traditions, and

---

[13] All of the resources of the earth, of course, are involved in the present and future welfare of the world's population, and the development of most of these and the ways and the areas in which they are utilized affect both population changes and the production and consumption of food in innumerable respects. For a concise treatment by a number of experts, see Hatt pp. 141-262. For extended treatments, in most instances with copious data, see especially M. K. Bennett; both Orr references; both Osborn references; Pearson and Harper; Russel; all four of the United Nations FAO reports; Woytinski; and Zimmerman.

techniques as they are involved at any given time and place. The fundamental elements are nature, man and culture. As Zimmermann points out, the meaning of "land" changes constantly "in response to the impact of changing human attitudes and actions and, above all, of ever-changing culture."[14]

It should also be recalled that the habitability of the land is a determining factor; people can only produce food in any volume where they can live satisfactorily year in and year out as biological and socio-cultural specimens.

The estimates given by different persons and organizations vary widely, because of variations in definition and use-evaluation of kinds of land, differences in the accuracy of the sources of data, differences in the time at which the estimates were made (estimates a decade apart, for example, of cultivable or potentially cultivable land might be quite different because of subsequent technological developments), and the fact that for some parts of the earth (for example, parts of Asia and Africa) bases for estimates are lacking.[15]

The total land area of the earth is estimated at from 51 to 57 million square miles, or 33 to 37 billion acres, depending partly on whether or not Antarctica is included in the land area of the earth. Since the earth's total area is estimated at around 197 million square miles, at most 28 or 29 per cent of its area is land.

At least half of all the land is practically uninhabitable because it lies in the polar regions, is extremely mountainous, or is desert waste. Such inhabitants as these areas have are numerically insignificant. The remaining land—some 25 to 26 million square miles, or 16 to 17 billion acres—that can be thought of as at present favorable to habitation by man, if equally divided by the 1950 world population of around 2.4 billion, allows only a little more than 7 acres for each human being.

Taking all land into consideration, the world density of population per square mile is about 44. But the land of the earth varies so in habitability, accessibility, and usefulness that about one-half of its people live on one-twentieth of the total land area, with an average density of around 430 people per square mile, while another

---

[14] P. 85.
[15] For estimates see Baker; Brown, pp. 117-122; Condliffe; Fawcett; Osborn (1948), pp. 36-37, 43-47; Pearson and Harper, pp. 20, 27-28, 50; Salter; Sax; Stamp (1952), pp. 48-84; Rechter; Whitaker; and Woytinski, pp. 470-476.

one-fourth of the people live on an additional 13 per cent of the whole land area at a density of around 90 per square mile.

The proportion of the earth's land area usable for agricultural purposes is decidedly limited. The agricultural use of land depends upon such characteristics as temperature, moisture, topography, and soil fertility. It is estimated that from one-fourth to one-third of the land area of the earth (depending upon the particular authority and the criteria used) is too cold either because of high latitude or high altitude to be given consideration as agricultural areas with present agricultural techniques. Approximately another one-fourth, acording to some estimates, receives on the average less than 10 inches of annual rainfall, and, of this, 12,000,000 square miles (of which 5 million are in Africa, 4 million in Asia, and 2 million in Australia) are at present not usable for food production. Or to put it the other way around, only about one-third of the earth's land area has entirely satisfactory rainfall year in and year out, but some of this lacks other essentials. Of the rest of the earth's surface that is neither too cold nor too dry, a considerable proportion is not under cultivation for various reasons, such as rugged topography, thin or sterile soils, swamps and excessive rainfall, rainfall in the wrong season of the year, and areas occupied by such cultural features as villages, towns, cities, highways, railways, airfields, and military installations. In brief, only a small proportion of the earth's land surface has all the essentials for crop production. Osborn has also pointed out that a very large proportion of the originally habitable areas have been so misused by man that they have lost their productive capacity.[16]

Table 8

	Acres (in millions)	Percentage of World Land Area
World	33,381	100
Arable land	3,039	9.1
Permanent meadows and pastures	5,405	16.2
Forests and woodlands	9,943	29.8
Built-on area, wasteland, and other	14,994	44.9

[16] 1948, p. 36. See also Brown, pp. 131-132.

The estimates of land *actually* under cultivation vary somewhat, ranging from 7 to 10 per cent of the land area of the world. The Woytinskys, adapting their figures from recent data of the Food and Agriculture Organization of the United Nations, give the following estimates of world land use as of 1947-1949:[17]

On the basis of the 1950 world population of 2.4 billion, there is an average of only 1⅓ to 1⅔ acres of cultivated land for each person on earth. Many countries have less than one acre of productive land per capita. At the same time, with the present state of the agricultural arts used in cultivating the present land, it is estimated that at least 2½ acres per person are required to provide a satisfactory level of nutrition. Students of world land use agree that the extension of agriculture by means of scientific and technological advances to the world's marginal lands such as those of the colder regions, the dry regions, and the tropical rain-forest regions might very considerably increase the total acres of arable lands. But they add that much of this would be precarious agriculture and that much of the land would be less productive than that now in use. Those who face the economics involved admit also that the cost per unit of output might be very much greater.

As we examine the increase of the world's food supply by extending the cultivated land and by utilizing more intensively the present arable land, we will be thinking mainly of the production of agricultural crops at present depended upon for most of the world's calories. It may be pointed out that food is the major objective of world agriculture; in fact, the production of food crops accounts for perhaps as much as three-fourths of all the efforts of the farmers and farm laborers of the world.[18] Among the food crops, grain, in turn, represents about three-fourths of the production. The eight crops which supply 85 per cent of the world's food intake are wheat, rye, oats, barley, rice, maize, sugar, and potatoes. Also important are the pulses and oil seeds. This does not mean that the production of meat, milk and milk products, poultry and poultry products, leafy and other root vegetables and fruits—the providers of proteins, fats, acids, and vitamins—are unimportant; they are exceedingly important. But today, for example, the con-

---

[17] Present data adapted from Table 215, p. 471.
[18] Woytinski, p. 538. See also pp. 290-291.

sumption of animal foodstuffs and other "luxury" (though nutritionally essential) items are confined to the wealthy peoples and nations and command relatively high prices. Furthermore, for each calorie obtained for human nutrition, it costs much more to produce animal foodstuffs than cereals. Pearson and Harper point out that there are not enough grain and forage in the world for livestock consumption to universalize the North American diet with its large meat content. If more agricultural produce is fed to livestock and if more land is used to produce other "quality" foods—and these sometimes produce low yields per acre—many people will be even more hungry than they are. The production of these crops should be accelerated at the most rapid rate possible. But the immediate and pressing task is to produce the staple, basic subsistence crops—those which produce calories abundantly, cheaply, and efficiently.

EXTENDING THE ACREAGE OF AGRICULTURAL LANDS

The unsettled or sparsely settled regions of the earth have attracted much attention during the present century as areas of possible agricultural development. Some people, operating on the notion that "science can solve all problems" or that "something will turn up," have been extravagantly optimistic about the possibility of vastly and continuously extending the world's agricultural domain and of thereby almost indefinitely increasing its food supply. So much of the discussion seems to be confined mainly to the *theoretical* possibility of extending acreage. This is very different from the *practical* possibility. Some of the students of the situation, however, have been soberly and cautiously scientific in their examination of possibilities, weighing not only the geographic, the agronomic, and other physical and biological-technological problems, but also the economic, political, and social ones.[19] There is no thought here of denying the possibility that science and technology will work unforeseen miracles in the future, and there is every likelihood that the agriculturally utilized acreage of the world will be very considerably expanded. The actual general

---

[19] For significant studies see Binns; both references to Bowman; Forsyth; Jeorg; Moore (1945); Salter; and Stamp (1952). For treatments of both food and agricultural problems see Clark and Pirie, and Tolley. For studies concerned specifically with the tropics see Brown, pp. 133-136; Pelzer; and Price.

situation regarding the present "open spaces" of the earth, however, is about as follows.

Thanks to the marked development of all kinds of transportation, to nonrestricting political conditions in recent times, and to the exploratory and pioneer spirit of men, there are no "dark" or "unpenetrated" continents or land masses anywhere. What is even more significant for us is that there are no very sizable land areas with even remote agricultural possibilities that have not been examined and perhaps even tried out. In the old and crowded portions of the earth, the usable land under prevalent forms of cultivation has been taken up and intensively used to the last square inch for centuries and even millennia. With the exception of certain large areas in South America held back from full settlement by owners of huge estates, and certain lands in interior Asia now held by pastoral peoples and capable of more intensive agricultural use, the vast open spaces are not necessarily being selfishly withheld from agricultural utilization. Almost none of the unused land is ready-made land for agricultural production as were the lands in almost all of the continents settled mainly by European stocks prior to 1900, that is, land appropriate as to latitude, topography, temperature, and moisture—land with soil well endowed as to essential texture and chemical elements and accessible to large populations and markets. These lands (in the United States, Canada, the U.S.S.R., southeastern and eastern Australia, southern Brazil, and central and northern Argentina) were, in most cases, virgin soil, waiting for easy and profitable cultivation with cheap and relatively simple equipment. With the present means of cultivation and transportation, about all of the "good earth" of the world is being utilized.

The areas which up to the present have not been agriculturally developed or have been developed only to a slight extent are in such a state for good reasons. They present a great variety of difficult "conditions." At best they have been, and still are, marginal areas; that is, the expenses of all kinds involved in their human settlement, their agricultural utilization, and their continuous, fairly satisfactory human inhabitance have been, on the average, equal to or greater than the possible returns under all present conditions and with present or readily foreseeable technological aids. Many of the lands frequently mentioned are, in fact, submarginal at present. In the future, as efforts are made to develop many of these areas, they are likely to be experimental zones. Their settlement and utilization involve a scientific and technological struggle with many unfamiliar, unpredictable factors. Investment of all kinds in them is likely to be somewhat risky because of the large number of unknown and inadequately known variables involved. It seems quite certain that the expenses and risks of all kinds in making productive even the most likely of these areas will be decidedly greater than those involved in putting the already cultivated areas into production.

We will briefly examine the most frequently mentioned types of potential agricultural land resources and note possibilities and problems that apply to all undeveloped lands or lands of very limited development.

THE TROPICAL RAIN-FOREST AREAS

The tropical rain-forest lands of South America (the Amazon Valley), Africa (mainly the Congo River basin), and some of the larger islands of the West Pacific are frequently mentioned as potentially arable lands totalling possibly as many as a billion additional acres. At present such agriculture as there is in these areas is of the primitive "shifting" type and consists largely of subsistence gardening on small clearings hacked or burned out of the forest and bush-plots; these must be abandoned for new ones after two or three years of use when the weak and thin soil has lost its crop nutrients. The local population must supplement the limited food by wild game, by tree foods, and by imported food.

To make these lands cultivable in some degree requires first of all the extremely difficult and expensive job of clearing the land of trees and dense undergrowth. But the task involves more than bulldozers. Extensive and expensive drainage may also be necessary. But the swamps when cleared and drained frequently prove to be sour. The lush vegetation often covers only second- and third-rate soil. Thousands of years of equatorial rains and heat have weathered these soils to the point where they are almost exhausted of mineral nutrient resources. Only the humus, constantly restored by the annual crop of leaves, has kept the soil alive and fertile.

When the forest is cleared, the high temperatures induce rapid chemical changes in the soil, notably rapid oxidation. The downward movement of the heavy rainfall leaches out or destroys further many of the essential plant food elements in the thin and disturbed humus cover, such as chemicals and micro-organisms, leaving mainly sterile mineral particles. Plowing, as against the native hoe culture, adds to the rapid impoverishment of the soil, and the clearings are liable to rapid water erosion. Some of the land when cleared is suitable for rice, yams, and a few other concentrated food crops for several years, but then the land is worn out.[20]

The continuous production of cultivated food crops in these areas requires the development of whole new techniques of agricultural engineering and of soil and farm management. Not only must the poorly constituted soil be conserved, but it must be supplemented and continuously built up with various kinds of chemicals, biological and physical amendments, as determined by soil surveys and continual soil analyses.[21] The supposedly universal boon of mechanization has to be examined very carefully. It is probable that special machinery is necessary—machinery being redesigned to suit the condition of good land management, and not farm land altered to accommodate high mechanization. While the tropical climate itself is monotonous with its humidity and limited variation in temperature and season, it in itself is no obstacle to greater human settlement. The most serious habitance problem consists of the many widespread debilitating diseases, such as yellow fever, malaria, dengue, typhus, dysentery, and hookworm, which, in spite of the fact that we know how to deal with most of these, still take their toll of life and efficiency in these areas. They will have to be eliminated before sizable populations can be accommodated. There are also the alarming pests and diseases of plants and animals.

There seem to be very good reasons why for millennia there have been forests—and only forests—in these areas. The climatic conditions were appropriate, and the forests provided their own humus for the thin, poor soil. Hence, the profitable production of

[20] Yet, as Stamp says, "The old myth that equatorial soils are of great fertility dies hard." 1952, p. 61.

[21] It has been pointed out, for example by Osborn (1953, p. 141), that almost any soil, even sterile beach sand, can be made to yield crops by the addition of various physical, chemical, and biological elements *if cost is disregarded*. With as thin and poor a soil as most of these, cost of sufficient additive elements to produce marketable crops is probably prohibitive, even if all of the needed essential elements were known.

field food crops in sufficient amount to add to the world's food supply seems to be problematical because of natural limitations, the lack of knowledge and techniques, and the tremendous potential costs involved. However, as Osborn points out,[22] "developments in the Belgian Congo have demonstrated that tropical forests can be successfully converted to *tree*-crop plantations without seriously upsetting the biological and nutrient complex of the soils." It would seem that the wisest use of some of this land would be for commercial tree-crops, such as those producing copra, rubber, cocoa, tonka beans, tagua, bananas, Brazil nuts, rosewood, and mahogany. Several of these, it should be noted, would add highly essential nutritive elements to the world's food supply.

THE SEMI-ARID GRASSLANDS

Also important among the lands often mentioned as potentially cultivable are the semi-arid savannas, bushlands, and grasslands with scattered trees in the tropics, especially in much of Africa. Here the main problem is water, particularly its highly seasonal supply. During the dry season of six to eight months there is little or no rain; the salts in the soil harden and the soil develops into hardpan. In the rainy season the soil is leached and due to heavy rain there is much erosion. At present these areas seem to be unsuitable either for extensive livestock production or for large-scale development of plant crops. The land is alternately sun-baked and rain-drenched. When the rains come the fodder is abundant, but when they cease it quickly becomes tough and loses its nutritive value. During the long dry season the cattle are exhausted in a constant effort to find water and nutriment in the vast stretches of parched and dried-up grassland or bushland. Serious problems are confronted when these areas are considered for cropland. The preparation of the ground for cultivation is often expensive and the results uncertain. Even bulldozers cannot get out some of the long roots of the brush growing on the bushland. Where the soil is sandy it packs when machinery is used on it. Little is known about the nature of the soils or what happens to them when watered and plowed, or what will grow on them. Much of the soil is laterite, which hardens when exposed and de-

[22] 1953, p. 141.

feats the plow and the cultivator. The water supply is always uncertain.[23]

THE DRY, IRRIGABLE LANDS

Every continent has areas, supposedly with good soil, which do
not produce crops at present because they are too dry or have very
irregular rainfall, or rainfall at the wrong season of the year. Some
of this land, it is thought, can be made cultivable if water can be
brought to it. The extension of irrigation is presented as the major
way of bringing this about. Irrigation is a very ancient technique
in making land cultivable. In most of the older, densely populated
areas of the world, irrigation has long been developed nearly to
the utmost limit with past and present technology. We are informed
that about a quarter of the world's population lives on irrigated
crops. India irrigates almost a quarter of its cropland, China about
one-half, and Egypt practically all of its land under cultivation.[24]
Elsewhere also, on every continent, where irrigation is physically
feasible and not too expensive in terms of capital outlay, it has
been carried on for centuries and even millennia.

There is an abundance of land that can be irrigated, and without
doubt a considerable amount of it will be. Especially is this true
with respect to some of the more recently settled and less densely
populated areas of the world (such as parts of the United States
and the Soviet Union, Australia, and some regions of Africa).
However, projects that show great possibilities, if both the engineering and the political problems can be worked out, are underway or
contemplated in some of the long-settled regions of the earth.[25]

[23] A classic example of the failure on a stupendous scale of a developmental
project on such land is the famous East African (Kenya, Tanganyika, and Northern Rhodesia) Groundnuts (Peanuts) Scheme. For details see Stamp, 1953, pp.
421-423; Osborn, 1953, pp. 91-93.

[24] Pearson and Harper, pp. 28-29.

[25] *Time* of July 19, 1954, reports the completion of the first link of the
Bhakra-Nangal hydroelectric-irrigation system in the Punjab of India-Pakistan,
deriving its water from the Sutlej River in the Himalayan foothills. When completed this will have more than 4500 miles of canals and, it is hoped, will irri-
gate an area twice the size of New Jersey, some of it now in chronic famine.
The same issue also reports water storage in Syria, Israel, Trans-Jordan, and
Iraq involving mainly the waters of the Jordan and the Tigris-Euphrates. Both
of these Asiatic projects pose enormous political problems, since the rivers
and the drainage areas do not confine themselves within given political boundaries. The possible extension of irrigated land in Egypt by converting Lake Vic-

In all of the extension of irrigation into and beyond the arid fringe of already irrigated areas and into areas heretofore unirrigated or deemed nonirrigable, it will be necessary to construct dams, canals, and ditches, and often carry out extensive earth levelling, terracing, and sloping. Technological developments also make possible the bringing of water to areas now unsupplied or very inadequately supplied under "natural" conditions, such as the shifting of river channels, the construction of tunnels through mountain ranges bringing surplus water from another slope, the construction of aqueducts and siphons. But most of this new irrigation will be much more difficult and infinitely more expensive than the construction of the present irrigation systems of the world; and the costs of continuous maintenance must also be taken into consideration.

Even then, unless competent and comprehensive land-use surveys are made and adequate experimentation carried on, it may be discovered that the land is useless even if watered; it may develop strong alkalis; it may harden when watered; its nutritive elements may leach out rapidly; it may readily become waterlogged and sour. In many regions of the earth, as the result of deforestation, overgrazing, and other improper land practices on the watersheds, the natural drainage systems are unmistakably dying. Sizable areas of land irrigated in the past, such as parts of Iran, the Tigris and Euphrates valleys, and parts of North Africa, have been abandoned for one reason or another.

No world survey of lands both good as to quality and potentially irrigable by natural waters has been made. Those lands that have been successfully irrigated in recent history, over and above those under irrigation for long periods of time, have been widely advertised and some have added significantly to the cultivable acreage and to the supply of agricultural products.[26] In general, however, it seems to be the conclusion of competent students that the total

---

toria into the world's largest storage dam to provide an ever-normal flow for irrigation is also reported. For the actual and projected increase of irrigated land in the last decade, especially in the Far and Near East, see the 1955 FAO report, pp. 55-57.

[26] The Gezira project in the Sudan, whereby with the help of some 5,000 miles of channels approximately one million acres were brought under cultivation, is an example of a notable success. See, e.g., Stamp, 1952, pp. 348-349.

expansion of good arable land by means of technically and financial-
ly feasible irrigation procedures is limited, even negligible.[27] In
vast areas with some water, rainfall and stream flow are too limited
and uncertain to assure continuous intensive use of the land. In
areas where irrigation now occurs, existing water supplies cannot
be indefinitely spread over wider sections, up the slopes, and up
and across the valleys of the watersheds and basins. Irrigation with
water pumped from underground has temporarily added to the surface waters, improving existing cultivation and making some new
cultivation possible. To be profitable this requires the availability
of cheap power, sometimes possible as the result of hydroelectric
development. In the end, however, ground water depends upon
the same sources as surface waters, and where pump irrigation has
been carried on in any considerable volume over a period of time,
it has had a serious effect upon the water table.

Some attention has been paid recently to induced rainfall by the
"rainmakers" as a possible means of extending cultivable areas and
also of regularizing rainfall in areas of fluctuating precipitation.
Moisture-bearing clouds must be present at the critical moments
even if successful means of precipitating the moisture exist. Where
rainmaking has been effective it seems occasionally to have caused
unfortunate meterological disturbances elsewhere in the general
area. There is little reason for believing that man-made rain would
not vary from place to place as does natural precipitation.[28]

There is also talk of desalting sea water and brackish water
(with a lower salt content, both for irrigation and for industrial and
domestic use. The ionization process for "demineralizing" salt or
brackish water, seems to offer great possibilities. It is reported
that a pilot project is to be started in Arizona.[29] While the Ionics
Laboratories of Cambridge, Massachusetts, have promised production of fresh water at between 10 and 20 cents per thousand gallons,
depending on the cost of electric current, the lowest figure now in
sight is 60 cents per thousand gallons. This would come to almost
$200 per acre-foot, as the cost of irrigation water is reckoned. While
hydroelectric power can be developed to a much greater degree

[27] Pearson and Harper, p. 30.
[28] Cf. Osborn, 1953, pp. 203-204; Bliven, pp. 92-99.
[29] Cf. Bliven, pp. 110-116; *Saturday Evening Post*, July 31, 1954, p. 68, and
October 23, 1954, p. 103.

than it has been, even as part of multiple-use projects, it can provide at best only a very small part of the electrical energy needed. It is commonplace knowledge that all of the advanced nations of the world are suffering extreme power shortages. Steam plants for producing electrical energy depend upon coal, oil, or gas, all of which are fixed in supply. Poorer and poorer grades of coal may become usable with improved techniques, such as converting coal into heat in the very strata where found. Solar engines, atomic engines, or means of utilizing subterranean heat might in time produce cheap and abundant electricity; but the materials of which they would be made would come from our "fund" resources. If the ionization process can be developed for large-scale use, and if electrical energy can be cheaply produced, possibilities exist for providing water for irrigating large desert or semi-arid areas now close to the sea, such as in Australia, North Africa, the Middle East, and California and Texas in the United States. This could supplement municipal water supplies, and also freshen brackish water, for example, in Florida, California, Bermuda, the Bahamas, Cuba, Hawaii, and the upper Nile region.

In general however it would seem that the greater proportion of the earth's 10 million square miles which now have less than 10 inches of rain and much of that with several inches more is beyond any conceivable range of artificial watering sufficient to produce plant food crops continuously and profitably.

THE COLDER AREAS OF THE TEMPERATE ZONES

Another possibility for extending the arable lands is to push cultivation into the colder areas at the upper fringes of the temperate zones, as for example in northern Asia and Canada. Here the elemental problems are two: the length of the growing season, notably the summer period between killing frosts, and the uncertainty of the soils as the timber or shrub-growth is pushed back or recourse is had to marginal plain or even semi-tundra belts. There is great likelihood, especially on deforested and tundra land, that the soils will have to be copiously supplemented. Furthermore, there is the necessity of discovering or developing strains of food plants that will mature to the point of producing a crop in 100 or fewer growing days.

It should be reported, however, that a natural development, possibly another alteration in the earth's temperatures, seems to be taking place which may provide a large amount of arable land in these northern latitudes. Many meteorologists think that the world's climate is getting warmer, and various data are presented to substantiate the claim. If this is the case, we do not know how long the change will last. There still remains the problem of cost in the development of the land for agriculture, and the problem of providing adequate transportation must also be faced.

LANDS FOR MEAT PRODUCTION

We have not examined the possibility of using semi-arid grass-land areas and mountainous and forested areas as grazing land to add to the food supply through meat-production, especially the raising of sheep and cattle. Needless to say, much of this land that offers any possibilities is already in use. Furthermore, certain serious problems present themselves. The semi-arid grasslands lack moisture much of the year, and the grass cover deteriorates. In various parts of the world (as in parts of Africa, Australia, Mxeico, and the United States) it is already overgrazed. This means reduction of plant growth and wind eroson in dry weather and rapid run-off and water erosion in the rainy season. There is also the danger (and the actuality in many areas) of too-close grazing in hilly and mountainous forested areas. This results in the destruction of the new forest growth and the diminution of grasses and other edible plants on the forest floor. This, in turn, means loss of ground cover and progressive failure to hold the winter moisture, with serious effects on both the surface and underground water supply upon which crop cultivation down the watershed depends.

COMMON PROBLEMS AND GENERAL CONSIDERATIONS

We have by no means exhausted the categories of potential crop lands. These various kinds of land differ widely in dozens of important aspects. However, at the present time they are all marginal lands, which means that they are problem lands. Certain difficulties stand out as characteristics of almost all of these potential crop lands. These will be briefly examined.

Most of these lands require expensive processes, often involving costly and elaborate equipment, in the physical preparation of the area for cultivation. Needed are such operations as forest or bush clearance, ground levelling, or control of the water supply, such as control of run-off and flooding, drainage, storage, and irrigation.

Most have soils that are structurally and qualitatively inadequate as they are, being deficient in chemical and bacterial elements essential as plant nutrients. They need green manures (which, incidentally, keep the land out of crop cultivation while the vegetable supplement is growing), animal manures (often wasted or used for other purposes in these areas), and expensive and often remote chemical fertilizers and mineral amendments.

Most areas require specially developed varieties of plant crops and animals that will do well. These marginal or submarginal areas do not, in their undeveloped or deteriorated state, support plants or animals that contribute appreciably to the food supply. The strains of plants that are likely to be profitable must be suitable to the peculiar soils, to the dominant moisture conditions, to the temperature and length of the growing season, to the topography, to the altitude, and to the pests and diseases that are encountered in the area. Similarly, the animal strains should give optimum returns for the kinds of forage and other foods that can be profitably fed in the area, be suitable for the climatic conditions, and, if possible, be pest and disease resistant.

Almost all of these areas present uncontrolled or only partially controlled health hazards for human beings, plants, and animals. Temperature, moisture, the seasonal cycle, and altitude may not be conducive to normal and secure human habitation. As already noted, the widely acclaimed tropical areas have been ridden with destructive and debilitating diseases, none of which are entirely under control in these marginal areas. Most have pests and diseases that are highly destructive of plant and animal life. The northern two-thirds of Africa, for example, is subjected to periodic devastation by locusts, which come in hordes that darken the sun. Those areas that go through the year without frost have difficulty in suppressing or eradicating numerous parasites of economic plants, domestic animals, and man. The tsetse fly makes large areas uninhabitable by man or beast; in fact, it has been said with good reason that it is still the real ruler of Africa.[30] It is perfectly

---

[30] Stamp, 1953, p. 164.

clear that all of these areas pose enormous problems with respect to human hygienic conditions, sanitation, endemic and epidemic disease control, and many other aspects of public health.

In general, any efforts at development should be preceded by the most careful and exhaustive land-use surveys and by experimentation and pilot operations in well-sampled portions of the larger areas. There should be careful surveys of soils as to characteristics, deficiencies, potentialities for different kinds of crops, and the ability of the soils to retain their essential content upon continued but careful use under local conditions. Very important is the determination of the long-time adequacy of the water supply and of its availability at the right time in the growing season. There should be careful study as to the effects upon the soil, in the form of loss of nutrients, oxidation, alkalization, and hardening, of forest and bush removal, irrigation, drainage, plowing and other cultivation techniques. The availability of suitable and profitable crops under the conditions of climate, altitude, and soil should be carefully examined. For example, it was found that tobacco introduced in some parts of Africa has a peculiar tang which rendered it of little commercial value. Another problem to be faced is the design and manufacture of agricultural tools and machinery suitable to the agriculture under principles of good land management. There has been a tendency, often with unfortunate results, to alter farmlands to accommodate machines used elsewhere under different conditions.

Almost all of these areas present problems of accessibility with available and economical forms of transporation, both for immigration of settlers with their equipment and regular supplies and for transportation of their products to outside markets. Since hardly any are easily accessible, extensive networks of highways and railways will have to be built. Because of the nature of the terrain and in some instances of climatic conditions, they will be difficult to engineer and expensive to construct and maintain, having to pass through jungles and swamps (as in the Matto Grosso of Brazil, the Congo, and possibly the Amazon Valley away from the waterways), across deserts (in Australia, Africa, and Asia), across tundra (in Canada and Siberia), or across mountains (in the highlands of Venezuela and elsewhere). Air transport for agricultural crops in sufficient volume at present prices is quite out of the question.

Because of their inaccessibility, these areas, even if they can be made to produce primary crops, are likely to be handicapped by long hauls and high freight rates which have to be added to the otherwise already high cost of production. This makes it difficult for their products to compete with those of the more favored areas in the world markets.[31]

There are nearly always human, social, and cultural problems that are inadequately faced. If the settlers are from other parts of the same country, they have a great advantage over foreign immigrants since they are familiar not only with the physical conditions of existence, but also with the system of government, the language, the commercial practices, and all of the other customs, traditions, and institutions of the area. As strangers, the immigrants may be discriminated against in various ways by both the local population and the government. If the indigenous population consists of preliterate or tribal people, how are they to be displaced? How is the land to be acquired from them? How are they to be treated as to land use and ownership, as to social and political rights? Is there likely to be social intermingling and cultural cross-fertilization, and if so, what are their effects on assimilation likely to be? Will the settlers have the funds, equipment, food reserves, and so on, to see them through the first critical year or two? Will they have the appropriate agricultural experience, and the technical, occupational, and managerial training? What pattern or patterns of settlement—individual farms, groups of farms, village-centered colonies—are likely to be most suitable? What kind of dwellings and sanitary conditions will be required and will the people be able to afford them? Will there be the provision of civilized living facilities, such as police, public health, medical care and veterinary services, schools and other educational institutions, other essential occupational, personal, and professional services, shops and stores, financial and credit facilities, storage facilities and marketing arrangements, communication and postal services, electricity, water, arrangements for religious life, and recreational facilities.[32]

----

[31] For a list of twenty criteria which determine the success of land settlement projects see the excellent treatment by Binns, pp. 4-5.

[32] For an extensive treatment of these human and social problems of settlement see the FAO study by Binns, pp. 7-23.

Finally, there are certain other considerations that must be faced in connection with the extension of cultivation among these lands which have been marginal.

Because of the magnitude and complexity of the operations necessary to bring most of these different types of areas under cultivation, many phases of the operations will have to be conducted by large organized groups. Almost invariably the state will be the organization of primary importance, and often the only one. Individuals or even small groups or organizations can do very little especially in the initial stages. Essential are such extensive operations as forest and brush clearance, land levelling, irrigation and drainage systems, widespread pest or disease control and other public health activities, research and experimentation along a dozen lines, soil development over wide areas, the construction of transportation networks, and town development. Only a huge organization with wide jurisdiction can provide or make arrangements for the provision of the equipment, know-how, organization, and finances. With respect especially to finances, only the state through its taxing or borrowing power or its ability to solicit and use gifts from other nations or international bodies is in a position to secure funds for many of these operations if they are to be sufficiently adequate in scope and quality to be minimally profitable.

It must also be pointed out that because of the huge costs frequently involved, the products may be too expensive to justify the projects. The justification in large part depends upon the economic limits of costs and returns. By the time the land has been made usable it has come to be high priced and should bring an adequate return on the investment. In most instances the per-unit cost of products will be higher than on better land, and the transportation and marketing costs will be above average. The food thus raised is almost certain to be more expensive than that now being consumed. Technology has made possible the raising of food in arctic regions, but the world is hardly in position to pay two dollars for every head of cabbage.

The peoples now in need of these potential food products are the poorest in the world. Can means be found of raising their individual and collective purchasing power? Do they have other resources that can be profitably exploited and sold in the markets of the world, or do they have the necessary materials, means, and proficiencies to modernize and thus develop the ability to purchase expensive foods from the ends of the earth?

In the end, such food extension projects have to pay their own way, and the people who utilize their products should be able to pay for them. The few countries and the international organizations that are now assuming the cost may not always be able to do so.

These elaborate and expensive projects should produce a commercial surplus of food which adds to the per-capita volume of food for the people of the world and which is a means of increasing the per-capita wealth and of raising the standard of living not only for the settlers but for the world population. If they are used simply for subsistence agriculture, the major purpose has been defeated. What we would have is simply more—perhaps many more—people living as poorly (at a mere existence level) as before, or even worse.

What has so often occurred is typified in the incident described by Sir Charles Galton Darwin:

> Not long ago the province of Sind (in West Pakistan) was mainly a desert; the ground was quite fertile but there was no rainfall. A great engineering undertaking, the Sukkur barrage, has spread the waters of the Indus over a very wide area, and turned much of the desert into a garden. According to the universally accepted standards this was a great benefit to the world, for it made possible the adequate feeding of a people previously on the verge of starvation. But things did not work out like that, for after a few years the effect was only to have a large number of people on the verge of starvation instead of a small number.[33]

Finally, if sizable new areas can be opened up to agriculture they are not likely to be available to the most hard-pressed peoples of the world, namely, those of Asia. Within Asia itself Salter estimates that it is possible to extend cultivation to about 100 million acres outside the Soviet Union. How much of a boon is this for more than 1300 million people? The uncultivated but potentially usable lands of Africa and South America, estimated by him at 900 million acres, may, under a complex of appropriate conditions, provide space for future expansion of the population now living on those continents and possibly for a certain number of emigrants from

[33] P. 37.

Europe; but at least under present economic, political, and social conditions such lands are virtually closed to the millions upon millions of Asiatics. Salter placed 300 million unused acres in the Northern Hemisphere; but these, too, are neither readily accessible nor physically or socially hospitable to the peoples of the earth's crowded regions. Such considerations cannot be glossed over lightly.

INCREASING THE PRODUCTIVITY OF LAND ALREADY UNDER CULTIVATION

While much land not now used for crops can be brought under profitable cultivation with modern means and techniques and under modern conditions, many of the students of the world food problem are of the opinion that the more scientific utilization of already cultivated lands, selected through successful experience and naturally favored with most of the essential conditions and qualities, offers much greater and more certain possibilities of increasing the food supply. Moreover, it would require no great and expensive shifting of population, as in the case of settling new agricultural frontiers, since labor supply in these regions exists in abundance.

The examination of the more effective use of existing cultivated land resolves itself into two parts: (1) halting soil depletion and other forms of mismanagement and waste in connection with crop production and marketing and the possibilities and necessities of conservation and restoration of deteriorated land; and (2) the increase of output on now successfully and profitably cultivated land. Needless to say, the two overlap somewhat.

HALTING DEPLETION AND DESTRUCTION OF THE SOIL

Although crop land is by all odds the most essential of the world's natural resources, it is in some respects the most neglected and abused. Soil is a mixture of organic and inorganic materials formed by the interaction of climate, vegetation, and animal organisms. Moreover, soil is a continuous product, and the "soil factory" must be permitted to operate effectively if the physical structure and nutrient content of the soil is not to be impaired. Over wide areas men, through ignorance or carelessness or greed, have violated these principles; millions of acres of once-fertile soil have been so depleted that they have become marginal crop lands or cannot be used at all. Semi-arid land that should have been left as grazing land and forest land that should never have been cleared have been put under the plow. Further depletion has resulted from wanton cutting and burning of forests and from overgrazing of mountainous forested areas with loss of the water-retaining capacity of the ground, greater danger of floods, silting of streams and reservoirs, and general impairment of both surface and underground water supplies. Through continuous cropping, lack of crop rotation, clean tillage of row crops, and mismanagement of water, essential nutrients have been lost—in many cases faster than they have been replaced. Improper water management has resulted in leaching, waterlogging, and souring.

In fact, according to Whitaker, instead of expansion of productive land, it appears that a net contraction is actually taking place. H. H. Bennett, former Chief of the Soil Conservation Service of the U. S. Department of Agriculture, has estimated that in the United States approximately 280 million acres of crop and range land have been essentially destroyed, and that 100 million acres have been so badly damaged by erosion that they cannot be restored.[34]

Much of this soil depletion or destruction resolves itself into erosion by water or wind. We are told that erosion has damaged at least 50 per cent of the arable land in the United States; that the annual cost of erosion in the United States is about four billion dollars; and that about one million acres are ruined each year for further cultivation. O. V. Willis, also of the Soil Conservation Service, has stated that there are over 50 million acres of land now in cultivation in the United States which should and probably will be retired to grass or trees during the next twenty-five years. During that period, we can add economically to our cultivated area about 20 million acres through various programs of reclamation. Once valuable agricultural lands in North America, Latin America, Australia, Africa, and even Europe—much of it settled since the beginning of the nineteenth century—have been rendered worthless by erosion due to overcropping, or other forms of destructive exploitation.[35] Some of this depleted and eroded land has deteriorated beyond repair; some can be restored in considerable part by quite expensive corrective procedures.

---

[34] Pp. 56-83. See also Sears, and Whyte and Jacks.
[35] Christensen. See also Woytinsky, pp. 477-480.

The soil structure and its nutrient elements must be restored by crop rotation or even occasional resting, periodic planting to green manures and soil-enriching crops (such as nitrogen-fixing plants), the use of animal and chemical fertilizers and the addition of other missing or depleted structural (organic and inorganic) trace elements, and by many of the other measures already mentioned in connection with the development of possible new agricultural lands.

Erosion control involves proper management of the water-retaining forest and other ground cover in the high portions of the watersheds, reforestation, possibly the return of some cultivated land to grazing land or forest, and in the eroded cultivated lands or those subject to erosion such practices as terracing of slopes, contour planting, stubble mulching, gulley planting, construction of grassed channel ways, meadow or other cover strips on slopes, and "shelter belts."

When the task of soil conservation the world over is viewed realistically several facts stand out. First, while most of the saving and corrective practices are finally conducted by the individual farmer on his fields and pastures, he must cooperate with all other soil-users in his basin or watershed. Though each farmer has his own means and his own particular land problems, all that each does must fit into the over-all integrated plan if it is not to harm the others. Erosion control, for example, can never be purely a private affair. Furthermore, sizable, expensive, and complicated public or semi-public projects, such as dam and ditch systems or tree nurseries to supply reforestation projects, must be carried on. Almost everywhere there must be extensive investigation and experimentation, the setting up of development programs, the establishment of training schools for advisers and supervisors, the conducting of pilot schemes, and widespread instruction, demonstration, and provision of other extension and aid services for the farmers. Usually it also involves the provision of credit facilities on a rather large scale. Such things can only be done by large, usually public, organizations. Invariably, therefore, soil conservation efforts to be generally effective require government encouragement, operation by government of some of the projects and facilities, a considerable measure of governmental control, and government subsidy and financing.

Secondly, some of these essential practices of soil conservation are not feasible in certain parts of the world because of the great poverty of the farmers and the country generally, that is, a lack of adequate and ready capital. The great pressure to produce continuously on the land does not permit any temporary loss of product due to land held idle for restorative purposes, or for land uses that might reduce crop acreage such as are required by terracing and meadow strips. It is also difficult to get illiterate peoples to use chemicals and other soil supplements intelligently. Finally, it will be necessary to overcome the deep-rooted traditions, prejudices, and distrust of farmers whose primitive methods have often remained unchanged for hundreds of years.

There are other wastes, quite apart from the waste and destruction of the topsoil, that directly affect the present food supply of the earth. About half of the world uses human fecal matter as fertilizer, but the other half wastes one of the most efficient means of replenishing lost soil materials, especially nitrogen, even though such matter can be made available in a manner quite inoffensive to Western sensibilities.[36]

We waste annually a sizable proportion of our potential food through preventable plant disease and insect and rodent infestation. After the food crop has been produced, and before it gets to the consumer, much of it is lost through spoilage and through insect and rat infestation. The FAO reports that even in the United States grain storage loss due to rats alone is estimated at about 7 million metric tons annually, and further losses of between 8 and 16 million metric tons annually is caused by insects. The rice and other grains destroyed by rats for the world as a whole probably equals the amount moving in international trade.[37]

Much produced food is lost through careless storage and preservation and through careless transportation. In some countries, notably the United States, where there has been overproduction there has been the deliberate destruction of the market surplus.

India, with some 200 million head, has between one-fourth and one-third of the total cattle population of the world. This is by all

---

[36] Note, for example, the very profitable production of "milorganite" by the sewage disposal plant of the City of Milwaukee. The City of Oakland, California, processes its garbage as agricultural fertilizer.

[37] *Second World Food Survey*, p. 30.

odds the largest cattle density of any area of similar size in the world; indeed, with only about half the land area of the United States, it has nearly three times the number of cattle.[38] Only about 25 per cent of the population of India eat meat at all, and beef is consumed only by the Moslems. These cattle add very little milk to the meager diet of the Indian people; their production of power is inefficient because of their famished, diseased condition; and though the hardworked soil needs replenishment by the dung, this is used as plaster or as floor surfacing for the myriads of huts, and especially as fuel. These cattle overrun the land and prevent the growth and use of vegetation essential to the tragically underfed people. In fact, the acreage they keep out of use for humans is fantastic. It is reported that the virtually useless cattle consume about three times as many calories as are consumed by the human population.[39] The overgrazing which they cause prevents the maintenance of protective vegetation for the soil and adds to both wind and water erosion.

Not only is a portion of the "good earth" used for so-called cultural purposes, for example, for villages, towns, and cities, and for cemeteries, but also the very growth of population causes an encroachment upon the habitable and agricultural land of the earth. Every additional million people means that a corresponding portion of the earth's surface must be used for residential purposes, for land transportation arteries and for airfields, as sites for warehouses and manufacturing plants. The very growth of population is usually greatest where population is already dense and where land is most intensively used. Furthermore, in the present world where peace is so insecure and where war has come to be carried on by technological means, frequently areas of high agricultural production are being devoted to military installations, such as airfields, atomic bomb and powder plants, weapon testing ranges, and ammunition dumps.

The very increase of population, especially in densely populated underdeveloped areas, may also lead, at least under some conditions, to a reduction in the productivity of the land. Efforts to make large crops meet emergency demands may permanently damage the

---

[38] *Ibid.,* p. 32; "Report on India," *Population Bulletin,* 1953.
[39] Brown, p. 124.

soil. When every possible acre needs to be cultivated to eke out a bare subsistence for the people, the possibilities of practicing conservation of the soil are negligible. Such overcultivation and impoverishment of the soil have been reflected not only in diminishing returns but also in crops deficient in essential minerals, and in soil erosion.

INCREASING THE OUTPUT OF GOOD LAND NOW IN USE

We have been briefly concerned with the correction of mismanagement of lands under cultivation as a means of increasing the food supply. The other side of the shield is to review the possibilities of the further increase of productivity on what is now deemed "good earth" by the utilization of modern science and technology in agricultural management practices. Many authorities contend that it is possible to produce much more food on our present farm acreage, even that already intensively cultivated. Stamp,[40] for example, points out how some of the countries of northwestern Europe by good land planning and land management have phenomenally increased the productivity of their crowded agricultural lands. He cites Denmark, once described as the smallest and poorest country in Europe, which now supports 4 million of the best-fed people in the world on 10½ million acres, only five-sevenths of which are productive lands. He discusses the results of land planning in England during and since the recent war under the "concept of the optimum use of every acre in the national interest." The essence of the concept can be indicated by concisely presenting the procedures most often mentioned for achieving increased output. Some of these apply also to the utilization of marginal and mismanaged lands. They are all thought to function with highest effectiveness on land which experience—sometimes very long experience—has shown to be good land.

Increasing the yield requires first of all the careful avoidance of mismanagement, by continually resorting to those practices (discussed above) that correct and prevent erosion, soil depletion, and other forms of waste and destruction. Beyond this are the positive procedures.

[40] 1952, pp. 147-174.

Maintaining and even improving the nutrient quality and the texture of the soil by use of fertilizers and other soil supplements will increase production. Since every crop reduces the productive capacity of the soil, the used elements must be restored. Furthermore, most soils upon laboratory testing show certain lacks, for example, in nitrogen, phosphate, or potash, in essential microorganisms, and in humus. Adding these by means of farmyard manure, commercial fertilizers and supplements, and by green manures occasionally rotated with the food crops, may considerably increase the productivity of existing crops or make possible even more profitable new ones.

Insecticides, fungicides, and other chemicals are increasingly available for the control of plant diseases and insect pests, which may greatly reduce crop yields and may, if not checked, persistently infest particular areas. Weeds need not be taken for granted. They take up space needed for fuller growth of crop plants and retard this growth by consuming plant nutrients and moisture in the soil; by shading they hinder crops in maturing, and they often harbor noxious insects. Certain mechanical and cultivation practices in weed control have long been used. Chemical killers have been developed recently, and methods and equipment for spraying, dusting, and fumigating have been improved. Flame has been successfully used in the weed control of cotton and may presently be used elsewhere.

Finding and developing new plants as food producers, introducing food plants from elsewhere into a given area, and improving regional plants through selection and cross-breeding supplement and diversify given food supplies and often greatly increase yields per acre. Tomatoes and sugar beets are superb food plants fairly recently "discovered." The pea (a good soil builder and rich in protein) spread all over the world from ancient Egypt; the potato spread from South America to North America, Europe, and Japan, greatly augmenting the calorie supply with its easily and cheaply produced yields; citrus fruits spread over the world from the Orient; and Turkey Red wheat spread from eastern Europe to North America. The possibilities of such "introductions," soil and climatic conditions permitting, are greater than ever before. Some of these transfers often do better in the new habitats than in the old.

By selective breeding and with no additions of labor or machinery, varieties of plants have been developed that produce considerable increases in yields even though the fertility of land in general has not increased and in some cases has even diminished (for example, hybrid corn in many parts of the United States). In recent years acre yields of corn, wheat, oats, barley, potatoes, sugar beets, and other vegetable crops have been greatly increased. It is estimated that the use of hybrid corn has nearly doubled the yield per acre, and has increased the total production in the United States about 20 per cent, and that the corn yield could be increased *several hundred per cent* in some countries.[41] By genetic manipulation, varieties may also be developed that will flourish in heretofore marginal or submarginal areas (such as the movement of corn production northward in the United States and into Canada by means of "90-day" corn). Another marked contribution is the development of strains or varieties of farm crops resistant to the more destructive plant diseases, to insect pests, and to drought.[42]

The quantity and quality of livestock can be improved by empirical crossbreeding, scientific feeding, and disease and parasite control. Livestock important for food, such as cattle, hogs, and poultry, by selection and cross-breeding, can be developed for greater efficiency in converting feed into meat, milk, and eggs, for greater and more regular reproductive capacity, for earlier maturity, and for disease and pest resistance. Scientific feeding based on new knowledge of content of feeds, knowledge of nutritional requirements for different purposes, and the use of newly devised feeds can obtain greater returns per head. The greater use of antibiotics and parasiticides has similar effects. It should be pointed out, however, that advances in livestock production have not increased man's food supply as much as has the improvement of crops, and that increased production of improved livestock will not feed many people.

These five aids in increasing output on existing acreages are applicable in all parts of the world, although the possibility of utilizing them varies greatly, due to variations in wealth, knowledge, and population conditions. Though often mentioned as aids, the

---

[41] Cf. Christensen, p. 98.
[42] Pearson and Harper, pp. 57-59. See also Jenkins.

last two factors—both controversial—are much more limited in applicability and profitable utilization.

The increased mechanization of farming operations is one of these aids. Power machinery (for good or ill) has brought under the plough vast acreages of grass and range land, and forest and brushland, that otherwise would not be cultivated today. Power equipment has also been a great help in drainage, ditching, terracing, and levelling. In some areas of the world, such as the United States, Canada, the United Kingdom, parts of Russia, and to a more limited degree in certain other areas, the wide use of machinery has helped increase food production by greatly increasing the yield per man-hour and by permitting farming on an extensive scale on good but not highly populated land and on land operated under appropriate tenure conditions. It may increase yields on lands with good soils and favorable topography by enabling farmers to fit the land better, to till the crops more thoroughly, and to harvest them more quickly and at the right time. By substituting machines (tractors) for draft animals, a considerable amount of land formerly used to produce feeds for these animals has been released for human food crops.[43] It is also a fact that countries with high technological development are today producing a considerable array of synthetic fibers which are substituted for animal and vegetable fibers, thus, in part at least, releasing for food production the land on which these natural fibers were produced.

But mechanized equipment does not increase agricultural output by improving the fertility of the soil. It may actually in time reduce yields by making possible the farming of marginal lands the fertility of which can only be maintained at considerable expense and by making possible ploughing in sections where hoe culture should have been retained to permit plant cover, thus hastening soil depletion and erosion. Furthermore, while total yields have increased through mechanization, in most cases the production per acre has not increased through mechanization itself, and the output per dollar input has not necessarily increased. In areas of mechanization where yields have greatly increased, it has been because the

---

[43] Draft animals still supply 85 per cent of the power used on the world's farms, though in North America and the United Kingdom they supply only about one-fourth. Woytinsky, p. 515.

other aids, discussed above, were carried on simultaneously. In fact, as Christensen points out, the world's highest crop yields per acre are still achieved in those countries practicing the simple hoe-oxen method.[44]

At the present time the use of power machinery is restricted to a limited number of countries and to a very small percentage of the farmers of the world. The use of machinery and mechanical power in cultivation depends upon favorable topography; the ground must be fairly level, and not hilly or stony. Of necessity, it usually implies extensive one-crop agriculture, producing a commercial crop for an extensive market. Since the fields and farms must be fairly large, the fragmentation of land found under the land-tenure systems in many parts of the world rules it out. It is confined to countries capable of producing or acquiring surpluses over and above subsistance needs—surpluses that can be translated into such expensive mechanical and power equipment and its maintenance. It is also confined to countries with a fairly high per-capita income, since it is expensive agriculture and requires a people able to pay higher prices for agricultural products. Furthermore, wages have to be high in terms of goods to support the kind of working force that can create such mechanical equipment. Finally, since it is labor-saving above all else, it is likely to be profitable only in countries already highly modernized—countries that have a continuous and possibly mounting market for labor released from agriculture to industrial, commercial, and service employment.

In most of the underdeveloped countries population is growing faster than resources and industrialization. Consequently they are poor, and growing poorer, and are not developing industrial-urban employment for the additional population, not to mention employment for the agrarian population that might be released by agricultural mechanization. In many instances the agricultural areas are densely populated, and the fields are small, with an agriculture based on intensive cultivation by redundant labor. In 1948 the British government appointed a mission of three experts to inquire into the problems involved in the mechanization of native agricul-

[44] Pp. 104-105.

ture in tropical Africa. This commission reported in 1950.[45] It pointed out that pressure of population on resources is so great in many areas that mechanization of agriculture would only be worth while if there were new and substantial demands for labor in non-farm work. Also, the substitution of tractors and other equipment demanding expensive fuel and expert handling by ordinary native farm labor would be the substitution of costly for cheap factors of production. The costs, in general, would be too much as compared with any net increase in production that the mechanization might bring. Therefore, it would seem that mechanization, even if feasible on other grounds, would so raise the cost of crops as to make them unavailable to the very people needing them most.

Finally, the use of more labor is sometimes proposed as a means of increasing man's food supply on the present acreage. This offers few possibilities. Pearson and Harper point out that in highly mechanized countries, such as the United States, increased use of human labor would be accompanied by a decreased use of machinery; a decrease in yields would result because, under the existing conditions, mechanization permits better preparation of seed beds, better cultivation, and better harvesting. It might be added that such an increased use of labor in agriculture would mean a proportionately diminished use of labor in industry and commerce; and this would imply a recession of the economy, reduction in levels and standard of living, and a marked reversion in the modern way of life.

At the other extreme, for example, is Asia, where little machinery is used. As Pearson and Harper point out,

> . . . there is little opportunity for increasing yields by the use of more human labor, since the maximum is already being used. The use of more labor per acre in Asia, though it would probably increase yields somewhat, would not sustain the additional laborers at their present poverty level.
> The application of additional amounts of human labor does not increase yields proportionately. Those who recommend this method of increasing food supplies, therefore, propose that the standard of living of the world would be reduced.[46]

[45] J. W. Y. Higgs, R. K. Kerkham, and J. R. Raeburn, *Animal Health and Forestry,* Publication No. 1, Colonial Office, Colonial Advisory Council of Agriculture (London: His Majesty's Stationery Office, 1950).
[46] Pp. 55-56.

It may be concluded that the lands which have been cultivated for centuries or even millennia do not offer great possibilities of increasing the food supply. In many instances the land is excellent in most respects—some of the best in the world, but by virtue of its excellence it is already overcrowded. It has the maximum application of labor, and a variety of physical, social, and economic conditions greatly limit the practicality of mechanization. The people on these lands and their governments are poor, and at least at the outset they will have to be assisted from the outside in the utilization of the other possible aids to enhanced cultivation.

It should be pointed out, however, that the underdeveloped and overpopulated people cannot afford to devote all of their cultivated and cultivable land to food production, however hard pressed they may be. They also need to produce agricultural cash crops for world industry in order to provide income for purchasing foods to supplement and diversify their own food crops to achieve a more balanced ration. Manpower should be used in other primary industries such as mining and forestry to the extent that resources permit, in order to provide funds for imports to be used in industry and other aspects of modernization.[47]

OTHER POSSIBILITIES FOR INCREASING THE FOOD SUPPLY

A third area of consideration in increasing the world's food supply involves a heterogeneous array of items such as the resort to more productive food crops, the inclusion in diets of foods not now used, the utilization of untapped food sources, and the technological production of food not directly involving agricultural land. Some of those more prominently mentioned will be briefly examined.

INCREASING CALORIE PRODUCTION

When the food problem in the world or in a nation becomes so pressing that sufficient calories to sustain life become the all-absorbing consideration, shifts to those crops with very high calorie productivity per acre will be of great assistance. Potatoes, for example, produce more food energy per acre than any other staple crop except corn. One hundred bushels of potatoes, which is the yield of one-third to one-half acre in many parts of the world, give

---

[47] See Chapter VI, pp. 122-147.

about as many calories as the wheat produced on two acres in the United States. Corn is a high-energy crop, and the opportunity for increasing the total yield per acre is very great, as is the possibility of extending its cultivation to new areas. In the United States, only about 10 per cent of the corn yield is used directly as human food. In general, the shift from lesser energy-producing and lower per-acre yield crops is rather promising.[48]

There is also said to be much green vegetation of the earth which is both edible and nutritious. But because of ignorance or existing food habits we ignore these potential food substances. Another possibility, if the world situation becomes even more tense, is to cease feeding to meat animals many of the food crops now consumed by both animals and men.

An animal diet entails the use of much more land than does a vegetable diet. The Population Commission report of 1953 points out that, other conditions being given, only about half as much land is required to provide a diet comprising only 10 per cent animal food as is needed to supply one including 30 to 40 per cent animal food.[49] The FAO in its first *World Food Survey*,[50] states that when crops are fed to animals instead of directly to human beings, they lose between 80 and 90 per cent of their caloric value before they re-emerge in the form of meat or milk or eggs. On the average, seven primary calories in crops are required to produce one calorie in food of animal origin. If corn, for example, is converted into meat, it should also be recalled that some animals do it more efficiently than others. It takes from 5 to 6 pounds of corn to produce a pound of pork, but 10 to 12 for a pound of beef. In an extremity, the raising of livestock to produce meat and other food products of animal origin could be confined to land that cannot be used for plant food crops. This, however, would mean the sacrifice of very important food elements greatly needed by most of the people of the world and the abandonment of the established nutritional targets for the world set by the FAO.

A further food-conserving possibility—used in some degree in wartime—is to sacrifice the industrial uses of certain food items. Ben-

[48] Cf. Christensen, pp. 102-103.
[49] United Nations, *Determinants and Consequences*, p. 212.
[50] P. 19.

nett points out that several of the grains, potatoes, and sugar in nearly every country go to some extent into the manufacture of alcoholic beverages; various edible animal and vegetable fats are made into soap, paint, and varnish; much laundry starch is made from grains or potatoes. The manufacture of such commodities could be curtailed, and the materials used for food instead, but again, certain standard-of-living features would be sacrificed.

CHANGING DIETARY CUSTOMS

Faulty food habits, based on deep-rooted tradition, prejudice, and ignorance, are responsible for much malnutrition. Social values and religious taboos may not only deny certain people essential foods but actually wear out their land and prevent it from producing other food. Thus in parts of Africa cattle are current wealth, not to be used for food, except as they die accidentally or naturally. Their increase is encouraged; the grazing lands are overstocked; erosion is occurring at a disastrous rate. Crowded India, as we have noted, has a huge, useless, and highly destructive cattle population; religious taboos prevent their consumption as food in a land desperately short of proteins. The Moslem world taboos the pig—about the most efficiently productive of all meat producers—as food.

Plants eaten as wholesome and tasty vegetables by the people of some regions or social classes are rejected by others as weeds and unfit for human consumption. The raising of vegetables is considered an inferior occupation in some areas. The difficulty of popularizing new, unfamiliar foods, often cheaper and superior from nutritional standpoint, is well known.

UTILIZING FOOD RESORCES FROM THE SEA

It is often contended that the waters of the earth, both oceanic and inland, offer vast untouched and undeveloped food resources. The extension of fishing is widely urged. As noted above, fish or marine animals now constitute only about 3 per cent of the human diet on a world-wide scale. Yet it is known that the oceans teem with vast quantities of edible animal life. Up to now oceanic fishing has been confined mainly to a few areas of the oceans, mostly in the cooler waters of the Northern Hemisphere and near the shores. Only certain fishes, mollusks, and crustaceans that are easily and profitably caught have been taken from the waters. People are accustomed to these varieties and deem them edible, to the exclusion of many other available ones. These waters have been fished, in most instances, for centuries, and some show signs of depletion.

Some believe that fishing operations are extendable to vast areas now practically untouched, for example, the waters of the Antarctic. Also, it is maintained that costs might come down though the use of new revolutionary technological equipment, such as electronic devices for locating schools of fish. Some believe that with proper equipment marine life far from the shores and at depths which heretofore could not be reached can now be fished. The peoples of the world would have to adjust their food sensibilities to these new items, assuming that they could be properly processed and profitably made available.

There is also talk about developing great salt-water "ranches," for example, in fenced-in portions of estuaries, where fish could be fed on sea plants and other fish food and produced in great quantities, much as we raise edible livestock on land.

While fish produced in the rivers, ponds, paddies, and ditches have in a small way supplemented the food supply in some parts of the earth, it is thought that fish production could be greatly extended by stocking the waters behind the great irrigation and hydroelectric dams, the irrigation and drainage systems developed in many parts of the world, the small ponds behind soil-conservation dams, and inland rivers. Garbage and other waste products could be used for feeding. It must be recalled, however, that fish have a more and more difficult time of it in the rivers and inland waters of the world because of the increasing loads of silt (due to erosion) and the increasing amounts of sewage and industrial waste which they carry.

In general, we have to face technical, locational, transportation, and processing problems, deep-seated and long-standing food habits and traditions, and the very real possibility of high costs of operation in considering the difficulty in introducing these potential forms of sea food to compete with the accepted sea or land foods.

Plankton is mentioned as a possible marine food in almost inexhaustible supply. It consists of the vast swarm of microscopic plants and animals representative of almost every known group of invertebrates that exist in the seas—the broad base of the "food pyramid" of the ocean. It is nutritious, being about 50 to 60 per cent protein, 5 to 15 per cent fat, and around 15 per cent carbohydrate, and is also rich in minerals and vitamins. People have eaten it—the Kon-Tiki crew, for example. It is proposed to harvest it directly and process it so that it is palatable, either as human food, as a feed supplement for land animals, or as food for fish which, in turn, would be added to the human diet. Thus far, however, no one has yet demonstrated how to catch it in a profitable manner or quantity, nor have the problems of processing it been solved.

Seaweeds have been used as food for men and animals, and have furnished fertilizers, vegetable gelatins, fibers, minerals, and so on. Some see the possibility of greater use, perhaps even cultivating some of the seaweeds for human food. It is known, however, that neither the carbohydrates nor the proteins in seaweeds are digestible by human beings and serve chiefly as bulk. Their human nutritional value lies wholly in their content of minerals. Seaweeds are a digestible and very beneficial food supplement for animals such as the ruminants, which are able to digest their carbohydrates. They are also useful as fertilizers and soil conditioners.

ARTIFICIAL FOODS

Occasionally this direction is mentioned as a means of increasing the food supply. By chemical synthesis grass, straw, and wood, especially sawdust, are to be turned into edible carbohydrates assimilable by human beings. It has been shown that water organisms such as the green algae, especially *chlorella,* can be grown in huge tanks on minerals and gas mixtures under optimum photosynthetic conditions, and can produce a food of high protein content and high vitamin potency. This, it is thought, can be done at as low a cost as ten cents a pound, or even less, for the dry product. This estimate was based on the pilot plant operations conducted by the Carnegie Institution. Experiments are being conducted on the production of artificial milk for consumption both by humans and young animals.

Scientists have found as the result of pilot plant operations in various parts of the world that certain kinds of yeasts can, efficiently and economically, turn carbohydrates such as sugar or molasses into true protein as nutritious as beef.[51] This has significance in view of the fact that many areas of the earth in which sugar-rich plants can be easily produced are very poor in protein foods.

HYDROPONICS

In great central "food factories" edible plants are to be grown in solutions of chemicals and water.[52] While this has been success-fully done, its practicality on any considerable scale must be questioned both on biological and economic grounds.

Most of these last three ways of increasing the food supply are definitely new and highly experimental procedures, and some are almost utopian ventures. They present a host of problems, some of which probably will be solved by modern science and technology. They require extended research. The capital equipment and the technical processes to produce them on any considerable scale have not yet been developed. Some are likely to be very expensive in themselves. Effective modification of present means is likely; ma-terials and energies now wasted or undeveloped may become avail-able for developing these items as foods. In the main, however, their development is likely to be quite expensive. Furthermore, significant human nutrient elements may be lost. It must be pointed out that most food has to grow in the soil. The elements of health, starting with vitamins and going on to other factors— for example, the "trace minerals"—are provided by plants that grow in good healthy soil spread out under the sun. Finally, these artificial foods cannot be made out of nothing; the materials have to be obtained somewhere, and not all of them will be waste items or readily accessible. Nothing is in indefinite supply; even some of the "flow" resources deteriorate and may disappear when over-used. Every discovery or invention with respect to the food supply uses some materials not used before for food.

---

[51] K. Sax, however, makes the comment: "The prediction that yeast may be produced to sell at 10 cents per pound seems unduly optimistic in view of the present retail prices of nearly a dollar a pound for baker's yeast and nearly two dollars a pound for brewer's yeast prepared for human consumption." P. 260.

[52] For a more extended and highly readable examination of these various means proposed for creating foods by technological means, see Bliven, pp. 47-69.

CONCLUSION

Can science increase the food supply indefinitely for an ever-increasing population? Can it solve the problem of food supply forever, as some imply?[53] Science has done wonderful things and will doubtless produce even more marvelous achievements in the future. There is every reason for believing that it will be able to increase the world's food supply greatly. Some see the possibility of increasing it ten or even twenty-five times with known technological means.[54]

But even the most sober and carefully reckoned estimates do not offer certainty, for the simple reason that too many stern variables and unknowns are involved. We can hardly be very realistic, even at a given time, with known land, known techniques, known food attitudes and habits, known economic and social organization, not to mention likely or possible changes in all these in the future. If it were only a matter of the use of science and technology, and we could assume that all other aspects of the situation would remain *neutral* as to influence, predictions could be made with some confidence. But *none* of the other factors—physical laws, economic laws, demographic facts, internal and international political conditions, psychological and social-psychological tendencies—are neutral.[55]

The earth is finite, and its agricultural land is limited quantitatively and qualitatively. All extensions of agricultural land will be to poorer land. All fertilizers and soil amendments used to increase yields will at best be substitutes for lost natural elements or artificial supplements to naturally inadequate soils. Almost everything that must be done will be more expensive than present processes. Ironically, the peoples of the earth in greatest need of

[53] Cf. Kirtley F. Mather, *Enough and to Spare: Mother Earth Can Nourish Every Man in Freedom* (New York: Harpers, 1944); C. F. Kellogg, "The Earth Can Feed Her People," *Farm Policy Forum*, Jan., 1949; E. P. Hanson, *New Worlds Emerging* (New York: Duell, Sloan & Pearce, 1949).

[54] Cf. Darwin, pp. 33-35; Brown, p. 146.

[55] For a thoroughly informed treatment, by Sir John Russell, of the task of increasing the food supply in India and Africa, not only from the point of view of the formidable technical and financial problems, but also of the obstacles in the form of religious beliefs and practices, other customs and traditions, shortage of technically qualified instructors and supervisors, lack of suitable appliances and implements, see "The Politics of Bread," *Saturday Review*, 38 (Mar. 26, 1955): 11-12, 29-31.

these additional food supplies are least able to carry on most of the processes and least able to shoulder the costs.

The machines and engines, the railways and pipelines, and the other technical equipment used in increasing the food supply, as well as in the production of many of the other gadgets and appliances deemed essential to a decent level of consumption, require great quantities of metallic ores. The machines are powered by energy derived from the geological fuels—coal, petroleum, and gas. The materials essential in the increase of agricultural yields, such as the soil builders and supplements, and those essential in the production of artificial foods—for example, those used in synthetic foods and hydroponics—come from the earth's supply of chemicals. These elements are all part of the world's irreplaceable or "fund" resources—its fixed capital. The possible utilization of solar or atomic energy and the extraction of all manner of materials from ocean water still depend in part upon this "geological capital." Some very important items, such as iron ore, are being consumed at an alarming rate; many deposits are on the verge of exhaustion; poorer and poorer qualities must be used; resort must be made to sources remote from the places of major use—all at increasing cost. What is equally alarming, as Boulding points out, is the fact that the present phenomenal rate of consumption of this natural capital is almost all the result of the activity of not more than a fifth of the world's population—what we have designated as the Group I countries. If and when the rest of the world uses them in productive processes to provide the items in the present American level of consumption, the problem of their exhaustion will be a matter of crucial urgency.[56]

Financial means will have to be increased for research organizations, agricultural colleges, experimental stations, and for schools and extension services to teach people how to use the more complicated agricultural methods and instruments. The ways and means of increasing the food by agriculture either on newly claimed land or by working the old cultivated areas more intensively sooner or later involve the law of diminishing returns and increasing costs. This means that more and more capital, effort, and ingenuity must

[56] Kenneth E. Boulding, *The Organizational Revolution* (New York: Harpers, 1953), p. 190.

be invested simply to prevent diminishing returns. The other potential forms of increasing the food supply—algae culture, plankton processing, hydroponic tank farming—are exceedingly experimental, and even if they turn out to be highly successful, as well they may be, it might still be necessary to use all the agencies of mass persuasion to get people to eat synthesized sawdust muffins, algae puddings, and plankton sausages—and to like them.

All sorts of social values attach to consumption, including that of food, and people have a tendency to cling to their customary patterns. In many instances, especially among the static societies, there is a tendency to lower the quantity or quality of the traditionally consumed items, but to maintain them, rather than to adopt the consumption of new ones.

In general, the continuous and possibly greatly accelerated increase of the food supply means an even more persistent encroachment upon ever-dwindling essentials and a search for substitutes; above all, it means an increasingly vast and interlocking system that becomes more precarious and expensive as to supply of resources, cost of equipment and techniques, transportation, and exchange and distribution—and more disastrously vulnerable to disturbing factors.

Demographically, the consumers of any immediately foreseeable additions to the food supply already exist, or will exist long before these techniques can reduce the proportion of human beings who are perpetually hungry, seriously malnourished, or actually starving. One of the most difficult aspects of the problem will be to get enough food, whether by increased local supply or by the difficult and expensive processes of distribution, to places where it is most urgently needed—to Asia, Africa, and Latin America. Here most of the essentials are in shortest supply, and all activities necessary to produce supplies are stifled by excessive and pressing population. Also, every additional billion people will not only greatly reduce the acreage of productive land per capita, but will require a proportionate amount of standing room. That standing room (place of good habitance) is likely to be where the earth is best for agriculture as we now think of it.

Increases in the production of food in all areas of the earth having considerable potential food resources are urgently required. The extension and expansion of international trade, international conditions permitting, should aid in equalizing the vast differences in per-capita food production and food consumption. For obvious reasons, Asia, for example, has been both a small importer and exporter. Only Europe has drawn heavily on other lands. But however large the food surpluses in the exporting countries may be, they alone can never bridge the gap between food requirements and the levels of food production. The entire scale of food production in the overpopulated and underdeveloped areas must be raised if this problem is to be met effectively. This means, among many other things, various national and international programs directed to this end. Unfortunately, much of this is still a hope and not a promise.

There may be a world of plenty in the foreseeable future, but, at best, to achieve it will be a struggle in which we will be ever more precariously crowding the margin of safety. We cannot afford to engage in careless thinking and absurd optimism. Scientists and administrators are not magicians. It would be folly for us to make plans on the assumption that they are. *All* the facts of this many-sided and progressively more complex problem must be faced. Finally, whatever is done to improve the food situation for the world as a whole must be done soon. The situation is deteriorating and time is running short.

BIBLIOGRAPHY

ADAMS, ROGER. "Man's Synthetic Future." *Science,* 115 (Feb. 15, 1952): 157-163.

BAKER, O. E. *The Population Prospects in Relation to the World's Agricultural Resources.* College Park: Univ. of Maryland, 1947.

BECKETT, W. H. "The Development of Peasant Agriculture," in Ruopp, pp. 132-152.

BENNETT, H. H. *Soil Conservation.* New York: McGraw-Hill, 1939. Pp. 56-83.

BENNETT, M. K. *The World's Food: A Study of the Interrelations of World Populations, National Diets, and Food Potentials.* New York: Harpers, 1954. Esp. Part III.

BINNS, SIR BERNARD O. *Land Settlement for Agriculture* (FAO Development Paper No. 9). Rome: UN Food and Agricultural Organization, 1951.

BIRD, JOHN. "Will Your Grandchildren Go Hungry?" *Sat. Eve. Post,* 227 (Oct. 23, 1954) : 30, 103-104.

BLIVEN, BRUCE. *Preview for Tomorrow: The Unfinished Business of Science.* New York: Knopf, 1953. Pp. 9-12, 36-133.

BOWMAN, ISAIAH (ed.). *The Limits of Land Settlement*. New York: Council of Foreign Relations, 1937.

——————— (ed.). *The Pioneer Fringe*. New York: American Geographical Society, 1931.

BRITTAIN, R. *Let There Be Bread*. New York: Simon & Schuster, 1952.

BROWN, HARRISON. *The Challenge of Man's Future*. New York: Viking, 1954. Pp. 95-99, 107-148.

BRUNNER, E. S., and DONALD ENSMINGER. *Farmers of the World*. New York: Columbia Univ. Press, 1945.

BURCHARD, J. E. (ed.). *Mid-Century: The Social Implications of Scientific Progress*. New York: Wiley, 1950.

BURLEW, J. S. (ed.). *Algal Culture: From Laboratory to Pilot Plant* (Carnegie Institution Publication No. 600). Washington, 1953.

CARSON, RACHEL. *The Sea Around Us*. New York: Oxford Univ. Press, 1951.

CHRISTENSEN, J. J. "Technologies of Increasing Food Production," in Hatt, pp. 94-107.

CLARK, F. L., and N. W. PIRIE (eds.). *Four Thousand Million Mouths: Scientific Humanism and the Shadow of World Hunger*. London: Oxford Univ. Press, 1951.

CONDLIFFE, J. B. *The Economic Pattern of World Population* (Planning Pamphlet No. 18). Washington: National Planning Assoc., 1942.

CRESSEY, G. B. "Land for 2.4 Billion Neighbors." *Econ. Geog.*, 29 (Jan., 1953) : 1-9.

DANIELS, FARRINGTON. "Solar Energy," in Hatt, pp. 246-262.

DARWIN, SIR CHARLES G. *The Next Million Years*. Garden City: Doubleday, 1953. Pp. 33-36, 181-186.

DOBBY, E. H. G. "Food and the Changing Function of Southeast Asia," in P. W. Thayer (ed.), *Southeast Asia in the Coming World*. Baltimore: Johns Hopkins Press, 1953. Pp. 126-139.

FAWCETT, C. B. "The Extent of Cultivable Land." *Geog. Jour.*, 76 (Dec., 1930): 504-509.

FITZGERALD, D. A. "World Food Needs and Resources," in Hatt, pp. 126-137.

FORSYTH, W. D. *The Myth of the Open Spaces*. Melbourne: Melbourne Univ. Press, 1942.

GALTSOFF, P. S. "Food Resources of the Ocean," in Hatt, pp. 108-118.

HATT, P. K. (ed.).*World Population and Future Resources*. New York: American Book, 1952.

HAWTHORNE, D., and F. MINOT. *The Inexhausible Sea*. New York: Dodd, Mead, 1954.

HENSHAW, P. S. *Adaptive Human Fertility*. New York: McGraw-Hill, 1955. Pp. 66-89.

JENKINS, M. T. "Genetic Improvement of Food Plants for Increased Yields." *Proc. Am. Phil. Soc.*, 95 (Feb., 1951): 84-91.

JOERG, W. L. G. (ed.). *Pioneer Settlement: Cooperative Studies*. New York: American Geographical Society, 1932.

KELLOGG, C. F. *The Soils that Support Us*. New York: Macmillan, 1941.

MEAD, MARGARET (ed.). *Cultural Patterns and Technical Change*. New York: UNESCO, 1953. Pp. 194-211.

MOORE, W. E. "Economic Limits of International Resettlement." *Am. Soc. Rev.,* 10 (April, 1945): 274-281.

————. *Industrialization and Labor: Social Aspects of Economic Development.* Ithaca: Cornell Univ. Press, 1951. Pp. 48-55.

NATIONAL RESEARCH COUNCIL. *The Problem of Changing Food Habits,* Report of Commission on Food Habits, 1941-43 (Bulletin No. 108). Washington, 1943.

ORR, SIR JOHN BOYD. "The Food Problem," *Scientific American,* 135 (Aug., 1950): 11-15.

————. *The White Man's Dilemma: Food and the Future.* London: Allen & Unwin, 1953.

OSBORN, FAIRFIELD. *The Limits of the Earth.* Boston: Little, Brown, 1953. Pp. 171-205.

————. *Our Plundered Planet.* Boston: Little, Brown, 1948.

PEARL, R. S. *The Natural History of Population.* New York: Oxford Univ. Press, 1939. Pp. 266-277.

PEARSON, F. A., and F. A. HARPER. *The World's Hunger.* Ithaca: Cornell Univ. Press, 1945.

PELZER, K. J. *Pioneer Settlement in the Asiatic Tropics: Studies in Land Utilization and Agricultural Colonization in Southeastern Asia.* New York: Institute of Pacific Relations, 1945.

PENROSE, E. F. *Population Theories and their Application, with Special Reference to Japan.* Stanford, Calif.: Food Research Institute, 1934. Pp. 121-151.

Population Bull. (Population Reference Bureau, Washington): "Can Science Win the Peace?" 5 (April, 1939): 9-15; "How Many People Can the World Support?" 4 (Dec., 1948): 37-43; "The 'Eat Hearty' Hoax?" 5 (Jan., 1949): 1-7; "Report on India," 9 (Feb., 1953): 1-9.

PRICE, A. GRENFELL. *White Settler in the Tropics.* New York: American Geographical Society, 1939.

RECHTER, J. H. "Population and Food Supply." *Soc. Research,* 20 (Autumn, 1953): 253-266.

RUOPP, PHILLIPS (ed.). *Approaches to Community Development: A Symposium Introductory to Problems and Methods of Village Welfare in Underdeveloped Areas.* The Hague: W. van Hoeve, 1953.

RUSSELL, SIR E. JOHN. *World Population and World Food Supplies.* London: Allen & Unwin (New York: Macmillan), 1954.

SAMKALDEN I. "Land Tenure and Land Reform," in Ruopp, pp. 153-170.

SALTER, R. M. "World Soil and Fertilizer Resources in Relation to Food Needs," *Science,* 105 (May 23, 1947): 533-538; or *Chronica Botanica,* 11 (No. 4): 1948.

SAX, KARL. "Population Problems," in Ralph Linton (ed.), *The Science of Man in the World Crisis.* New York: Columbia Univ. Press, 1945. Pp. 258-281.

SCHANTZ, H. A. "Agricultural Regions of Africa." *Econ. Geog.,* 18 (July, 1942): 229-246; 18 (Oct., 1942): 343-362.

SCHULTZ, T. W. (ed.). *Food for the World.* Chicago: Univ. of Chicago Press, 1946.

SEARS, P. B. *Deserts on the March.* Norman: Univ. of Oklahoma Press, 1935.

SHAW, W. J. "Food, Famine and the Future," *Eugenics Rev.,* 29 (Jan., 1953): 216-219.

SMITH, F. G. WALTON, and H. CHAPIN. *The Sun, the Sea, and Tomorrow.* New York: Scribners, 1954.

SPOEHR, H. A. "Clorella as a Source of Food." *Proc. Am. Phil. Soc.,* 95 (Feb., 1951): 62-67.

STAMM, A. J. "Production of Nutritive Substances from Inedible Carbohydrates." *Proc. Am. Phil. Soc.,* 95 (Feb., 1950): 68-75 (includes extensive bibliography).

STAMP, L. Dudley. *Africa: A Study in Tropical Development.* New York: Wiley, 1953.

————. *Land for Tomorrow: The Underdeveloped World.* Bloomington: Indiana Univ. Press, 1952.

TOLLEY, H. R. "Farmers in a Hungry World." *Proc. Am. Phil. Soc.,* 95 (Feb., 1951) : 54-61.

ULMAN, W. A. "How to Make Sea Water Tasty." *Sat. Eve. Post,* 227 (June 25, 1955): 43, 123-126.

United Nations Conference on Food and Agriculture, Hot Springs, Va., 1943. Washington: U. S. Government Printing Office, 1943.

UNITED NATIONS. *Defects in Agrarian Structures as Obstacles.* New York, 1951.

————. *Economic Survey of Latin America, 1948.* New York, 1949.

————. *Report of the Food and Agricultural Organization of the United Nations.* Mimeo., E/2195, 7 April 1952.

————, FAO. *Second World Food Survey.* Rome, 1952.

————, FAO. *The State of Food and Agriculture: Review and Outlook.* Rome, 1952.

————, FAO. *The State of Food and Agriculture, 1955: Review of a Decade and Outlook.* Rome, 1955.

————, FAO. *World Food Survey.* Washington, 1946.

————, Population Division, Department of Social Affairs. *The Determinants and Consequences of Population Trends: A Summary of the Findings of Studies on the Relationships between Population Changes and Economic and Social Conditions* (Population Studies, No. 17). New York, 1953. Pp. 163-177, 181-193, 220-222, 267-275.

VOGT, WILLIAM. *Road to Survival.* New York: William Sloan Associates, 1948.

WALFORD, L. A. "On Increasing the Exploitation of Aquatic Resources for World Food Needs." *Proc. Am. Phil. Soc.,* 95 (Feb., 1951): 77-83.

WEISS, F. J. "Chemical Agriculture." *Scientific American,* 187 (Aug., 1952) 15-19.

————. "Useful Algae." *Scientific American,* 187 (Dec., 1952): 15-17.

WHITACKER, J. R. "World Land Resources for Agriculture," in Hatt, pp. 75-83.

WHYTE, R. O., and G. V. JACKS. *Vanishing Lands.* New York: Doubleday Doran, 1939.

"World Population and World Food Resources." *Eugenics Rev.,* 45 (July, 1953): 71-75.

WOYTINSKY, W. S. and E. S. *World Population and Production: Trends and Outlook.* New York: Twentieth Century Fund, 1953. Pp. 312-348, 451-594, 630-681, 715-746.

YATES, P. L. "Food and Income," in Schultz, pp. 177-186.

ZIMMERMANN, E. W. *World Resources and Industries.* New York: Harpers, 1951.

8

Migration As a Possible
Solution of Population Pressure

MIGRATION AS AN ADJUSTIVE PROCESS,
PAST AND PRESENT

Migration has been one of the great demographic and social adjustive procedures throughout human history. Man has devised
continually more efficient ways of moving across space. He has
the ability to survive and even flourish in many regions and climates.
Consequently, the members of the human race—unlike most other
species of higher animal life—have spread to almost every portion
of the earth.

The migratory currents are evidence of recurrent tendencies toward redistribution of human beings, and they have had elemental
forces behind them because neither natural nor man-influenced
conditions of life are equal everywhere over the face of the earth
at any given time. The natural features of regions—resources,
climate, hazards—are different, and natural conditions may change
as a result, for example, of changes in the rainfall and climatic
cycle, and of related natural catastrophes such as famine and
epidemic. Great differentials exist in man-made, or at any rate
man-influenced, economic levels of living due to variations in the
techniques of utilizing resources. The less tangible but increasingly
important rights and freedoms and the intellectual and spiritual
opportunities are very unequally distributed and are continually

changing. These differentials mean a lack of opportunity to satisfy human wants and realize human values somewhere, and the possibility of satisfying them elsewhere. In the main, it means that demographic and socio-economic ratios vary greatly. The incentives to migration will exist as long as the conditions of human life are, or are believed to be, less hard in one region than in another.

Migration is a "flow" tendency analogous to that which exists where there are differences in atmospheric pressure, and air of the higher-density area tends to rush into the space of lower density. In brief, the human populations of the earth live under varying conditions ranging from those of "high" to "low" pressure. But the "flow" of human beings in space is never a "free" flow governed solely by high or low pressure. There are always such obstacles as ignorance of alternative opportunities, attitudinal and evaluational factors, ethnic antagonisms, political barriers, limitations of facilities, and especially economic costs. Furthermore, the very expansion of population, the closing of settlement areas, and the changes in scientific-technological-economic development and in international political relations mightily modify from era to era the possibilities and the nature of migration.

In view of the *past* significance of international migration in population redistribution, and also in view of the fact that it is advocated by many at the present time as a means of relieving population pressure in some of the overpopulated areas, it is essential that we briefly examine its possible effects and efficacy in the pressure areas, the nature of the likely targets for immigration, and the general economic, political, and cultural conditions in the world of 1955 that affect the international movement of any considerable volume of people.

NINETEENTH- AND EARLY TWENTIETH-CENTURY EMIGRATION-IMMIGRATION

Many people of the world, including some Americans, are still operating mentally on the basis of the emigration-immigration philosophy and the comparative geographic-economic-political conditions prevailing during the nineteenth century and the first decades of the twentieth century. Between 1820 and 1932, according to the estimates[1] as many as 65 million persons from Europe alone left for other continents; the world intercontinental migration amounted to some 67 million; and from two-thirds to three-fourths of these migrants stayed abroad. What were the conditions under which this movement of human beings—most certainly the greatest in history in terms of numbers—occurred?

In Europe a variety of "push" factors were operative. In the first half of the nineteenth century northwestern and central Europe were in the first flush of the Industrial Revolution. The plight of both the urban masses and the surplus rural population was great, the condition of the latter being further aggravated by a succession of agricultural crises. The death rates were falling rapidly, while the birth rates remained high, thus making for unprecedented population growth in no wise abated by the emigration. It was also a century of revolutions and internal national disturbances, of developing nationalisms, and of European international wars. Finally, all manner of discrimination existed—political, racial, national and religious.

The "pull," or permissive, factors were most imposing and unique. New, virgin agricultural land (in North America, South America, southern Siberia, Australia, and parts of Africa) became accessible. This land was not "waste" land, but "best" land; it was free or cheap and gave immigrants of farm origin a chance to carry on agriculture with increasing returns. This good land provided a ready opportunity for a man with little capital (other than his two strong hands, some common ingenuity, a willingness to work, and, as soon as possible, a coterie of sons) to make good. The lands, moreover, were in climates and zones not too unlike those of the homelands of the migrants.

The indigenous populations, in the main, were sparse, of primitive culture, politically and regionally unorganized, and incapable of offering effective resistance.

In some parts of these new worlds, especially the United States—the chief recipient of the migrants—there was also a rapidly developing industrialization with a tremendous capacity for absorbing labor. In fact, there was a great *demand* for cheap new labor

---

[1] Carr-Saunders, pp. 46-58; Ferenczi (1933); Forsyth; Staley, pp. 287-288; Woytinsky, pp. 66-77.

as the older stocks moved up the social ladder. All of these new lands had a rapidly expanding economy. The immigrants aided the expansion of both agriculture and industry by opening up new territories, developing new resources, and creating new markets. In the United States, for example, each wave of immigrants created favorable conditions for additional newcomers.

Both technical and political conditions favorable to widespread movement existed. Steam had made possible cheap and rapid transoceanic and transcontinental travel. It was the only known epoch in history in which people were relatively free to cross international political boundaries—free to leave and enter with only formal requirements. For a while human beings circulated more freely than merchandise. There was also relatively easy hospitality for population surpluses from elsewhere.

There were all kinds of superior opportunities in the newly opened areas in addition to the economic, such as political and ethnic freedoms, educational opportunities, religious tolerance and freedom, internal peace (except for occasional interludes), ready internal physical mobility, and flexible class systems and opportunities for social mobility. In these new areas higher economic levels of living and greater cultural and humane possibilities could be achieved without great difficulty.

But this easy and favorable movement was almost exclusively the privilege of the white race, whose members alone had the means, due to their growing wealth; the target lands were European conquered, European controlled, and mainly inhabited by European stocks. The whites monopolized and exploited the new, rich lands of the earth, and there were no more lands nearly so good.

An array of factors which put an end to the great volume of migration from Europe began to be effective in the late nineteenth century and continued with increased effectiveness in the twentieth. These have been summarized by Stephen W. Reed. The industrialization and urbanization, especially of the northwestern European countries, created wider opportunities at home through higher production, better levels of living, and greater economic and social security. The redundant rural populations tended to be absorbed in their own metropolitan areas. The reduced rates of natural increase provided fewer potential emigrants, and expanding economic systems were increasingly able to cope with the natural increase. The waxing strength of economic and political nationalism reduced the desire to seek new national homes. Finally, restrictive legislation in some sending countries and in almost all the former receiving countries following World War I greatly reduced the possibility of international "flow."[2]

INTERNATIONAL MIGRATION IN THE
SECOND HALF OF THE TWENTIETH CENTURY

With respect to migration the present and the near future present a very different world situation as compared with that prior to World War I. By way of introduction it may be said that many people are more aware than ever before that migration is not a way of appreciably solving population pressure anywhere; a major shift in the areas of potential emigration has come about; easily exploited developmental territories do not want or need the kind of immigrants they might receive in volume if free international movement prevailed; and, finally, easy hospitality for population surpluses from elsewhere—the "open-door" or laissez-faire policy—has largely ceased to exist, with the most favored countries exercising the most rigorous control over immigration.

POTENTIAL EMIGRATION AREAS

In general, most world demographers believe that the population of the former areas of intercontinental emigration are less and less likely to contribute to any possible or likely migration of the future. There is a marked stabilization of their populations.

The European Situation.

Most of the portions of Europe contributing the great volume of nineteenth and early twentieth century emigrants have now a matured or rapidly maturing industrial economy. The growth of population shows much evidence of its being controlled, and the general tendency is for the rate of growth to decline. Some of the countries, often the most closely settled, try to retain their populations, have arrangements for importation of selected labor, and resort to pro-natalist policies. The "modernizing" of Europe has weakened the drive to emigrate, and declining birth rates are drying up the stream of emigration at its source. The great atten-

[2] See United Nations, *Determinants and Consequences*, pp. 98-111.

tion paid to potential emigration from Europe at the end of World War II has almost disappeared with the remarkable economic and political recovery made by most of the countries.

This is not to imply that there is no actual or potential emigration from Europe. In a recent highly significant study, Kirk and Huyck found an "identifiable net outward movement" from Europe in the period 1946-1952 of about 3.2 million, or roughly 450,000 per year. They point out that this "overseas migration drained off approximately one-eighth of the natural growth of population in Europe since the war, as compared with one-fifth removed by maximum movements in the years 1900-1914."[3] In net *emigration* during the period 1946-1952 the leading countries were the United Kingdom and Italy with over 600,000 each; Poland with 460,000; Germany with 290,000; the U.S.S.R. with 230,000; Spain and Portugal with 180,000 each; and Rumania with 160,000. However, of the eight countries supplying over 100,000 emigrants since the war, six were in eastern and southern Europe.

Almost all of the post-war migrants of eastern European origin— about one million—were either displaced persons or refugees from Communism. Furthermore, and contrary to the situation prior to World War I, since World War II two-fifths of all European emigrants have been moved with governmental or international financial and physical assistance. The typical post-war migrants from Europe have not been farmers, and only a small portion have sought agricultural land in the areas of immigration. They were predominantly urban workers with specialized training and professional qualifications, and they went primarily to the urban areas in the receiving countries.

With respect to "Future Prospects" the authors state:

Most of Western Europe has now passed the demographic stage which brought about the great swarming of Europeans overseas in the 19th and early 20th centuries. Declining birth rates in the 1930s have so reduced the size of cohorts entering the labor force that pressure to seek opportunities has been slightly reduced . . . even in Germany there is much less pressure to migrate from demographic causes than a generation ago. The lower birth rates now prevailing in Southern Europe assure that pressure from

[3] P. 447.

this source will also shortly recede in that region, especially in Italy, where the birth rate is now quite low, lower even than in France, the classic country of depopulation, and much lower than in the United States.[4]

There are, and probably will continue to be, "distressed" peoples —those discriminated against and persecuted, those who are victims of the dislocations and destruction of production and markets due to war and rebellion. They deserve the right to go elsewhere. In times of economic depression, however caused, there will be the unemployed with the urge to leave. There are also the restless, the curious, and the adventurous. But, in view of the high efficiency of European agriculture, the high degree of industrial development, and the well-established position of most of the countries of Europe in world trade both in importation of raw materials and in exportation of finished products, in fairly peaceful times there is a point to Carl O. Sauer's famous statement: "Europe is perhaps of all parts of the world the best suited to support a large population."[5]

Kirk and Huyck point out that the underemployed rural populations of southern Italy, Spain, Portugal, Greece, and to a lesser extent the Netherlands will furnish the basis for overseas migration for a decade or more; but further economic improvement and observable demographic trends will reduce, if not completely eliminate, this pressure.[6]

The Asian Situation

Demographically speaking, the potential migration pent up in Asia is enormous. Here are mammoth populations operating under Malthusian principles, living at the subsistence level and suffering malnutrition, recurrent starvation, and epidemics. Many regions of Asia are glutted with people and are showing signs of even greater glut in the future. While most of the people of India and China are still embedded in a rigid "cake of custom" and of institutions, the cake is beginning to crumble. They note other areas of the earth that are rich, and they see that the differences in the levels of living between their own and these areas are almost fantastic. Con-

[4] Pp. 455-456.
[5] "The Prospect for Redistribution of Population," in Bowman, p. 24.
[6] P. 456.

stantly present is the pressure—economic and psychological—to cause the destitute masses of these underprivileged regions to swarm across international and continental boundaries.[7] The actual migration, however, is also governed by the availability of outlets in other areas, the economic costs of migration, the possibility of physically moving appreciable numbers, the limited horizons of the potential emigrants, prevailing ethnic attitudes in the potential target countries, political barriers to free movement, the development of internal changes in the economy, and related demographic changes. To what extent are these factors operative?

Centripetal Population Movement

Many politicians and students of world affairs still look to the vast "open spaces" and those subjected to very limited agricultural exploitation as places for settlement by the overflow people of the overpopulated countries. Since most of these people are at present peasant farmers, they would doubtless prefer to engage in agriculture since that has been their traditional way of life. As we have previously noted,[8] most of the profitably exploitable agricultural areas of the earth, with the present state of development of the technical arts and present world economic conditions, are now being intensively utilized. The physical world has been rather well explored and tested, and most of the areas of the world where the latent agricultural resources are close to the surface have been settled. The so-called "pioneer lands" that remain today, while some of them are not without possibility of cultivation in the future as prices increase and technology advances, are under present conditions marginal or even submarginal with respect to climate, terrain, soil fertility and cultivability, and transportation. Their exploitation, even for mere subsistence, requires much more than mere human capital. And if the agriculture is to be better than subsistence farming in these undeveloped areas, the products must

---

[7] The actual demonstration of the migration drive among a people, when sufficient improvement among them occurs to show them how badly off they are by comparison, is evident in the case of Japan: her surge into Formosa after the Sino-Japanese War, into the islands of the Pacific after World War I, into Manchuria from 1931 on—not to mention her actions before and during World War II.

[8] Chapter VII, p. 174.

sell in the world markets and compete with the products of the well-developed agricultural areas. In view of the many unknowns and the relatively huge expenses involved in producing and transporting the possible products, exploitation will not be profitable until vastly greater world scarcities, with correspondingly higher prices, prevail. With some exceptions, possibly in some parts of southeastern Asia (Indo-China) and Brazil, only extremist subsidization from foreign or international sources would make these areas available as satisfactory migration outlets.

Furthermore, over against these possibilities stands the important fact that *the main tendencies in population movement in the present century have come to be centripetal rather than centrifugal.* With the technological development of agriculture and of the extractive industries generally and with the ever greater development of industrialization and urbanization, there has been a noticeable tendency for population to move toward and concentrate in the industrial areas—the already densely settled centers of secondary and tertiary production—and not to disperse to the peripheries of agricultural settlement. In the early stages technical advance favors, indeed requires, concentration of population. In the latter half of the latter nineteenth century most of Europe had already experienced the rural-to-urban "drift" within countries and the movement of population from the agricultural central and southeast areas to the industrialized northwest. The industrialized-urbanized areas frequently were in need of labor. This tendency has been a commonplace in the United States and Canada, with even the immigrants showing a much greater tendency to settle in the cities. In South America, the overflow peasants from the underdeveloped lands have tended to settle in the cities rather than become farmers. In Japan, in the present century, there has been this centripetal drift both on the part of its own population and of the rural Korean immigrants of the 1930's. The same tendencies are perceptible in China, India, the Carribbean countries, and also, generally, Siberia. Even during the nineteenth century migration did not tend to spread population more evenly. It rather accentuated the crowding of mankind into lands already considered good. Since then the migrants from one continent to another have gone increasingly into areas of concentrated population.

The potential emigrants, whether from Europe or Asia, are not so likely to be interested in the "open spaces" as areas of entry and settlement, except for special and rather small groups (religious or political refugees and occasionally nationality or racial groups intending to establish colonies). Generally the migration targets are the rich, highly developed countries with their advanced technologies and economies and already high levels of living. When people move they want to improve their "life chances." They want to go where they can be most productively employed; they want to raise their *level* of living and have a chance at a higher *standard* of living; they want an easing of burdens and an improvement of life; and they want the gains to exceed the costs—physical, psychical, economic. Nowadays agricultural "pioneering" involves risks, hardships, sacrifices, and the possibility of defeat and failure.

The main target areas today, if free movement existed, would be the United States, Canada, Australia, New Zealand, the increasingly industrialized areas of the temperate zone of South America (Argentina and southern Brazil), and, to a lesser extent, the areas in process of industrialization and urbanization in eastern Asia and South Africa. The people with the high "migration potential," as we have noted, are those of the underdeveloped countries of the world. A series of almost insoluble problems grows out of this situation, only a few of which can be examined.

There are, first, certain stern economic considerations. The potential migrants are in the main illiterate rural peasantry with very limited, if any, industrial training and skills and even very little, if any, knowledge of and skill in modern agriculture. Most of them are without experience in urban living. The target countries, as a rule, have mechanized agriculture, requiring less and less manpower. Their rate of population growth (involving both birth and death rates) is under a considerable degree of control, and hence flexible and adjustive in relation to economic and social conditions. If, at certain times, these advanced countries require additional labor supply, they need technically skilled industrial, commercial, and professional workers, or persons from areas sufficiently advanced culturally to be readily educable and trainable. Furthermore, all elements of the population of the advanced countries are very much concerned about protecting their standard of living against reduction due to the inundation of their country by immigrants with markedly lower standards of living, and the reduction of their wage scales through competition with "cheap" labor.

There are numerous ethnic problems. The potential emigrants are largely "yellows," "blacks," and "browns"; the people of the target areas mainly "whites." The latter fear racial conflict, miscegenation, potential racial or national minorities, unassimilable elements, or elements which they fear to assimilate, and complications of their class system. The respective peoples involved have markedly different cultures. The target countries are in fear of cultural confusion, distortion, and dilution by the potential migrants. There is the likelihood of linguistic difficulties, religious differences, and other dissimilarities so striking and profound as to create sharp cultural conflict, isolation, and separation of culture groups. Politically, there are questions of franchise and civic participation among people of a lower level of political development, and there is the possibility of the immigrant elements retaining foreign loyalties. Aside from educational problems, there are demographic problems relating to imbalance of the sex and age-group ratios, and the possibility of complicating effects on the various crucial vital rates. In many instances, on the basis of past experience with these potential emigrants as *immigrants,* many may be only temporary sojourners, skimming off the economic cream, then returning to their old country and clan. Consequently, the potential receiving countries do not want or need the kind of immigrants they are likely to receive in any volume if free movement of peoples existed.

In view of these recognized facts, there has been developing among most of these target areas, since World War I, an array of immigration controls in the form of legislation which sets up both restrictive and highly selective procedures. This legislation is mainly directed against peoples of the more "backward" areas of the earth, especially Asiatics. It is found in the United States and Canada, in Brazil, Argentina, Guatemala, Bolivia, Peru, and the Caribbean countries, in Australia and New Zealand, in South Africa, and in the U.S.S.R., which, with a few exceptions, is closed to both emigration and immigration. Important in most of this legislation are ethnic and "national" requirements, educational ("literacy") requirements, health requirements, and occupational requirements giving preference to artisans, skilled farmers, and professionals. Noticeable also is the tendency to set up absolute annual admission quotas, which are usually very low, reducing the immigration to a barely perceptible trickle.

In brief, political frontiers are again important in migration. The most advanced countries have reacted sharply against laissez-faire immigration policy. There are no freely-swinging "open doors." There are even sharp restrictions on the rights of temporary resident aliens. The admission of refugees is carefully guarded, and even plans for resettling limited numbers of displaced persons meet strong opposition. There is no noticeable disposition to relax or depart radically from these nationalistic controls over immigration, either as to their quantitative or qualitative restrictive features; in fact, it is quite realistic to anticipate their accentuation within countries and extension to others. As E. M. Kulischer puts it, "To plead for the reopening of migration opportunities seems to be preaching in a wilderness."[9] In this connection H. P. Fairchild states, ". . . It must be recognized that the right to determine who shall pass its boundaries is one of the very last items of independence that will be relinquished by any autonomous state." In the same connection he says, "Unless we envision a postwar world organization where the component groups will have practically abandoned all pretense at self-regulation we cannot imagine a system of enforced hospitality to world immigrants."[10]

THE ULTIMATE FUTILITY OF VOLUME MIGRATION

Regardless of the fact that migration in the modern world is considerably restricted by the political actions of some of the most important countries of the world, a realistic view of the situation points to the fact that migration in any considerable volume—especially transoceanic migration—of the overflow peoples of the underdeveloped countries is both impossible of execution and futile as to desired demographic-economic results, even if favorable resettlement opportunities existed elsewhere in sufficient degree to justify a large movement.

[9] P. 319.
[10] Fairchild, 1944. See also United Nations, *Determinants and Consequences*, pp. 111-123, 128-133; and Eldridge.

ECONOMIC EXPENSE

In the first place, most of the people cannot afford the economic expense involved both in transportation to a possible destination and in resettlement with effective means of livelihood. The people most needing relief are quite without even the most limited financial resources. The governments of these people are certainly in no position to give any financial or physical assistance. Nor are there any international agencies fitted to provide for the movement and settlement of more than mere thousands of people, whereas the situation actually implies the possible movement of millions upon millions. Furthermore, the movement of any considerable number of them would markedly upset social and economic conditions in both the emigrant and immigrant countries, not to mention the disturbance of world demographic and economic balances.[11]

PSYCHOLOGICAL AND CULTURAL FACTORS

The most likely migrants from the overpopulated areas are the unschooled lower classes with very limited perspectives and horizons. These are, however, neither mentally nor technically and culturally prepared to assess adequately the risks and tasks involved in settlement in either widely different new agricultural regions or in industrialized areas. Due to ignorance and low physical tone, a lethargy and apathy prevails among many of them. Coming from ancient, long-established static agrarian cultures, they have powerful ties to clan and community and to beliefs and institutions; breaking them exposes the people to "culture shock." In addition, because the migrants would be invading countries with quite different cultures, they would be looked upon by the recipient populations as people of great "alienness," and they would themselves keenly feel their alien ways. In the light of almost all experience up to this moment these people would for several generations be living in ecological and cultural agglomeration, mainly in segregation. Only the most effectively conducted program of diffusion on the part of the receiving country would prevent this. The immigrants in the meantime would be a people apart, living, as nearly as possible, their old-country institutional life and pursuing their old-country fertility practices. Finally, if

[11] Cf. United Nations, *Determinants and Consequences*, pp. 216-217, 299-300.

the movement were in sufficient volume to relieve, even temporarily, population pressure at home, the sheer numbers entering other countries would almost amount to tribal invasion, and tribal invasions have seldom been peaceful for long, since there is both the threat of vast cultural confusion and the replacement of one people by another.

THE PHYSICAL IMPRACTICABILITY OF VOLUME TRANSPORTATION

If enough people were to be moved from India or China to eradicate the necessity of famine (which has afflicted some part of these countries almost annually for 2000 years), or better still, sufficient numbers to create, even temporarily, such a balance of numbers with present resources and productive practices and facilities as would provide a humane way of life conformable to the standards of the more advanced countries of the world, the numbers involved would be fantastic. It is impossible, of course, to propound a categorically convincing number. India, and probably China also, has annual increases of around 5 million per year. Would an exodus of 20 or 50, or 100 million be adequate? If it were 100 million from each, it should be recalled that the population of South America south of the equator or of the United States east of the Mississippi is about 100 million. Japan in recent years has been increasing at about 1,500,000 per year. It might be necessary to move at least 15 million, which is approximately the population of the American Pacific Coast states. What is true of India, China, and Japan is equally true of any other densely crowded countries. Even if we assume welcoming destination countries, to transfer sufficiently appreciable numbers is quite beyond the bounds of practicality. The situation is simply but dramatically stated in the report of the Red Cross Commission to China for study of the famine conditions of 1928-1929:

> If all the ships that sail the seven seas were withdrawn from their regular routes and devoted henceforth exclusively to carrying emigrants out of China they would not keep up with the procession.[12]

[12] Cf., on this contention, Fairchild, 1939; Thompson, 1946, pp. 321-324; Davis, pp. 224-225.

Furthermore, it is questionable whether the unused but usable land in the Pacific Basin or in Africa, even most optimistically considered, could absorb and support the annual natural increase of these countries for more than a few years.[13] Also, if immigration were permitted into all of these areas they could do little to relieve the actual pressure of population in the more crowded Asiatic countries, for, as Thompson points out, ". . . the population needing outlets is five or six times that of Europe of 1800, and the lands available are relatively small and not so richly endowed as the Americas."[14] Finally, he also calls attention to the fact that there is no organization powerful enough to direct and control such a migration, nor is there likely to be.

THE FUTILITY OF EMIGRATION IN PERMANENTLY EASING POPULATION PRESSURE

Emigration has for centuries been recommended and, when possible, used as a favorite nostrum for the evils of overpopulation. The procedure has been naively thought of as simple arithmetic subtraction: the emigration of a certain number of people supposedly has meant that many fewer people in the area. In the main, this has only been true when the emigration was due to natural or social catastrophe which made the area unlivable. Under any other conditions, the cumulative historical evidence, especially of the last century, points to the fact that the phrase "on the day of departure" should be added, for seldom has the subtraction had a permanent or long-time effect. Usually the gaps at home were quickly filled, and, in notable cases, the rate of population increase has been accelerated.[15] Even the emigration of very considerable numbers does not do a great deal to relieve population pressure unless industry develops fast enough to absorb the major portion of the natural increase, or unless for other reasons natural increase is

[13] "There simply is not enough land in the Pacific Region (and tropical Africa combined) to accommodate the more than 2,000 million people that would result during the next five decades from a 15 percent decennial increase among the more than 1,100 million now living there [i.e., eastern and southeastern Asia]." Thompson, 1946, p. 332.

[14] 1946, p. 13.

[15] The most notable exception is Ireland, where the reduction in population by emigration (and the potato famine of the 1840's) has been maintained through efficiently implemented prudential motives.

checked by prudential motives and practices. According to Thompson's analysis,

> What happens in a povery-stricken population . . . where new industry is developing slowly, is that, while the birth rate is little changed by emigration, any temporary relief of pressure on subsistence reduces the death rate so that more of the children born survive, and the gaps caused by emigrants are quickly filled by those children saved from an early death.[16]

Or as Fairchild explains it:

> Some of the people remaining at home do not die who otherwise would; some young people get married who otherwise would not have; some married couples relax whatever precautionary measures they have been following. The death rate falls slightly, and the birth rates moves up a bit, and the gap is soon filled.[17]

This tendency toward increase, even at an accelerated rate, goes on as long as emigration continues.

While one is not always safe in predicting future trends on the basis of past experience, in the light of the demographic and economic conditions and the attitudes and values regarding fertility which prevail among the overpopulated peoples of the world, it looks very much as though emigration, even if feasible on other grounds, would not be simple subtraction but rather a matter of multiplication.

As noted above, from the early nineteenth century to 1932 some 65 million people emigrated from Europe, yet during that time the population of Europe itself increased from 180 million to about 480 million, and the number of persons of European stock overseas increased beyond 160 million. Almost all of the European countries that have produced a considerable number of emigrants during the last century and a half demonstrate the point. Italy, however, has been a particularly significant example. In summarizing the experience of Italy, Cook states:

[16] 1946, p. 13.
[17] Fairchild, 1939, pp. 231-232.

Between 1880 and 1920, four and a half million Italians emigrated to the United States and over twelve million to other lands. But the birth rate remained high, so the population at home grew from 29 million to 39 million. . . . numbers actually increased faster in Italy during the years of greatest migration than they had before or since. The small island of Sicily experienced the heaviest out-migration of any part of Italy, yet Sicily increased in numbers nearly twice as fast as the population of the Italian mainland.[18]

It may be pointed out that the Italian birth rate has fallen only *since* emigration has practically ceased, though the cessation of emigration has by no means been the only factor in this decline. The emigration of northern Chinese into Inner Mongolia and Manchuria since 1920 is estimated as being in excess of 30 million, with nearly two million leaving in some single years. Yet the out-movement has had hardly a momentary effect on population stabilization.[19]

The great bulk of the evidence points to the fact that emigration can never solve the problem of population pressure while the birth rate remains high. In all honesty, it should be recalled that in the case of the European examples above, there was a general downward trend of the death rate while the birth rate remained stationary or declined slightly but much more slowly. But it is significant that the temporary improvement of economic and social conditions occasioned by the reduction of population through emigration *did not decrease the birth rate;* in some instances the birth rate actually increased. It is almost axiomatic that only when population increase is reduced to zero can migration begin to affect population pressure.[20] But when a country has reached this point there rarely *is* population pressure or migration potential.

The effects of migration on the receiving country are less clear. In the last several centuries, where there has been migration into new or relatively undeveloped countries, and where the indigenous population has been practically negligible in numbers and in ability

---

[18] R. C. Cook, *Human Fertility: The Modern Dilemma* (New York: William Sloane Associates, 1951), p. 90. See also Fairfield Osborn, *Limits of the Earth* (Boston: Little, Brown, 1953), pp. 36-38; Bruce Bliven, *Preview for Tomorrow: The Unfinished Business of Science* (New York: Knopf, 1953), pp. 25-27.

[19] Young.

[20] Cf. Cook, *op. cit.,* p. 91; Thompson, 1946, p. 328.

to resist the immigrants in a sustained manner, the immigrants have been a clear addition to the population. Moreover, pioneer conditions have invariably been accompanied by high birth rates and very high rates of population increase. It seems quite likely that if the possible resettlement of the few remaining "open spaces" by peoples from the present overpopulated countries should take the form of subsistence farming, it would be a case of the rabbits taking over the Australias. Soon all of these open places would be filled to capacity, there would be no gains in the sending or the receiving areas, and the world as a whole would be pressed nearer to the Malthusian limits.

If, assuming the possibility, the migrants entered a settled and modernized country, the immediate effect would be some increase of population. If the immigrants should bring high fertility habits with them, the next effect would most likely be some *displacement* of the old stocks by the new. After several generations the long-time effect would probably be a reduction of the birth rate of the immigrant stocks to the same fertility performance as the rest of the population.[21]

It would seem, then, that emigration from overpopulated countries is at best only a temporary palliative for those countries. In the kind of world we live in it is a stop gap procedure, simply transferring to some other country the responsibility for effectively solving a local or areal population problem. For the world as a whole, any considerable free movement of peoples would soon tend to fill up every nook and cranny; and this in turn would bring about the progressive deterioration of the levels of living of even the more favored countries, not to mention the international tensions that would be created.

CONCLUSION

It is quite apparent that the migration of people in any considerable volume is (1) impracticable as even a partial solution of population pressure in the underdeveloped and/or overcrowded countries, both from the point of view of favorable timely effects at home and of the availability of population-absorbing areas of settlement; and (2) practically impossible, because of the lack of

[21] For an extended discussion of these points see United Nations, *Determinants and Conseqeunces*, pp. 136-141.

physical facilities and the huge economic costs of moving sufficient numbers to produce even temporary relief at home.

In the first place, the people of the overpopulated countries usually have to meet their demographic-economic problem *not by flight from home, but by reorganization at home.* Specifically, this implies agricultural improvement, including, if possible, commercial agriculture and the production of materials for world exchange, the development of other possible extractive industry, and the accelerated and intensified development of urban industry, producing for both the home and the world market. Such improvement implies the development of local raw materials and commercial access to usable ones from abroad, as well as available exchange and transportation facilities for both raw materials and marketable products. It implies also the importation of capital funds and capital equipment and of technical instruction, advice, and assistance, and the temporary emigration of students, future technicians, supervisors, and other experts and specialists for training abroad. On a world scale this would mean free movement of funds and equipment, of technical knowledge, skills, and advisers, and of raw materials and processed commodities. For if people cannot come and go in sufficient volume, ways of developing a regimen of adequacy and prudence must. Thus, international *trade* is at least a partial substitute for international *migration.* Furthermore, the ability of the underdeveloped peoples to trade more freely in the markets of the world would very likely have a beneficial effect upon their demographic-economic balance. Almost without exception in history, if the general level of economic productivity, the general level of life, and the standards of living can be raised more rapidly than the rate of population increase, the rate of natural increase tends to be reduced, both fertility and mortality come under a growing degree of control, and the emigration potential is reduced and may cease altogether.[22]

Secondly, however, international migration will not and should not cease entirely. New or partly developed agricultural and extractive areas without a surplus of population experienced in extractive industry will create a demand for immigrants. The same will be true in some areas undergoing rapid industrialization. The

[22] Cf. United Nations, *Determinants and Consequences,* pp. 172, 189-192.

people thus utilizable, however, will not in most instances be the peasant overflow of "backward," overpopulated lands, but people with some technical preparation for either modern agriculture or manufacturing industry. The selection of these migrants as to fitness for either frontier or urban-industrial life and the checking as to acceptability of the settlement conditions (climate and health, financial and capital resources, housing, political and cultural conditions) will have to be a matter of bilateral or multilateral arrangement among the countries involved, or be managed by an international authority like the International Labor Organization.

As in the past, labor shortages are likely to develop, for a number of reasons, in various commercialized agricultural areas and in highly industrialized areas. A pattern for the movement of such appropriate labor supply has been developed in Europe since World War I through bilateral arrangements between the sending and receiving countries. Further international policies and facilities will doubtless be developed.

Finally, as long as there are great physical catastrophes and as long as there is man's gross inhumanity to his fellowman, humane people will have to permit and facilitate some movement of the captives, the homeless and stateless, the displaced, oppressed, discriminated against, and persecuted, and those facing possible liquidation to safe harbors either in the form of feasible colonies in new lands or, what is more likely and desirable in most instances, to culturally and industrially advanced countries (since, especially in the case of political and religious refugees, the people often have widely usable skills and services to offer) .[23]

[23] On the resettlement of refugees and displaced persons see United Nations, Department of Public Information, *What the UN is Doing for Refugees and Displaced Persons* (New York: 1948); I. Ferenczi, "Relocation of Europeans," *Annals Am. Acad. Pol. and Soc. Sci.,* 237 (Jan., 1945): 172-182; E. M. Kulischer, "Displaced Persons in the Modern World," *Annals Am. Acad. Pol. and Soc. Sci.,* 262 (March, 1949) : 166-178; P. M. Malin, "The Refugee: A Problem of International Organization," *International Org.,* 1 (Sept., 1947): 443-460; Marjorie Villiers, "The Displaced Person: A Twentieth Century Phenomenon," *Quarterly Rev.,* 286 (Jan., 1948): 83-93; G. L. Warren, "Refugees and Displaced Persons," in *The New International Yearbook: A Compendium of the World's Progress for the Year 1948* (New York: Funk and Wagnalls, 1949) , pp. 472-474; "Finding Homes for Europe's 600,000 Refugees," *UN Bulletin,* 5 (Aug. 15, 1948) : 685-686; "International Refugee Organization," *UN News,* 3 (May, 1948): 38; "What Future for the Refugees?" *UN News,* 3 (Oct., 1948): 72; "International Refugee Organization," *UN News,* 4 (Feb., 1949): 16.

In the kind of interlocking world in which we live the facilitating of all kinds of population movement across international political boundaries, whether of settlers for undeveloped territories, of workers to relieve labor shortages, or of refugees, exchanges, and displaced persons, is increasingly the responsibility of some international authority. The International Labor Organization, first of the League of Nations and now of the United Nations, has played a partial but notable part thus far. Its ability and responsibility, along with other temporary and permanent international and United Nations organizations, in selecting migrants, facilitating and safeguarding the actual movement, and securing satisfactory economic settlement and social treatment in the receiving areas, are likely to increase.[24]

[24] Cf. "International Migration," *Population Index* (Princeton Univ.), 14 (April, 1948) : 97-104. The Interdivisional Committee on Migration of the Economic and Social Council of the United Nations, in cooperation with the International Labor Organization and other specialized agencies, issued a report on the *Allocation of Functions Among the Various Organs Concerned in the Field of Migration* (Social Commission, Third Session, Item 4f of the Draft Agenda, Economic and Social Council E/CN.5/40. 10 February, 1948). The fundamental assumption of this Committee was that ". . . migration, if properly directed and organized, can be of great economic and social usefulness as a part of the economic and social policy of the countries concerned" (p. 11). The Report points out that the proper allocation of international responsibilities and the coordination of programs and activities in the field require a larger measure of international cooperation in fulfilling the following functions: (1) information; (2) advising on migration schemes and their financing; (3) international placement of manpower; (4) simplification of formalities and reduction of costs; (5) protection of the social and economic rights of migrant workers; and (6) protection of the rights of migrants as citizens and aliens. On "Regulated Migration" see also Kulischer, pp. 318-325.

BIBLIOGRAPHY

BERNARD, W. S. *American Immigration Policy: A Reappraisal*. New York: Harpers, 1950. Pp. 199-231.

BORRIE, W. D. *Population Trends and Policies*. Sydney: Australian Pub. Co., 1948, Pp. 237-244.

BOWMAN, ISAIAH (ed.). *The Limits of Land Settlement*. New York: Council on Foreign Relations, 1937. Introduction, pp. 1-5.

CARR-SAUNDERS, A. M. *World Population*. Oxford: Clarendon Press, 1936. Pp. 46-58, 145-225, 306-319.

CHANDRASEKHAR, S. *Hungry People and Empty Lands*. New York: Macmillan, 1955.

CLARK, GROVER. *A Place in the Sun*. New York: Macmillan, 1936. Pp. 85-91, 109-110, and Chaps. VII-VIII.

DAVIE, M. R. *World Immigration*. New York: Macmillan, 1936.

DAVIS, KINGSLEY. *The Population of India and Pakistan*. Princeton: Princeton Univ. Press, 1951. Pp. 93-123.

DIXON, R. B. "Migrations: Primitive." *Encyc. Soc. Sci*. New York: Macmillan, 1933. Vol. 10, pp. 420-425.

ECKLER, A. R., and JACK ZLOTNIK. "Immigration and the Labor Force." *Annals Am. Acad. Pol. & Soc. Sci.*, 262 (March, 1949) : 92-101.

ELDRIDGE, HOPE T. *Population Policies: A Survey of Recent Developments*. Washington: International Union for the Scientific Study of Population, 1954. Pp. 78-96.

FAIRCHILD, H. P. *People*. New York: Holt, 1939. Pp. 227-240.

————. "Postwar Population Problems," *Soc. Forces*, 23 (Oct., 1944): 1-6.

————. "Public Opinion on Immigration." *Annals Am. Acad. Pol. & Soc. Sci.*, 262 (March, 1949): 185-192.

FERENCZI, IMRE. "Migrations: Modern." *Encyc. Soc. Sci*. New York: Macmillan, 1933. Vol. 10, pp. 429-440.

————. "New Factors in Migration and Settlement," in *Regionalism and World Organization*. Washington: American Council on Public Affairs, 1944. Pp. 129-146.

FORSYTH, W. D. *The Myth of the Open Spaces*. Melbourne Univ. Press, 1942. Pp. 5-9.

GLASS, D. V. *Population Policies and Movements*. London: Oxford Univ. Press, 1940.

GRATTAN, C. HARTLEY. "Postwar Migration: A Mirage." *Harper's*, 118 (Dec., 1943) : 24-33.

FLUGEL, J. C. "Population Policies and International Tensions." *Sociological Rev.* (Brit.), 44 (1952); Sec. 1.

HALPHEN, LOUIS. "Migrations: Ancient and Medieval." *Encyc. Soc. Sci*. New York: Macmillan, 1933. Vol. 10, pp. 425-429.

HANSEN, M. L. *The Atlantic Migration: 1607-1860*. Cambridge: Harvard Univ. Press, 1940.

HUTCHINSON, E. P., and W. E. MOORE. "Pressures and Barriers in Future Migration." *Annals Am. Acad. Pol. & Soc. Sci.*, 237 (Jan., 1945): 164-171.

ISAACS, J. *Economics of Migration.* New York: Oxford Univ. Press, 1947.

KIRK, DUDLEY, and EARL HUYCK. "Overseas Migration from Europe since World War II." *Am. Soc. Rev.,* 19 (Aug., 1954): 447-456.

KUCZYNSKI, R. R. *Population Movements.* New York: Oxford Univ. Press, 1936.

KULISCHER, E. M. *Europe on the Move.* New York: Columbia Univ. Press, 1948. Pp. 8-29, 318-325.

LORIMER, FRANK. "Issues in Population Policy." *Annals Am. Acad. Pol. & Soc. Sci.,* 237 (March, 1945): 193-195.

MEADOWS, PAUL. "The Right to Migrate." *Soc. Science,* 27 (Jan., 1952) : 23-26.

MOORE, W. E. "Economic Limits of International Resettlement." *Am. Soc. Rev.,* 10 (April, 1945) : 274-281, esp. 277-281.

PENROE, E. F. *Population Theories and Their Application, with Special Reference to Japan.* Stanford, Calif.: Food Research Institute, 1934. Pp. 173-305.

Postwar Problems of Migration. New York: Milbank Memorial Fund, 1942. See especially: Irene B. Taeuber, "Migration and the Potential Population of Monsoon Asia," pp. 7-29; Kingsley Davis, "Future Migration into Latin America," pp. 30-48; Dudley Kirk, "European Migrations: Prewar Trends and Future Prospects," pp. 49-73; Carter Goodrich, "Possibilities and Limits of International Control of Migration," pp. 74-81; E. P. Hutchinson, "The Present Status of our Immigration Laws and Policies," pp. 82-94; W. S. Thompson, "The Demographic and Economic Implications of Larger Immigration," pp. 95-109; M. R. Davie, "Recent Refugee Immigration from Europe," pp. 110-123.

REED, S. W. "World Population Trends," in Ralph Linton (ed.), *Most of the World: The Peoples of Africa, Latin America, and the East Today.* New York: Columbia Univ. Press, 1949. Pp. 131-137.

RIPLEY, JOSEPHINE. *Peoples on the Move.* Geneva: Office of Public Information, Intergovernmental Committee for European Migration, 1955.

SAUER, C. O. "The Prospects for Redistribution of Population," in Bowman, pp. 7-24.

STALEY, EUGENE. *World Economy in Transition.* New York: Council on Foreign Relations, 1939. Pp. 187-294.

TAFT, D. R., and RICHARD ROBBINS. *International Migration: The Immigrant in the Modern World.* New York: Ronald, 1955.

THOMAS, BRINLEY. *Migration and Economic Growth: A Study of Great Britain and the Atlantic Economy.* New York: Cambridge Univ. Press, 1954.

THOMPSON, W. S. *Plenty of People.* Lancaster, Pa.; Jacques Cattell Press, 1944. Pp. 132-151.

————. *Population and Peace in the Pacific.* Chicago: Univ. of Chicago Press, 1946. Pp. 11-14, 319-343, 462-467.

UNITED NATIONS, Population Division, Department of Social Affairs. *The Determinants and Consequences of Population Trends: A Summary of the Findings of Studies on the Relationships between Population Changes and Economic and Social Conditions* (Population Studies, No. 17) . New York, 1953. Chap. VI, "Economic and Social Factors Affecting Migration," pp. 98-133; Chap. XVI, "Effects of Major Migratory Movements in Modern Times," pp. 288-315.

————, Population Division, Departmnet of Social Affairs, *International Research on Migration.* New York, 1953. Cites and briefly describes the

extensive array of studies of international migration issued by, and the problems treated by, various regional and special commissions of the United Nations, and by the International Labor Office, UNESCO, the International Bank
for Reconstruction and Development, the Food and Agricultural Organization,
and the World Health Organization.

————, Population Division, Department of Social Affairs. *Population Bull.*,
No. 1 (Dec., 1951). New York, 1952. Pp. 13-20. Bibliography on migration,
pp. 29-30.

————, Statistical Office, Department of Economic Affairs. *Demographic
Yearbook, 1951.* New York, 1951. Pp. 38-39, 540-564.

WANDER, HILDE. *The Importance of Emigration for the Solution of Population
Problems in Western Europe.* The Hague: Martinus Nijhoff, 1951.

WIGNY, P. "Migratory Movements in Underdeveloped Countries in Course of Industrialization." *Int. Labour Rev.,* 68 (July, 1953): 1-13.

WOYTINSKY, W. S. and E. S. *World Population and Production: Trends and Outlook.* New York: Twentieth Century Fund, 1953. Pp. 66-110.   An especially
detailed treatment with much pertinent statistical material.

YOUNG, C. W. "Chinese Immigration and Colonization in Manchuria," in W. L. G.
Joerg (ed.), *Pioneer Settlement.* New York: American Geographical Society,
1932. Pp. 333-359.

9

World Fertility Reduction

THE BACKGROUND SITUATION

There is a growing groundswell of concern regarding the balance between world population on the one side and world resources, technological capacities, and institutional facilities on the other. The torrential rate of population increase threatens a great distortion of the elements of the relationship. The numerous persons and organizations concerned are seeking both an improvement of conditions among the countries so obviously suffering from this lack of balance and an easing of world population pressure with its persistent menace of unrest and conflict.

We have examined modernization both as a means of greatly extending and improving the utilization of the world's resources and as a very important factor in bringing death rates under a considerable degree of control over much of the world. We have also noted that to a lesser extent it has been a factor in bringing about an occasional reduction of birth rates through the operation of motivations stimulated by modernization and through controls implemented more effectively by its accompanying technology. Such fertility control, however, has been confined mainly to certain Western nations, especially those whose modernization processes started first. And, as noted, the effects of modernization in the form of fertility control in the West came very slowly, with a century or more elapsing before there was noticeable evidence of such control.

— The various possibilities of increasing the food supply for the ever-expanding population of the earth have been examined. Granted were the possibility and even the likelihood of a very considerable extension of agriculture to lands at present unusued or used only in a limited degree, and of a greater output from present agricultural land by means of more intensive and efficient utilization and the extension of conservation practices. Also of some promise were additions to the food supply of substances not now included as such, more extensive and intensive use of only partially tapped sources, such as the waters of the earth, and resort to foods synthetically created by modern science and technology. But we had to admit that such possibilities and probabilities were not unlimited. All such expansions would ultimately mean increasing costs, and in many instances they would accelerate the exhaustion of the supply of essential resources. No increases of food supply, however achieved, could forever take care of an ever-growing population. The intellectual and creative powers whereby men have produced the miracles of science and technology are limited. At any rate, such improvements can be only temporary in effect. Attempts to compensate indefinitely on the economic and technological side are bound to fail because resources are finite, even with the considerable extension to be had from better stewardship. We are in no wise, however, suggesting any relaxation of the efforts to increase the food supply.

We have also examined emigration as a possible means of reducing population pressure in the overpopulated and underdeveloped countries of the world. There is the possibility that certain countries can absorb, even encourage, the influx of the *right kind* of immigrants. Canada, Brazil, and some of the other Latin American countries have been doing this since World War II. But such migrants are carefully selected, come mainly from Europe, and at most amount to only several millions. The real problem is the surplus peasant peoples of the overcrowded Eastern lands, and their migration, as noted, would have to run to tens and scores of millions to offer any relief. At best, migration would be only a temporary palliative in the emigrant country. It was pointed out that migration on any adequate scale is impracticable, even impossible, primarily on physical and economic grounds, though also for cultural reasons. All likely target areas are exercising rigorous immigration control. Attention might also be called to the fact that if international migration were free and feasible in any considerable volume in the present world, it would doubtless tend to fill up the "good" places in a short period of time and hasten the *world-wide* appearance of M (Malthus) Day.

Parenthetically, it might be remarked that if population goes on increasing and if diminishing returns and increasing costs in a finite world become more and more acute, the standard of living and of well-being in Western civilization, as well as in all the rest of the world, will inevitably decline.

Since a potential and progressive worsening of world population conditions is something to be avoided at all costs, it behooves us to examine one other possible alleviative, if not corrective, namely, the limiting of fertility and the resultant slowing up of the rate of population increase. This is an approach to the whole matter from the other side of the equation. It would seem that *something must also be done on the population side* if the worsening is to be halted. As we have already noted, a redundant and rapidly growing population has a decidedly adverse effect on modernization and food-increase programs. A fact of specific pertinence is that increasing the food supply by whatever means is at best only a *temporary* way of alleviating hunger in the overpopulated countries and offers no way of improving the per-capita quantitative and qualitative food situation of the world *unless birth rates are stabilized.* The same holds true with respect to any of the other tried and suggested means of appeasing persistent population growth. It seems almost axomatic, all factors considered, that the control of population is a prerequisite to the promotion of present and future welfare.

It should also be pointed out that the problem of population growth, especially in the overpopulated areas of the earth, is not a matter that can be worked out leisurely through several centuries, but one insistently requiring treatment here and now. It is very questionable whether particular countries or the world as a whole can wait until modernization and prosperity bring down the birth rates in the most overpopulated countries, because, as Sir Charles

Darwin has said, "Everything happens in the wrong order."[1] There is more than a lurking danger that unless fairly direct and expeditious action is taken soon, nature will act in a characteristically ruthless manner by matching increasing birth rates with increasing death rates.[2]

Demographic theory, with its well-established facts and principles, points out that there are only three ways of retarding the growth rate in any particular country or area, namely, raising the death rate, encouraging and effecting emigration, and lowering the birth rate. For the world as a whole only the first and third ways are effective. Deliberately raising death rates or permitting them to rise if avoidable is unthinkable. Health and longevity are ends in themselves. To reduce either is to violate the fundamental ethical aims relating to the sanctity of life and to counter many of the arduously bought gains of humane endeavor. Both are inherent aspects of a high standard of living, and upon them depends an array of other precious social and cultural objectives. Particularly abhorrent is the thought of increasing the death rate in order to improve the standard of living and the amenities of life for the survivors. Therefore, the problem in the underdeveloped countries is how to stop population growth before a rise in mortality automatically halts it. The only humane alternative is, if possible, to bring about some limitation of fertility.[3]

POPULATION CONTROL

Contrary to widespread belief, the concept of population control is not new. Such control involves both population policies and population practices. A population *policy* consists of a body of population objectives of a quantitative and/or qualitative nature, usually divised and declared by political agents. It is designed to

---

[1] P. 143.

[2] Paul B. Sears has pointedly presented the situation. "The curve of population growth in an inexorable thing—either we control it or nature does . . . . Morality entails responsibility for all foreseeable consequences, a heavy burden when science enlarges the scope of our vision.

"Better stewardship alone can only buy us time to face the ultimate problem of a rational adjustment between population and the resources which must sustain it." In P. K. Hatt (ed.), *World Population and Future Resources* (New York: American Book Co., 1952), pp. 124-125.

[3] Davis, *Population of India and Pakistan*, pp. 222-224. See also Brown, pp. 86-87.

produce a more satisfactory situation with respect to population in relation to other prized ends—social, economic, political, military, ethical, religious, and others. This array of population objectives is usually accompanied by a whole complex of political measures which are resorted to in order to attain them. Population *practices* are what the people actually *do* in the form of reproductive behavior in conformity with, or in spite of, such formulated policies as may exist. Frequently the policies and practices are far apart. The practices may also be employed with or without the sanction of the mores or the religious dictates of the people. Various peoples of ancient, recent, and modern civilizations have had and still have population policies. These policies, and practices, have been both restrictive and expansive. The policies have been predominantly expansive and the practices often restrictive.

RESTRICTIVE PRACTICES

The restrictive practices, as Thompson has pointed out,[4] have constituted the more important element in population control in human history. Various primitive peoples engaged, knowingly or unknowingly, in practices which tended to keep numbers within the limits not only of the food supply during the worst season of the year but also with in the worst phase of their climatic cycle. These have consisted of practices which reduced the likelihood of conception, such as certain mutilations of the genital organs during the initiation ceremonies, taboos on sexual intercourse at certain times, and crude, though sometimes fairly effective, efforts at contraception. Much more efficient in keeping down numbers were the practices which made for elimination after conception or after birth, such as abortion, infanticide, and the killing or abandoning of the aged, the crippled, and the sick. The people of the great ancient civilizations—the Egyptians, Hebrews, Hindus, Chinese, Greeks, Romans, Teutonic tribes—all resorted to abortion and infanticide, often on a rather wide scale. Some had fairly effective ways of preventing, or at least interfering with, conception. In later times, including the present, abortion has been widely practiced and contraception has achieved increasing vogue, especially during the last three-quarters of a century. Infanticide still seems

[4] Pp. 9-10.

to be rather widely resorted to among some of the over-populated peoples.[5]

These restrictive practices, in many instances, were aspects of folk life. The customs and the mores sanctioned or at least did not violently oppose them. Even the most inhumane from our point of view, such as infanticide and abortion, were publicly recognized and socially condoned in Greece and Rome. However, all of these means were practiced privately by the people on their own initiative; hence, they were not systematically or consistently engaged in, especially by the segments of populations that needed limitation most. There was little, if any, publicly expressed desire for the use of the means or for the ends served by them, no established policy regarding them, and no programmatic action of governmental or semi-public organizations to encourage or force the people to conform. In fact, where there was any perceptible public action, it was most likely to be critical or prohibitory in intent.

There is no evidence that any independent nation or imperial power ever seriously undertook measures to check excessively rapid population increases.[6] Thompson states that he knows of no country which is now following deliberate policies intended to *reduce the size* of the population, although the emigration policies of England and the Netherlands seem to indicate a belief that smaller populations would be better. He also points out that there have

[5] On the prevalence of these restrictive practices see H. Aptekar, *Anjea: Infanticide, Abortion, and Contraception in Savage Society* (New York: W. Goodwin, 1931); A. M. Carr-Saunders, *The Population Problem: A Study in Human Evolution* (Oxford: Clarendon Press, 1922), pp. 135-242; S. F. Cook, "Survivorship in Aboriginal Populations," *Human Biology* 19 (Feb., 1947): 83-89; G. Devereux, *A Study of Abortion in Primitive Societies: A Typological, Distributional and Dynamic Analysis of the Prevention of Birth in 400 Pre-Industrial Societies* (New York: Julian Press, 1955); M. S. Handman, "Abortion," *Encyc. Soc. Sci.* (New York: Macmillan, 1930), Vol. 1, pp. 372-374; F. H. Hankins, "Birth Control," *Encyc. Soc. Sci.* (1930), Vol. 2, pp. 559-565; Himes; A. M. Hocart, "Infanticide," *Encyc. Soc. Sci.* (1932), Vol. 8, pp. 27-28; Ludwig Krzywicki, *Primitive Society and Its Vital Statistics* (London: Macmillan, 1934); Lorimer *et al*, pp. 91-114; E. B. Reuter, *Population Problems* (Philadelphia: Lippincott, 1937), pp. 132-138; Thompson, pp. 10-14.

Among ancient Jews, on contraception see *Genesis* 38:8-9; on infanticide see *Leviticus* 18:21; *Deuteronomy* 12:31; *II Kings* 3:27, 16:3; *II Chronicles* 28:3, 33:6; *Psalm* 106:38; *Isaiah* 57:5; *Jeremiah* 19:5; *Ezekiel* 16:20-21.

[6] See, e.g., Lorimer, 1945.

been only a few, and rather exceptional, tentative official efforts *to reduce the rate of growth.*[7]

EXPANSIONIST POLICIES

On the other hand, population *expansion* and the effort to stimulate increase has been a matter of widespread public policy since early times. Throughout the historic period the ruling groups, especially the political and military leaders, have desired large and growing populations as abundant manpower for engaging in war and expanding over wider territory, as a redundant and submissive labor supply, as a body of consumers, and for other obvious dynastic, nationalistic, imperialistic, and economic reasons. Religious bodies have with few exceptions sought a larger number of adherents, both by proselyting and reproduction. Religious support has undergirded pro-natalism with presumed spiritual and ethical sanctions.

As illustrations of these attempts by precise policy to encourage increase, mention might be made of the efforts of some of the Greek city-states, notably Sparta and Athens, certain laws of Caesar, Augustus, Nerva, and Trajan in Rome, the expansionist policies of the Cameralists and Mercantilists, epitomized, for example, in the Spanish Edict of 1623 under Philip IV and the French Edict of 1666 under Colbert, and the almost universal policies of nineteenth and twentieth century European nations—not to mention the specific efforts of recent totalitarian regimes, such as those of Mussolini, Hitler, and the Soviet Union. At the present time the pro-natalist inducements, among most of the countries employing such policies, consist of various easements and bonuses, taking such forms as family allowances, home-furnishing loans and even grants, measures intended to reduce the personal or family expenses associated with childbirth (such as state maternity insurance and maternity relief), graduated income taxes and property taxes to ease the family financial burdens of the less wealthy classes, preferential government employment of heads of large families, taxes on bachelors, legislation prohibiting abortion and the giving of contraceptive information, marriage and birth premiums, and special educational assistance for the children of large families.

[7] P. 457. India has been governmentally concerned since 1947 with the reduction of the rate of population growth, as will be noted below.

Reproduction, however, is a matter of private inclination and practice—something quite apart from directives, decrees, and inducements. While in a few historical instances some population increase could be specifically attributed to the policies (with their attendant reward systems), in the main the conclusion as to the effectiveness of pro-natalist policies must be that of the Englishman Joseph Townsend after he had examined the effect of the Spanish Edict of 1623: "In vain!"[8] Generally, the population of given peoples has not only maintained itself but invariably tended to grow into every "gain" quite without incitement from pro-natalist policies.

FERTILITY REDUCTION AS A MEANS OF RETARDING POPULATION INCREASE

Death rates are falling everywhere among the peoples of the underdeveloped countries. Individuals of all social and economic levels are most enthusiastic about efforts to reduce deaths; semi-public and governmental policy supports such measures; and public action is effective in bringing about such reductions. We can anticipate still more marked reductions in the near future through the efforts of such semi-public organizations as the Rockefeller Foundation and such international agencies as WHO, FAO, UNESCO, UNICEF (UN International Childrens' Emergency Fund), UN Technical Assistance Administration, and certain organizations of the Economic and Social Council. These international agencies aid and cooperate with those of the various countries in the eradication of mass diseases like malaria, yaws, syphilis, tuberculosis, dysentery, diarrhea, and enteritis, and in the control of the epidemic diseases like typhus, cholera, yellow fever, smallpox, and bubonic plague by means of the ever-improving antiseptics, insecticides, rodenticides, and especially the antibiotics. More widely diffused knowledge regarding simple sanitation, hygiene, and feeding principles will continue to lower infant and child mortality rates—the area in which the greatest gains in reducing death rates appear.

We also can anticipate the reduction of mortality from famine through the further development of agriculture, transportation, and methods of international trade; through the improvement of housing, clothing, and other physical aids to improved health;

---

[8] On expansionist practices and policies see the classic works by Glass, 1936 and 1940.

through the general extension of community health facilities and services (such as refuse removal and sewage disposal and purification of water supply), hospitals, and medical research; and through general education and health training.

All this means an even further gap between birth and death rates and an accelerated rate of population increase. The only possibility of countering this situation is to bring about a corresponding fertility limitation. In the modern world death control must be paralleled by birth control. Yet everywhere, even in Western society, fertility control lags behind mortality control. The fact of the matter, however, is that in the long run the control of mortality is impossible without the control of fertility. But fertility limitation is not easy—on a world scale; the problems are numerous and vast.

THE IMPORTANCE OF FERTILITY CONTROL

In most of the Group II and all of the Group III countries extensive fertility control leading to stationary or declining numbers offers the chief immediate possibility of raising the scale of living, or even of preserving the traditional levels. In the end, these peoples have only one choice: if numbers are not limited by exercising control over birth rates, they will be limited by mounting death rates.

ITS RELATIVE DESIRABILITY

Fertility limitation by contraception is *the only acceptable means* of reducing the rate of increase, and thus of avoiding the Malthusian Dilemma. The other means most widely used by the depressed classes, abortion and infanticide, while they are extremely effective in reducing numbers, are physiologically most expensive and dangerous, produce suffering and hardships, and cannot be condoned morally. Both are frightful acts of desperation on the part of those practicing them. Sterilization, while desirable as a means of preventing the reproduction of defectives, and while eagerly sought, especially by the women of overpopulated countries,[9] cannot be

---

[9] Note, for example, the widespread resort to sterilization as a means of avoiding fertility among the women of Puerto Rico. See P. K. Hatt, *Backgrounds of Human Fertility in Puerto Rico* (Princeton: Princeton Univ. Press, 1952) ; J. M. Stycos, "Family and Fertility in Puerto Rico," *Am. Soc. Rev.*, 17 (Oct., 1952):

acceptable as a general limitation policy or practice, for the reason that those sterilized have lost choice in reproduction. In the case of contraception, on the other hand, reproduction is not abolished, and its practice seldom renders a woman less likely to conceive when a child is desired The number of children produced is to a considerable degree a voluntary matter; the size of the family is planned; the pregnancies can be spaced in the interests of maternal health, family economy, and child health and opportunity It simply means that by the exercise of care unwanted pregnancies can be avoided before they occur

Contraception is a relatively easy, humane, and apparently effective means of adjusting reproduction to the means and ends of living. There is considerable evidence that *the practice of birth control and the use of other historical means of keeping numbers in check exist in inverse ratio to each other.* In Western countries, among those population segments or classes or special interest groups that do not have a knowledge of, or an effective means of, birth control, or among whom the practice is forbidden, the incidence of abortion is higher than among those where this is not the case. Among the more underdeveloped countries this relationship seems to prevail with respect to both abortion and infanticide. The situation seems to resolve itself into *a choice between contraception and some kind of murder.*

Contraception is also an inexpensive means of keeping population within resources. The costs of teaching birth control methods to the most illiterate and poverty-striken peasants of the most "backward" countries and of supplying them with the relatively simple devices would be infinitesimal compared with the really fearful cost of feeding, clothing, educating, housing, and employing unwanted millions of people for whom food and other stark necessities are now in short supply and who are likely to die young. Says Bliven: "It would be interesting to speculate on what would have been the result if, say, one-half of all the Marshall Plan and Point-Four money had, from the beginning, been devoted to the teaching of contraception." [10]

572-580; J. M. Stycos, "Female Sterilization in Puerto Rico," *Eugenics Quart.,* 1 (June, 1954): 3-9; R. C. Cook, "Puerto Rico's New Look," *Population Bulletin,* 11 (April, 1955): 17-29, esp. 25-27.
[10] P. 35.

A GREAT HUMAN BOON

While population growth is finally determined by the natural limitations of the means of survival and the agents of death, in the more advanced societies both births and deaths are controlled in large part not by nature or by predeterming biological factors, but rather by social and cultural factors. As Landis has put it, "Man is a self-domesticated creature; his biological behavior with regard to vital processes is a product of this domestication as well as of natural laws."[11] His reproductive practices reflect, not always public, but folk values, and they regulate and define his behavior. Sooner or later most of them get into the mores and even become institutionalized.

Contraception is one of the man-made instrumentalities for well-being. Increasingly people are coming to regard it as one of the major events of human history.[12] This ability to control population growth through conscious, deliberate, humane, and physiologically economical restriction of the birth rate is now one of the great human powers. Its potentialities for human welfare are measureless. It makes possible an intelligent, painless, and hygienic direction of human families. Wise, realistic, consistent, and socially minded people accept it as such.

IS CONTRACEPTION UNNATURAL, UNSOCIAL, OR IMMORAL?

One of the contentions that often arise in the controversy over birth control is that it is "unnatural" and hence undesirable. If birth control as a means of rationally controlling population growth is "unnatural," then the direct and effective techniques that medical science has developed for controlling epidemics, plagues, and diseases, the technological means of manipulating plant and animal growth, and the development of means of transportation which reduce the incidence of famine are also "unnatural." Disease, epidemic, and famine are "natural"; they have been reduced only through human contrivance and artifice. This is true of almost every boon that man has enjoyed in adjusting himself satisfactorily to nature. Birth control is an equally "unnatural" and artificial method of ameliorating human suffering, forced upon men because

[11] P. 51.
[12] Thompson, pp. 197-198.

of the efficacy of the other great and successful "unnatural" procedures. It simply means that the size and growth of human communities can be brought under the control of the distinctly human faculties of foresight, reason, and self-control.[13]

Man, in the self-assumed role of manipulator and controller of natural phenomena, has the stern *dual* responsibility of balancing *death* control and *birth* control. He cannot allow nature to resolve the issue.

Contraception is also sometimes said to be unsocial or antisocial. The fear is expressed that a general knowledge of contraception would lead to "race suicide," that is, to population decline so rapid and general as to destroy or endanger the existence of the societies in which it is practiced. A very widespread experience with birth control among the Western countries, amounting in some cases to nearly a century, among Eastern countries, notably Japan, and among some members of the upper classes of other countries demonstrates the utter folly of such a contention. To approve it or practice it is in no sense a revolt against parenthood; in fact, since it gives control over conception, it becomes an expression of fine parenthood—the instrument of parents who love children, who have the number they want, and who nurture them according to the needs and values and conditions of their community.

Finally, it is occasionally referred to as "immoral." But we have seen that too many people for resources means masses of people living at a mean physical and cultural level; it means relative degradation and misery; it means large-scale, though indirect, murder for many. Can modern methods whereby man has the means of avoiding or ameliorating such conditions as malnutrition, starvation, famine, and endemic disease really be considered "immoral"? Is a humane means of balancing the equation immoral? The aura of immorality around contraception, often crystallized in ethical, religious, political, and legal opposition, has caused it to make its way, especially in Western society, secretively and shamefacedly. But it has made its way as a widespread private practice. In recent years here and there (the Netherlands, Sweden, Britain, India) it has been openly recognized, by authoritative public recommendation, as permissible and desirable.

[13] Cf. Fairchild, p. 141; Brown, pp. 236-238; Field, pp. 322-324.

While there is strong opposition to some kinds of contraception by certain great religious bodies, it should be recalled that the practice has survived two thousand years of religious condemnation in the West. Today the Roman Catholic Church condemns vigorously all artificial means for preventing conception. However, priests have been giving absolution in the confessional for some time to couples resorting to the rhythm method of fertility control, which consists of using the presumably "safe" period in the menstrual cycle. A number of books on the rhythm method have been published with imprimatur within the present decade.[14] Furthermore, it is the experience of birth control clinics in the United States that Catholic women attend the clinics in about the same ratio as non-Catholic women; and various studies, by both Catholics and non-Catholics, indicate that the Catholic birth rate fluctuates in about the same manner as that among other groups of the same educational and social status, though running about one point higher. There also is some reason for believing that the great religious bodies that oppose communism may soon begin to look more favorably on birth control as a means of relieving the poverty and land pressure in the crowded areas of the earth. In recent years in the United States many Protestant and some Jewish groups have not only come to accept the current mores on birth control, but have reversed their older stand of opposition and rallied to its support. Such knowledge cannot be suppressed, once it is abroad among intelligent people, in spite of antagonistic legislation or religious officials. Sooner or later religious and moral objections wither and disappear.

Contraception is an adjustive response to a stern problem. It has spread in the Western world because it supplies a crucial human need, and it will spread elsewhere, since the need is continuous, universal, and imperative.

THE NECESSITY FOR WORLD-WIDE FAMILY LIMITATION

In this world of interdependent and interlocking nations and peoples population problems anywhere are world problems. The present crisis in human fertility in relation to existing resources and falling death rates involves all people. Hence, questions of

---

[14] Regarding the Catholic position see Bliven, pp. 29-35; Brown, pp. 93-95.

population policy and procedure can only be dealt with realistically in the light of their world-wide effects. This principle applies no less to family limitation. The countries exercising some degree of effective fertility control need to hold such gains as they have made in general well-being. The countries showing little or no fertility control need to advance as rapidly as possible in this respect in order to raise themselves to world standards of well-being. The nations that restrict their increase have reason to fear their crowded, hungry, and prolific world neighbors. Moreover, they are ready targets for those who encourage philosophies and activities that are subversive of world peace. The countries in which population is controlled cannot forever appease the overpopulated countries by contributing gifts of various kinds to their maintenance. In the end the equalizing of conditions depends in very considerable degree upon world-wide family limitation and upon all of the scientific, technological, economic, cultural, and social procedures that contribute to this end directly or indirectly. But this is not a small or an easy task.

OBSTACLES TO FAMILY LIMITATION

Not only many people of the Western world, but also some special segments of Eastern peoples have some appreciation of family limitation and practice it. Its wide diffusion, however, especially among the great masses of overpopulated peoples, is blocked by a variety of obstacles in the form of organizational viewpoints and activities and adverse physical and socio-cultural conditions.

ORGANIZATIONAL VIEWPOINTS AND ACTIVITIES

Some of the obstacles inhere in the ideologies and activities of various large groups and organizations. There are certain economic groups that desire large populations and cheer mounting population statistics. Among some of these groups there is the industrial demand for a cheap and abundant labor supply, though this demand is rapidly disappearing because of mechanization in advanced countries. Among others there is the mercantile desire for more customers. The more astute realize, however, that this argument is without validity in the heavily populated and rapidly increasing countries, where low incomes create very limited purchasing power. By such reasoning, India should be at this moment one of the best markets in the world, not only for food, but for all sorts of capital equipment and a great volume of other consumer goods.

Nations, not only in the past, but right now, seem to identify size and growth of population with national greatness and strength, including especially strength in military manpower. There has even been a tendency to equate national vitality with the size and diversity of population and the rapidity of breeding. Hence, according to this viewpoint, to control parenthood would mean a decline in national greatness and military proficiency. As noted, to the extent that politically organized groups have population policies, these are preponderantly pro-natalist. The spread of birth control information has been made difficult by making it illegal, even in some of the most advanced countries. Only recently, as will be noted below, some attention has been given by nations to qualitative and restrictive considerations. If this political contention is carried to its ultimate conclusion, it contemplates the achievement of national greatness by the nation's eventually overrunning and inundating the earth with its population torrent. That such thinking is inconsistent with the precious notions of world brotherhood and equalization of opportunity and well-being is apparent.

Certain religous bodies, such as Roman Catholicism and some Islamic sects, carry on organized opposition to at least certain forms of birth control. It must be pointed out, however, that some of the great world religions which include among their nominal adherents vast portions of the overpopulated peoples of the earth, such as Hinduism and Buddism, seem to be passive rather than directly antagonistic to birth control.[15]

Repeatedly, race or nationality groups, dominated by their tribal feeling of superior worth, have encouraged their people to increase and multiply and hence inherit the earth. Needless to say, restrictive suggestions are coolly received by those maintaining such ethnocentric notions. Most of these viewpoints offend our present-day sense of decency and fair play; they violate many of our most precious values regarding freedom, well-being, and brotherhood;

---

[15] On the relation of different religions to fertility in general, including especially the different Christian groups, see Lorimer *et al.*, pp. 183-198.

most of them are specious when examined realistically. Above all, they violate the notion of a *quality* of human life.

ADVERSE PHYSICAL AND SOCIO-CULTURAL CONDITIONS

The very poverty and economic backwardness of most of the people of the overpopulated countries create a host of unfavorable conditions. Because of the low economic level of living and the present sharply limited economic "reach" of the people, there are lacking among them those social-economic objectives that have been the prime motivating factors in family limitation. The apathy, ignorance, and lethargy that so often accompany poverty induce a sense of indifference to the possibilities of economic and social progress and hence reduce the possibility of its achievement.

As has been noted repeatedly in other connections, the population of the underdeveloped countries consists mostly of peasant-agrarian peoples. Farm living and peasant life are generally conducive to large families. Sexual activity is a continual preoccupation among them. Often it is one of the few forms of recreation afforded by the impoverished life, and it is usually looked upon, especially among the men, as a sign of vitality and manhood. High-fertility, pronatalist values and beliefs are deepseated in the socio-cultural way of life. The perpetuation of traditional folkways and mores inhibits the spread of family limitation. In addition to these factors, the traditional, self-contained agrarian life and the solidarity of rural peasant groups tend to make them impervious to strange new ideas and practices.

Among some of these peoples, especially in India and China, the group or extended-family system prevails; this is not only an obstacle to modernization in general, as noted in Chapter VI, but also to fertility restriction. The emphasis on perpetuation of lineage, in China taking the form especially of a desire for sons— sons to fulfill a man's obligation to his father and his father's lineage, sons to administer the land and other property—provides a powerful motivation for high fertility and causes many of the people, particularly the males, to be very sceptical of fertility control.

Closely related to this is the traditional fear of barrenness among the women of many of these countries and the dependence of female esteem upon male offspring. The seclusion of these women, along with their general shyness and deepseated conservatism, has made instruction in contraceptive techniques very difficult. Furthermore, family limitation involves the sexual sphere, in which emotion, tradition, and superstition outdistance reason to an even greater extent than in most other fields. And these irrational viewpoints and the attendant compulsions and taboos usually are more prevalent among the large lower-economic classes and the rural segments of the population.

Several very practical difficulties present themselves. A great variety of contraceptive techniques exists; they differ greatly in effectiveness; the best are not necessarily one hundred per cent efficient even in the hands of the most intelligent and cautious; at present the best techniques are, in the main, the most complicated, the most difficult, and the most expensive. What is needed are devices and methods that are simple and practically fool-proof in the hands of ignorant, careless, and improvident people, that are suitable for all climates, and that are so cheap that they can be made available to those living at a bare subsistence minimum. Such a means may be the recently proposed "anti-fertility factor" embodied in a "foam tablet" that can be taken orally and which produces temporary, harmless reproductive ineffectiveness in husband or wife or both. More research is needed along biochemical, physiological, medical, and industrial lines to discover improved techniques of universal applicability. Such research is much less complicated and expensive than that involved in producing atomic bombs. Its possibilities, in a world in which population is "exploding," are as constructive as those of the atomic bomb are destructive. However, in the United States far less money has been spent on research on human reproduction, not to mention fertlity regulation, than has been spent on research on either bovine or plant reproduction.[16]

Flugel wisely points out that while the "perfect" birth control technique has not yet been discovered, there is no reason why the best of the techniques should not become as widely available as possible.[17] Fortunately, the probability that an excellent con-

[16] Cf. Brown, pp. 89-90.
[17] 1952.

traceptive will be in existence within the next few years appears to be very high.

Other serious obstacles to the use of contraceptives, until, for example, the perfected orally taken pill arrives, are inconvenience and lack of privacy. The homes of the poor everywhere are usually small and the living quarters crowded. Among large portions of the overpopulated peoples the homes often consist of only one room. Lack of private sanitary facilities, such as running water and bathrooms, and other conditions that go with congested living interfere with contraceptive practices.

THE DIRECT EFFORT TO INDUCE MORE WIDESPREAD FAMILY LIMITATION

The world population-resources equation, the general lag in the decline of birth rates in relation to declining death rates, and the obstacles to family limitation just noted point to the desirability—in fact, the pressing necessity—of direct and immediate methods of social action in the form of family limitation.[18] Thus far, of course, the change of attitude among a people toward fertility and the increasing practice of birth control have had to wait upon the gradual unfolding of modernization. It has come as an almost automatic effect of the component revolutions. To attempt to introduce birth control in the early stages of modernization would be the reverse of the whole course of development through which the rest of the world has gone in its movement toward fertility control. Therefore, it would seem at first glance to be audacious, even foolish, to propose a deliberate attack upon the problem of family limitation in Group III and Group II countries, and possibly even in some of the less advanced portions of the population of Group I countries. But time is short. It seems extremely hazardous to wait until the effects of the modernization revolutions—technological, industrial, agricultural, urban, democratic—work themselves out in the form of slow, automatic adjustment of the birth rate to the rapidly falling death rate.

[18] The term "family limitation," as often used, implies the use not only of contraception, but also the practices of sterilization and abortion, and the deliberate abstention from sexual intercourse. In this study we are ruling out the latter for the reasons mentioned above. As used here, "family limitation" means the control of family fertility (or reproductive performance) by means of contraception.

Industrialization, the key process of modernization, is itself difficult, involved, and slow. Birth control on a fairly wide scale, however, might be something that could be brought about within the lifetime of the present generation of reproducers. In many of the underdeveloped countries it would seem necessary to have birth control *first,* in order to make possible both the private and community economic easement which is essential if there is to be an economic surplus available for capital development and technological advance. What are the possibilities of a direct attack?

Davis has pointed out that from a purely physical and technical point of view birth control is easier than death control:

> It involves the management of only one type of germ and only one kind of contagion, as against hundreds of types in health work. It involves only one period of life, as against all periods subject to disease; and only one type of medical specialist, as against dozens in fighting sickness. It involves relatively simple and easy principles that the layman can grasp, as against complicated ones that he cannot grasp in general medicine. The money it requires cannot compare to that required for other kinds of medical attention. Indeed, so simple is the process of contraception, so clear the principle, that it is absurd to think that science, which has accomplished so much in so many more complex matters, cannot find suitable techniques for accomplishing this goal. In fact, we know that when there is a will to limit family size, even crude techniques will greatly reduce fertlity.[19]

The greatest obstacles to direct attack are thus not primarily technological but sociological. Is it feasible from the sociological point of view? The social sciences during the present century have accumulated experience and knowledge that may have considerable bearing upon the task of directly and quickly facilitating family limitation. Even though this as pioneering task of a kind and scope not previously engaged in successfully, what kinds of social action promise some degree of success?

It must not be thought that this advocacy of a direct attack ignores the importance of modernization or is offered as a substitute for it. It is suggested as a heretofore untried accompaniment. As rapidly as possible, all possible aid must be given and efforts made

[19] *Population of India and Paksitan,* p. 226.

that will increase the wealth, elevate the standard of living and the level of health, and enhance the quality of life of the less privileged families and peoples of the earth. As we have noted repeatedly, modernization alone has created the over-all physical, social-economic, and social-psychological climate favorable to population control.

GOVERNMENTAL APATHY TOWARD FAMILY LIMITATION

Max Adams, in an unusually astute article which is recommended to the reader, states, "No national or international organization is at present devoting any serious consideration to even pilot experiments to develop ways that might afford direct action to balance births and deaths."[20] There are a few partial exceptions, as will be noted. In the main, however, governmental agencies have not been and are not now interested in bringing about effective family limitation on any considerable scale.

The national legislation that does have some relationship to family limitation in the different countries where it exists is often a rather tangled skein of laws referring not only to prohibited or permitted practices in contraception, but also to abortion and sterilization. National legislation usually opposes abortion as a means of family limitation, but there are differences among the countries as to the degree to which it is actually tolerated and the methods adopted to control it. The legislation which permits sterilization does so mainly on the grounds of eliminating serious hereditary defects, or of protecting health. In general, the legal acceptance of abortion and sterilization rests on medical or eugenic grounds. Also, quite generally, where grounds for abortion or sterilization are recognized, the actual operations require authorization by a stated body, or at least a concurring opinion, before pregnancy may be legally interrupted or a sterilization operation performed. Nevertheless, abortion is widely resorted to privately as a means of family limitation, and sterilization is used in Puerto Rico and Japan for such purposes.

The legislation affecting contraceptives, where not prohibitory, is largely of a regulatory or permissive nature and only occasionally provides positive assistance in the form of information or facilities.

[20] Pp. 173-174.

Sweden is an exception among Western countries. The handling of contraceptives by chemist shops was made obligatory in 1945. Beginning in 1946, information and advice on contraception were made available to women through the maternal welfare centers and to men at venereal disease control centers. The sale of contraceptives is subject to administrative controls that set up minimum standards and prevent the sale of ineffectual or dangerous substances and appliances. The abortion laws were also eased in 1946, enabling women contemplating abortion to come to health and welfare agencies for special advice and assistance.

Japan and India provide the only instances of positive governmental efforts to reduce the rate of population growth. In Japan, the Eugenic Protection Law of 1948, framed in terms of eugenic and therapeutic objectives, extended the grounds for sterilization and abortion considerably beyond those allowed by the Act of 1940 (which permitted abortion only in case of hereditary defect or to save the life of the mother). The total frequency of abortion seems to have increased very considerably. The Diet in 1949 amended the law to provide for the extension of birth control information, and this action was accompanied by a burst of birth control propaganda. In 1952 the discretionary power of physicians in the matter of abortions was extended, and provision was made for the training of midwives, social workers, and nurses in contraceptive techniques. The steady decline of the crude birth rate from 34.3 in 1947 to about 21.5 in 1953 to under 20 in 1955 would seem to indicate that these measures, along with other conducive factors, were having some effect.

The most significant recent governmental development designed to curb fertility is to be found in Group III India. In its First Five Year Plan, adopted in December, 1952, there is full recognition of the need for population control as an aspect of social and economic development. It sets up a program for family limitation, including, among other items, provision in government hospitals and health centers for advice on methods of family limitation; field experiments to determine the suitability, acceptability, and effectiveness of different methods of family planning in various sections of the population; the development of suitable procedures for educating the people on family planning methods; and the collection of information on reproductive patterns and on attitudes and motivations affecting the size of the family. Funds have been allocated for the program.

This plan advocates the rhythm technique, and, it is contended, the instructions and aids have been so worked out that even illiterate women can keep track of their menstrual cycle. This governmental experiment does not conflict with any religion now widely practiced in that country, and the government is planning a tremendous educational campaign along American advertising lines employing the radio, movies, posters, newspaper advertisements, and pamphlets. This experiment will throw light on three important problems: (1) the effectiveness of a governmental family limitation program among a population largely illiterate; (2) the possible success in managing the psychological problems involved in introducing the idea into a particular culture; and (3) the possible efficacy and feasibility of the rhythm method itself.

It has been reported recently that since the Communist leaders of China are becoming worried that China's population may become too big, they are calling for a campaign to spread medical theories and guidance for the practice of birth control.[21]

Are *national* family limitation policies likely to occur soon and on a wide scale? Consciously devised and actively promoted restrictive population policies on the part of governments are conspicuous for their rarity. The reason for this is apparent. Except in totalitarian countries effective public policies and public programs come as an *effect* of a very considerable change in old mores or of the development of new ones on the part of a considerable portion of the public. These changes in mores grow out of new insights and values developed at first among small groups and organizations—usually very decided minorities—and then spread to larger portions of the population. In fact, such fairly far-reaching modification of public attitudes and opinions, especially those favorable to a marked innovation in the life of the people, should precede legislation and official governmental action; otherwise, the action is deemed arbitrary, even absolutist, and is condemned to opposition, divergence, and failure. Such legislation might—as it often has—

---

[21] On the above, and other governmental policies and practices relating to fertility control, see Eldridge; Bliven, pp. 10-12; "India's Basic Need: Population Control," *Population Bulletin*, 8 (Nov., 1952): 37-47; "Asian Population Roundup," *Population Bulletin*, 11 (March, 1955): 1-12, esp. 9-11.

become a dead letter. In the long run, governments of free people, while they may do some educating and leading, get their directives, or at least the approval of their actions, from the people. As Mr. Dooley pointed out with respect to the decisions of the Supreme Court: "They follow the illictions." Fertility control also, in most instances, cannot be expected to be instigated by the state. Even though the state is the organization that we call upon to do for us what we cannot do for ourselves as individuals and lesser collectivities, it can only do what we want it to do; and even in an era of increasing statism the world over not everything can be done by government.

Can a world political organization inaugurate and enforce family limitation? A world-wide policy and program of limitation engaged in by all or a considerable number of the nations is occasionally mentioned. But it would be unwise and unsound at present to place undue reliance upon the possible achievements of international organizations created by governments. Neither the League of Nations nor the United Nations has been able to achieve anything in the form of *military disarmament*. International *demographic disarmament poses problems of equal complexity and gravity*. International governmental agencies consist of representatives of sovereign national governments. These national governments are in the state of mind and of action just discussed. Each government represented has to consider its own national majority attitudes and values, interests and opinions, its comparative industrial and military manpower situation, its economy, and its international economic relations. All act with great and understandable caution.

Even if a restrictive policy could be agreed upon, a host of problems would arise in instrumentalizing it. As Sir Charles Darwin points out, "How would the nations settle the respective numbers admissable for their populations?" Would it be on the basis of existing populations, and if so, for how long? If the quota where exceeded, what kind of sanctions would be used? (For there would have to be sanctions.) Economic sanctions have been found to be difficult to administer and enforce, and military sanctions would precipitate many of the grave international evils of war, jealousy, and disorder which the world is seeking to eliminate. Even if seemingly effective measures along these lines could be devised, it would still be an arduous task for the rulers of the respective countries to enforce them internally. Dissentiing nations might readily become the source of fanatical opposition.[22]

This does not mean that the United Nations and its related bodies such as the United Nations Educational, Scientific and Cultural Organization (UNESCO), the World Health Organization (WHO), the Food and Agricultural Organization (FAO), the International Labor Office (ILO), the International Monetary Fund, the World Bank, the Population Commission, and the Statistical Commission cannot make valuable contributions to the various nations. They can carry on extensive research, present a vast array of critical comparative data, and give much valuable advice and administrative assistance in planning and executing both national and multilateral contributory procedures.

Not only these international organizations, but also the various appropriate national organizations should be encouraged to create better social, economic, and political conditions, create an atmosphere favorable to incentives to restriction, and provide direct as well as indirect facilities to these ends.[23]

That these international organizations are hampered by the conservatism of the member governments is illustrated in the work of the United Nations Mission of Technical Assistance to the Republic of Haiti in 1949. Though this technical mission included representatives of FAO, WHO, the International Monetary Fund, and UNESCO, and while it recognized the condition of grave overpopulation, it made only one brief, and in the present world almost innocuous, recommendation: ". . . the Mission recommends that serious consideration be given to the possibility of emigration as a means of relieving the acute population pressure. . . ." Nothing whatever was said about the crux of the matter, curbing population increase. Social pioneering by national governments or by international bodies created by governments in the form of policies and programs of family limitation can hardly be expected at this time. They tread on too many governmental toes.[24] Furthermore, for a

---

[22] Pp. 148-150.

[23] In this connection see Myrdal.

[24] It should not be implied that we are objecting to or ruling out the possibility or the desirability of governmental action in national or international programs of planned parenthood. The point is that they are not likely to occur on any adequate scale at present.

number of obvious reasons restrictive procedures by governmental agencies are even more likely to meet the quiet resistance of the people than have pro-natalist pressures.

A WORLD-WIDE SOCIAL MOVEMENT DIRECTED TO FAMILY LIMITATION

If there is to be an early and effective attack upon the task of diffusing and accelerating family limitation, it would seem to be most expedient to begin with the individuals and smaller groups who are the component elements of government and whose combined interest and opinion eventually become the basic dynamic for all acceptable and successful governmental action. In the United States, in Europe, among people of European stock elsewhere, and among those classes everywhere where the knowledge and practice of birth control have come to be rather widely diffused, it has been a private affair. 'Interest in it must be developed among the rank and file of the people. This interest precedes public discussion and agitation and must be substantial before there can be any formulation of public policy. This means, in the last analysis, that family limitation must first be got into the people's heads— into their thinking, their values, their objectives, their personal aspirations./ The concern about the smaller, planned family and the convictions as to its desirability and necessity must first be created; and then these interests and convictions must be developed at the individual, family, village, and local community level, and among the lower classes.' The strategy should be to start by building effective minority beliefs and actions and then to expand them to majority proportions. The essential procedure, therefore, would seem to be to arouse curiosity and fix attention, to bring about a change of values and beliefs and mores, and to aid and induce the actual practice of contraception among more and more of the common people in more and more countries/ Even though the social-economic incentives that come in the advanced stages of moderization do not necessarily exist among many of the most needful peoples, perhaps the simple but overwhelming facts can be presented, the common humane goals illuminated, and the deepseated hopes of betterment aroused in such a manner as to circumvent the slow, automatic development of restrictive incentives. This sort of action in connection with this demographic problem has never been tried on any considerable scale. It could be an immediate and feasible next step—a direct attack along with all of the flank movements that have been examined in this book. It may also be the cheapest and most efficacious way of offsetting Malthusian conditions in much of the world.

Such action is not without precedent in other important problem areas of human life. History affords an impressive list of accomplishments by such means, though few have ever been tried on a world scale. The procedure here suggested is the ancient one of conducting a social movement, specifically a social reform movement. The social movement has been the means of bringing about changes in other areas of social life involving sharp prejudices, archaic values, and sanctified actions—crucial changes which brought great social benefits to large numbers of people. Notable are the abolition of slavery, the abolition or sharp regulation of child labor, the equalization of rights for women, the acceptance of the principle of mental health and mental treatment instead of castigation of devils.

Before examining the essentials and potentialities of such a movement with respect to the specific objective of extending and accelerating planned family limitation, let us briefly note the principles and typical characteristics of that reorganizational activity known as social movements which sociology has established on the basis of numerous and varied instances.

THE GENERAL THEORY OF SOCIAL MOVEMENTS

"Social movement" is a general term for collective actions, involving small or large numbers of human beings and having dynamic reorganizational effects. They have appeared in all areas of social life where man-made operations are possible. As human manipulative procedures, they seek to develop, in some degree, new systems of values, new schemes of behavior, new relationships, new organizations, new institutional forms, and new or revised societal operations to meet the needs in those areas of social life where conditions have been intolerable.

In the course of development of a social movement needs, wishes, and hopes become articulated in the form of relatively specific values and ideas; objectives are clarified; principles and mechanisms of action are vaguely or clearly developed; the personnel is organized through leadership and systematized structuring. A social movement in any recognized or demonstrated "need area" attracts attention, arouses curiosity, invites private cogitation, produces group discussion and examination. It spontaneously brings about adjustment procedures compatible with the peculiar environmental views, needs, and abilities of the people, and it usually develops voluntary conviction and acceptance, often stimulating a considerable degree of mass response.

The typical characteristics of social movements can be set forth as follows:

1. They have their bases in untoward social conditions.
2. They are consciously and purposively engaged in as correctional procedures.
3. They consist of functional operations.
4. They have a developmental pattern, which includes the accession and participation of more and more members.
5. They have objective embodiment as specially formed private and semi-public organizations. These organizations are the foci of the movement, the vehicles for carrying it into effect, and they function as originating and modifying agents. Social movements also, as far as possible, use existing organizations and institutions.
6. They seek certain new or modified mores, action patterns, and possibly even institutions.
7. They have techniques or procedures to realize their goals. They engage in agitation and they propagandize and educate; they try to develop an *esprit de corps* and morale among the participants; they develop procedural tactics.
8. They may be carried on both by outsiders *for* the distressed population elements and by the affected elements themselves. The more successful movements usually get representatives of the affected elements into the movement as leaders as soon as possible.[25]

In recent times the successful social movements, having built up an effective majority opinion and created a demand for universal practice along some line, have been taken over by the state and transformed into government policy and government action.

[25] For a more extended presentation of the theory of social movements see Hertzler.

An incidental advantage of a social movement is that there is in it no element of bureaucratic governmental pressure or regimentation from above which might invite resistance. It grows from the grass roots.

A WORLD-WIDE FAMILY LIMITATION MOVEMENT

A world-wide family limitation movement does not need to start from scratch. The desire for family limitation is widespread, especially among the women of the underdeveloped countries; there is among many an awareness that something can be done; in some countries there are nuclear movements already under way. There is evidence of both interest in contraception and a degree of successful practice among the more industralized-urbanized segments of the population in Latin America, North Africa, India, China, Japan, the Philippines, and the U.S.S.R. There is evidence of sporadic movements. Cook points out that in El Salvador, in spite of official and clerical opposition, an organization called the Friends of the Land is carrying on a campaign of education which teaches the people that excess fertility is the crucial factor in their poverty.[26] In Japan the birth control movement is a people's undertaking manned and financed by the Japanese themselves. Present legislation allows but does not encourage birth control clinics. In India there has been an interest in birth control, though among a very limited portion of the population, since 1911. There have even been clinics in some of the larger cities.[27] In 1933 the All-India Women's Conference passed a resolution recommending that birth control be included in municipal health services, and in 1938 the National Planning Committee resolved, in effect, that family planning and the limitation of children were essential for both family and national interests.[28] The present governmental action in India may be based in part on these earlier private and semi-public activities. The significance of deliberate birth control agitation is borne out in the statement by Flugel:

[26] P. 337.

[27] A press statement (from the Chicago *Daily News* Foreign Service of March 21, 1954) reports that Bombay alone has thirty family-planning agencies and a corps of social workers who explain how women can space their children.

[28] Davis, *Population of India and Pakistan*, p. 227; Flugel, 1952, p. 14.

The reports of the extensive lecture and demonstration tours in eastern countries by Margaret Sanger, Edith How-Martyn and Eileen Palmer indicated that in many countries their birth control propaganda encountered far less opposition and far greater interest than they had been led to expect.[29]

These and similar movements have been partial, sporadic, and in most cases they have lacked financial backing; but their spontaneity and the seriousness and devotion of the participants constitute grounds for optimism. Though fertility control is most widespread in the West and among European peoples, the interest in it is not solely Western; obviously, it does not seem to be racial or race-bound phenomenon any more than industrialization.

Many of the people of overpopulated countries show a keen interest in population restriction and wish to bring it about. As soon as they understand something of the simple and humane nature of contraception, and the planning, choice, and control it makes possible, they see its multiple advantages over infanticide, abortion, and even sterilization. Perhaps the world is ripe for a family limitation movement, enlisting, and promoted and conducted by the alert and concerned "citizens of the world"—a movement bearing down especially where the needs are greatest.

DESIGN AND TACTICS

It is suggested that the principles of inaugurating and conducting social movements be utilized and that all of the modern facilities for such a deliberate and accelerated telic procedure be tried out. What then, in broadest outline, would be some of the more important aspects of the design and the minimal tactics in organizing and vigorously promoting a world-wide family limitation movement?

The content of the appeal. It is necessary at the very outset to create or to enhance a state of mind favorable to family limitation, to effect a desire for it, and to build up motivation, recognizing full well that in many instances this means bringing about revolutionary changes in values and objectives. Attention should be focused on the dire conditions of the people, their inferior status in comparison with the envied people of the world. These conditions should

[29] 1952, p. 13.

be related to the vast numbers of human beings in the world and to their rapid rate of increase. Stress should be put upon the national, family, and individual social-economic and humane gains to be derived. In the larger perspective, as Adams points out, it should be stressed that the objective ". . . is not simply to whittle down the number born every year, but to seek ways of balancing resources and population, and through these means raise the standards of living and life so that mankind need not destroy himself violently and painfully."[30] However, the more intimate and personal appeals should be especially resorted to, indicating how contraception contributes to the acquisition and enjoyment of the simple "good things" of life. The arousal of the general but powerful desires for safety, well-being, and opportunity is important. Attention can be called to the general and individual gains in health through a slowing up of the growth of population or, conversely, to the perils of disease among an overcrowded people suffering malnutrition, starvation, inadequate housing, and other sharply limited physical and economic resources and facilities. The simple arithmetic of having more economic goods and more house space per person if the family is smaller should be pointed out. The women, especially, will be impressed by the gains in maternal health and the lower maternal mortality through the better spacing of pregnancies, not to mention reduced infant deaths, better home conditions, and more attention per child. The widespread notion that large families are a form of insurance, an investment against old age, or a sign of vitality or prosperity needs to be overcome.

Finally, it is important to get across the idea that contraception itself is relatively easy and private; that it causes no physiological perils, as in the case of abortion; that it is not a form of murder, as is infanticide; and that it does not produce permanent childlessness, as does sterilization. Even the humblest will be impressed by the notion that it rests upon the dignity of the individual human being—a special, superior kind of creative and manipulative creature on the face of the earth—that it is an ingenious and available procedure, and that it permits choice in planning the number and the timing of children.

[30] P. 176.

If controversy should occur as these appeals are made, it is all to the good; in fact, it is wise to encourage controversy as an aid to any social movement that has any merits whatsoever. In the recent past, whenever and wherever contraception has met opposition—religious, political, or otherwise—by furnishing publicity it has created a curiosity about it, focused attention upon it, spread information about it among the people normally most difficult to reach, delineated the situation and its factors, and promoted its use. In general, opposition gives the proponents a "press" and other public opportunities for explaining and teaching, for diffusing facts and putting a program across.[31]

Research and experiment. The movement must be more than propaganda and indoctrination. Research and experiment, conducted by capable and responsible private, semi-public, national, and international bodies, are absolutely necessary. Some of this research should be of a general nature, concerned with population conditions and trends as they relate to nutrition, ecology, health, conservation, and increase and distribution of the food supply. Questions as to how many people the earth can reasonably support with physical-economic adequacy and political-military safety, now and in the foreseeable future, must be considered.

Specific research also is necessary with respect to: (1) simple, cheap, and effective methods of contraception, and (2) the devising and improvement of techniques, adapted to the peculiar conditions among particular peoples, areas, and countries, that are likely to be most satisfactory in diffusing population facts in general and contraception facts in particular. This is simply another way of saying that the social movement will have to take on certain *special* features for each people (or area) depending upon their cultural (especially literacy) level, the nature of their religious beliefs and practices, their family attitudes and patterns, and their economic means. The importance of a regional and even a world-wide clearing house for the fruits of such research is obvious.

Personnel and organization. As in every social movement, leadership and early personnel are of vast importance. Needed are leaders

---

[31] The effects, in this respect, of the Bradlaugh-Besant Trial in 1877 all over the Western world are generally known. For a typical recent instance in Puerto Rico of the effects of Church opposition see Cook, p. 338.

of various kinds for the different levels of the undertaking. At the upper world-wide and country-wide level the movement needs people of great vision and contagious enthusiasm, people who are adept at social strategy and blessed with great organizing ability. There should be scientists and scientific practitioners, especially in private and public health, skillful educators and propagandists, journalists and other publicists and organizers of mass communication programs. At the national level the personnnel, at first, may be heavily loaded with outsiders; hence, they must be the kind of persons who do not arouse suspicion and hostility.

At the national and at all lower levels indigenous persons should be enlisted and used as soon as possible. At all levels the personnel of the movement should be people who, because of reputation and position, are looked up to and respected. The movement should not be dominated by "intellectuals," since they are often suspect and occasionally inept along lines of practical action. The more leaders, promoters, teachers, and practitioners who can be recruited from the lower or middle classes the better. At all levels, however, the movement will need what are coming to be called social engineers—persons equipped to design, construct, and carry into effect social action programs.

This personnel will, of course, have to be organized at all levels— but as private and *not* as governmental bodies. There should, of course, be as many local nuclear and national organizations as possible. In each country the character of organization should be determined by socio-cultural conditions and pragmatic procedures and carried on in the most efficacious way. The importance of the "team" in arousing response and in training potential leaders should be stressed.

As Adams points out, planned parenthood organization, or whatever they will be called locally or nationally, should not be women's organizations, as they have been too largely in the past, but composed of both men and women who have the interest and imagination to understand this boon to mankind and to give it their support.

Periodic world congresses of the many like-minded organizations would provide an opportunity for review and collaboration. Possibly, some sort of loose, world-wide coordinating organization might be desirable. But the popular nature of the movement should be preserved. The various constituent organizations should function not as subordinates in a world hierarchy or under the paternalistic influence of some one nation or world area, but as world-wide partners acting toward a great human end.

The funds will have to be derived from all possible sources, both foreign and national. At first, the wealthier countries will have to be the major contributors. The great philanthropic foundations, especially of the United States, might be prevailed upon to contribute toward the solution of at least certain problems—and as part of a humane cause not unlike those they have been supporting. All potential private and organizational contributors should recognize that here is a cause with a program offering direct and fairly rapid relief at a relatively low cost and in such a manner that millions and perhaps billions of the world's common people can profitably and privately participate in it themselves, thereby relieving some of the most ominous and explosive demographic and political-military pressures on our planet. It might also be acknowledged that if the world spent only one billion dollars over a period of several years—which would be only a fraction of one per cent of what it has expended on atomic research, and used in the construction of atomic and hydrogen bombs—on contraceptive research, on the spreading of information about its importance and use, and actual devices given away at first, there is every likelihood that it would have tremendous results. It might, quite conceivably, relieve much of the pressure for atomic bombs and all the other military expenditures which solve no problems of peace, order, and prosperity even temporarily.

Techniques and instrumentalities. Before any major progress is possible, there is, above all, the necessity for conveying a basic understanding of the population problem and its possible solutions, including especially family limitation, to the millions upon millions of people whose support is required. This is a tremendous job of education which must be carried on at all levels. At the university and college level Adams suggests professorships, graduate fellowships, and undergraduate essay contests devoted to population-resources problems in general. Colleges and universities should also train personnel for all levels of the social movement—promotion and administration, research, economics, propaganda, and so on—down to extension agents, nurses, and social workers functioning at the family and village level. For the general reader there should be books, magazines, and pamphlets appropriately prepared for each people by top-flight writers and journalists. The power of the spoken word in influencing people, both literate and illiterate, and in molding opinion, when spoken by the right person, should not be overlooked. The amazingly successful action of Gandhi and his disciples shows what can be done.

It must be recalled, however, that the great masses of the people most directly involved (perhaps as high as 80 per cent) are illiterate rural peasants. The world cannot, and need not, wait until these become literate. There is first of all the desirability of using direct face-to-face indoctrination and instruction, including clinical aid. Today we have available for the underdeveloped and illiterate peoples agencies of mass communication and general instruction that the West did not have when its control over either births or deaths began to be effective. The small battery radio in the most remote African or Indian or Chinese village is coming to be a commonplace. Motion pictures, including the small, inexpensive portable machines, sound trucks, and an increasing array of other visual and audio-visual instructional aids are becoming available. It may not be long before television is available in the remote and crowded areas of the earth. In the United States especially, we have had much valuable and successful experience in developing educational programs conducted by means of these audio-visual techniques.

Because of the vast numbers that can be contacted directly over a short period of time by these modern devices of mass communication, it is possible that indoctrinating materials can now be diffused more effectively among the untutored masses in a week than could be done in a period of years a half century ago. One can also only surmise what the effects upon the world would be if its mass communication facilities devoted as much daily time for a year to family limitation as was given to the McCarthy-Army controversy in the spring of 1954.

Cooperation with public services. Finally the family limitation movement should work with the various public health programs and organizations wherever these are to be found. The wise practice is to relate contraception with wider hygienic services, with family and child care, with improved housing and other aspects of physical well-being. It should not be treated as an isolated measure, but as an integral part of a healthy, cautious, satisfying way of life. Beyond this immediate strategy, of course, is the fact that as soon as public opinion accepts and approves contraception, its salient features should be incorporated in the public health organizations of the various peoples as part of the national program of safety and well-being.

POPULATION UNLIMITED?

Most people still, consciously or unconsciously, accept the idea that a continuous and persistent increase in the number of human beings is not merely inevitable but somehow desirable. As a matter of philosophic orientation, then, we might finally ask ourselves whether we actually believe in and want "population unlimited." If we subscribe to this notion, it means, as we have noted from various angles, that we must envisage the future of our species as a constant effort to satisfy the material needs of this ever-increasing swarm of people, as a continual and desperate race between resources and numbers of human beings, in short, as "Operation Treadmill."

There is much evidence of tragic preoccupation with mere numbers. Our economic system tends to measure everything by the quantitative yardstick; we desire more persons to make more things to sell to more customers. We want more persons and equipment to conquer more enemies, or to resist being conquered by them. We want more persons in our nation, or our religious organizations, or our race, or our ideological group as compared with other groups—often, even, to the exclusion of all other groups. But this demand for large numbers is an expression of greed—material greed, political-military greed, the greed of religious organizations and ethnic groups. Furthermore, "giantism" is always a diseased condition.

Why should we fill the earth with two, four, eight, or sixteen times the present number? What point is there in applying almost every technological advance, in straining every resource, simply to provide subsistence for ever greater numbers? Need man condemn himself to the futile race of producing more and more food under conditions of diminishing returns for more and more people? Should he blithely multiply until the whole earth is overpopulated, all adjustive techniques strained to the utmost, and all resources in process not only of utilization, but also of exhaustion? Or, does he have some kind of humane obligation to his grandchildren and great-grandchildren?

Perhaps we must reassess our view of human destiny and of human ends? Are great *quantities* of persons and things our main ends? Or is *quality* of human life—the "good life" for each individual and for mankind as a whole—the ultimate objective?

This question rests upon the assumption that human beings are the highest beings in the world, the end-products of all developmental and control processes. If this has validity it means that the major objective is fully developed personalities; this, in turn, means the fullest and most harmonious exercise of human facilities and powers and the fullest utilization of the richness of culture; it means achieving an ascending scale of values from the material and biological to the intellectual and the spiritual; it means the richer and wider flowering of the higher qualities that make up man's uniqueness—his intelligence, his creative powers, his moral sense. We have the vision of *Humanitas*—the promotion of human worth, for all races, creeds, classes, and climes.

Such a quality of living cannot be achieved in a beehive. It is vastly more than breeding, grubbing, and feeding. The world must be looked upon as a good place for human beings through the ages to come. To achieve this "goodness' the world needs surpluses instead of deficits, general security, freedom, opportunity, cooperation, peace—now and a millennium hence.

Hence, there is much to be said in favor of a restrictive policy making for a relatively stationary population as a world guide for the immediate future. This would enable the peoples of the earth not only to move toward a universalized physical optimum, but also to realize and enjoy the highest known reaches of social well-being and opportunity and of intellectual and spiritual development. This is surely the kind of society old and young would like to see prevail in the future.

BIBLIOGRAPHY

ADAMS, MAX (pseud.). "Balancing Population and Resources: The Greatest Challenge of Social Engineering." *Jour. of Heredity,* 43 (July-Aug., 1952): 173-180.

BATES, MARSTON. *The Prevalence of People.* New York: Scribners, 1955. Pp. 94-109.

BLIVEN, BRUCE. *Preview for Tomorrow: The Unfinished Business of Science.* New York: Knopf, 1953. Pp. 10-15, 29-35.

BROWN, HARRISON. *The Challenge of Man's Future.* New York: Viking, 1954. Pp. 86-95, 236-243, 259-265.

COOK, R. C. *Human Fertility: The Modern Dilemma.* New York: William Sloane Associates, 1951. Pp. 334-341.

DARWIN, SIR CHARLES G. *The Next Million Years.* Garden City: Doubleday, 1953. Pp. 148-154.

DAVIS, KINGSLEY. "Population and the Further Spread of Industrial Society." *Proc. Am. Phil. Soc.,* 95 (Feb., 1951) : 8-19, esp. 16-19.

————. *The Population of India and Pakistan.* Princeton: Princeton Univ. Press, 1951. Pp. 221-231.

ELDRIDGE, HOPE T. *Population Policies: A Survey of Recent Developments.* Washington: International Union for the Scientific Study of Population, 1954. Pp. 97-118.

FAIRCHILD, H. P. *People.* New York: Holt, 1939. Pp. 288-294.

FIELD, J. A. *Essays on Population and Other Papers.* Chicago: Univ. of Chicago Press, 1931. "The Early Propagandist Movement in English Population Theory," pp. 91-129; "The Beginning of the Birth-Control Movement," pp. 206-214; "Reflections on the Case for Birth-Control," pp. 307-328.

FLUGEL, J. C. *Population, Psychology and Peace.* London: Watts, 1947. Pp. 110-122.

————. "Population Theories and International Tensions," *Sociological Rev.* (Brit.), 44 (1952): Sec. 1, esp. pp. 8-15.

FOLSOME, C. E. "Progress in the Search for Methods of Family Limitation Suitable for Agrarian Societies," in *Approaches to Problems of High Fertility in Agrarian Societies.* New York: Milbank Memorial Fund, 1952. Pp. 129-138.

GLASS, D. V. *Introduction to Malthus.* New York: Wiley, 1953. Pp. 47-49.

————. *Population Policies and Movements in Europe.* Oxford: Clarendon Press, 1940.

————. *The Struggle for Population.* Oxford: Clarendon Press, 1936.

HENSHAW, P. S. *Adaptive Human Fertility.* New York: McGraw-Hill, 1955. Pp. 124-269.

HERTZLER, J. O. *Society in Action: A Study of Basic Social Processes.* New York: Dryden, 1954. Pp. 360-371.

HIMES, N. E. *The Medical History of Contraception.* Baltimore: Williams & Wilkins, 1936.

LANDIS, P. H. *Population Problems: A Cultural Interpretation* (2nd ed. by P. K. Hatt). New York: American Book, 1954. Pp. 47-51, 187-191, 239-276, 490-509.

LASZLO, H. DE. "Oral Contraceptives." *Eugenics Rev.,* 44 (Jan., 1953): 244.

274 *The Crisis in World Population*

LEWIS-FANING, E. *Family Limitation and Its Influence on Human Fertility during the Past Fifty Years.* London: Royal Commission on Population, 1949. Vol. I.

LORIMER, FRANK. "Issues of Population Policy." *Annals Am. Acad. Pol. & Soc. Sci.,* 237 (Jan., 1945): 193-203.

————, *et al. Culture and Human Fertility: A Study of the Relation of Cultural Conditions to Fertility in Non-industrial and Transitional Societies.* Paris: UNESCO (New York: Columbia Univ. Press). 1955. Pp. 91-150, 183-198.

MOORE, W. E. "Attitudes of Mexican Factory Workers toward Fertility Control," in *Approaches to Problems of High Fertility in Agrarian Societies.* New York: Milbank Memorial Fund, 1952. Pp. 47-101.

MYRDAL, ALVA. "Population Trends in Densely Populated Areas." *Proc. Am. Phil. Soc.,* 95 (Feb., 1951): 1-7.

NOTESTEIN, F. W. "Problems of Policy in Relation to Areas of Heavy Population Pressure," in *Demographic Studies of Selected Areas of Rapid Growth.* New York: Milbank Memorial Fund, 1944. Pp. 138-158.

————. "The Reduction of Humna Fertility as an Aid to Programs of Economic Development in Densely Settled Agrarian Regions," in *Modernization Programs in Relation to Human Resources and Population Problems.* New York: Milbank Memorial Fund, 1950. Pp. 89-100.

OSBORN, FAIRFIELD. *The Limits of the Earth.* Boston: Little, Brown, 1953. Pp. 168-170, 215-219.

RILEY, JOHN W., and MATILDA WHIE. "The Use of Various Methods of Contraception." *Am. Soc. Rev.,* 5 (Dec., 1940): 890-903.

SAX, KARL. *Standing Room Only.* Boston: Beacon Press, 1955.

SOVANI, N. V. "The Problems of Fertilty Control in India: Cultural Factors and Development of Policy," in *Approaches to Problems of High Fertility in Agrarian Societies.* New York: Milbank Memorial Fund, 1952. Pp. 62-73.

STIX, REGINE, and F. W. NOTESTEIN. *Controlled Fertility.* Baltimore: Williams & Wilkins, 1940.

TAEUBER, IRENE B. "Some Recent Research on Fertility in Africa and Asia." *Population Index,* 21 (April, 1955) : 76-87.

————, and M. C. BALFOUR. "The Control of Fertility in Japan," in *Approaches to Problems of High Fertility in Agrarian Societies.* New York: Milbank Memorial Fund, 1952. Pp. 102-128.

THOMPSON, W. S. *Population Problems* (4th ed.). New York: McGraw-Hill, 1953. Pp. 9-19, 197-204, 446-467.

UNITED NATIONS, Population Commission, Department of Social Affairs. *The Determinants and Consequences of Population Trends: A Summary of the Findings of Studies on the Relationships between Population Changes and Economic and Social Conditions* (Population Studies, No. 17). New York, 1953. Pp. 283-287.

Index